Hitler's high seas fleet

The author of Hitler's High Seas Fleet: Richard Humble

Richard Humble joined the editorial staff of Purnell's *History of the Second World War* in 1966, after reading Military History at Oriel College, Oxford. He became Editor of Purnell's *History of the English-Speaking Peoples* in January 1970, and has written several articles on military and naval subjects.

Editor-in-Chief: Barrie Pitt
Editor: David Mason
Art Director: Sarah Kingham
Picture Editor: Robert Hunt
Designer: David A Evans
Cover: Denis Piper
Special Drawings: John Batchelor
Photographic Research: Jonathan Moore
Cartographer: Richard Natkiel

Photographs for this book were specially selected from the following archives: from left to right pages; 4-5 US Navy; 6-7 Suddeutscher Verlag; 8-9 Popperfoto; 10 Foto Druppel; 11 Mansell Collection; 12 Ullstein; 12 Sudd Verlag; 13-4 Bibliothek fur Zeitgeschichte; 15 Foto Druppel; 15 Imperial War Museum; 16 Sudd Verlag; 18 Ullstein; 18 Foto Druppel; 20 Bundesarchiv; 21 IWM; 21 Sudd Verlag; 23-4 Ullstein; 22 US Navy; 24-5 Foto Ferninand Urbahns; 26 Sudd Verlag; 26 Ullstein; 27 Foto Druppel; 30-2 Sudd Verlag; 34-5 Urbahns; 35 Sudd Verlag; 36-7 Urbahns; 39 Keystone; 42 US Navy; 47 Foto Druppel; 47 Popperfoto; 51 Bundesarchiv; 51 Urbahns; 54-5 Ullstein; 56 IWM; 58-61 Foto Druppel; 62-4 Ullstein 65 Druppel; 65 IWM; 67 Bundesarchiv; 72 Foto Druppel; 72 Bundesarchiv; 74-5 Sudd Verlag; 77 Urbahns; 80-1 Camera Press/IWM; 92 IWM; 93 Urbahns; 97 US Navy; 97 IWM; 99 Urbahns; 101 Ullstein; 101 IWM; 104 US Navy; 105 IWM; 109-113 IWM; 114 Bibliothek fur Zeitgeschichte; 117 IWM; 119 US Navy; 120 Urbahns; 123 Popperfoto; 124-5 US Navy; 126-7 IWM; 130 US Navy; 133 US National Archives; 134 Ullstein; 135 Urbahns; 138 IWM; 139 Urbahns; 144-5 Foto Druppel; 146 Keystone; 146 Popperfoto; 149 IWM; 150 Her Majesty's Stationery Office; 152-5 IWM; 156 Keystone; 157-9 IWM; Front Cover: IWM; Back Cover: IWM

Copyright © 1971 Richard Humble

First Printing: July 1971
Printed in United States of America

Ballantine Books Inc.
101 Fifth Avenue New York NY 10003

An Intext Publisher

Contents

8   Legacy of glory

24   Rebirth

36   From Graf Spee to Narvik

58   The surface raiders strike

76   Battleship Bismarck

94   Scharnhorst and Gneisenau

108   Arctic menace

124   The last battles

144   Lone queen of the north

154   Eclipse

160   Bibliography

Hitler's high seas fleet

Richard Humble

Neglected power

Introduction by Barrie Pitt

'Hitler was landsinnig (land-minded)', is the conclusion of one of the closest students of his character and to possess a great fleet of the sort which had been the pride of the Kaiser to create, was not an ambition of his. Thus the Kriegsmarine did not benefit on any scale comparable to the Wehrmacht or Luftwaffe during the great expansionist phase of 1935–39.

All this was quite natural, for while Hitler was not unaware of the rôle that sea power played in the politics of Britain or America – or had played in German policy during the time of the Kaiser – he considered such a rôle inapplicable to the strategy he planned for the Third Reich. This was to be primarily a land strategy, designed to secure for Germany possession of the Euro-Asian 'heartland', and sea power could contribute little to its fulfilment. On the other hand, the great sea powers – Britain and America – could do much it they so chose, to frustrate such a strategy – and Hitler's original intention was therefore to avoid conflict with both by refraining from offering a challenge to either at sea.

Nevertheless, some very fine and powerful ships were laid down during the pre-war years, notably the *Scharnhorsts* and the *Bismarcks*, and these were to provide a potent surface striking power for the German navy during the Second World War. Hitler's final pre-war decision over naval strategy was slowly to build up a small but select force of super battleships which, when the British navy was sufficiently overstretched by commerce protection, would break out over the great sea routes to track down and destroy their dispersed and weaker opponents.

The outbreak of war came too soon, however, for the German navy to have achieved the force levels which this strategy demanded. The surface fleet was too weak to commence raiding, as the destruction of the *Graf Spee* in

the Battle of the River Plate demonstrated, and later on the crippling losses in destroyers during operations in support of the army in Norway underlined the Kriegsmarine's unpreparedness.

Even Hitler's U-Boat force was too weak to initiate immediately any damaging campaign of merchant sinkings, but in 1940, the capture of the French ports changed all this. Suddenly, at a moment when Germany's submarine building programme reached a new peak, opportunities for U-Boat warfare on an unprecedented scale occurred – a situation of which full advantage was taken.

And the same opportunities were, in fact, offered to the surface fleet but it proved incapable of taking them – for to reach the vital French ports meant sailing through the net formed by the British home fleet, a desperately risky venture which, though brought off by the *Bismarck* in the spring of 1941, culminated in her pursuit and sinking.

Thereafter Hitler tired of the great ship strategy of his admirals. The battle cruisers *Scharnhorst* and *Gneisenau* were to humiliate the British navy by passing unscathed through the Channel defences in 1942 and the super battleship *Tirpitz* was to exert a worldwide influence on naval operations from its anchorage in the Norwegian fjords, but with the destruction of the *Bismarck* the high seas rôle passed from the German surface navy.

It might, but for Hitler's inflexible land-mindedness, have been otherwise. The young German navy had now a sound recognition for courage and seamanship and its ships were among the strongest, most powerful and most handsome in the world. A squadron of *Bismarcks*, protected by their own aircraft, might have swept the Northern seas.

Legacy of glory

When Nazi Germany went to war in September 1939, the modern German navy was exactly thirty-nine years old. Compared with the British Royal Navy, the strongest in the world, whose tradition dated back to before its defeat of the Spanish Armada in 1588, Hitler's small and uncompleted Navy seemed, on the face of it, to have had little chance of playing a decisive rôle. Yet this was far from the case. The British Admiralty in 1939 remembered the performance of the German navy of 1914-18 with undisguised respect and considerable apprehension. The German U-boat campaign had all but strangled Britain's war effort in 1917; and the hitting-power of

the German surface ships – the High Seas Fleet – had made itself painfully obvious every time the Iron Cross and the White Ensign had met in battle at sea.

The German navy of 1939 was built upon the legend created by its Imperial predecessor. Its formidable new warships were named with justifiable pride after the statesmen, commanders, and warships which had forged the German empire and navy and upheld the honour of both, earning undying battle honours in so doing, in the First World War. Just how strong was this legend? And what were the realities behind it?

'The new German navy has come in-

A battle squadron of the German Imperial High Seas Fleet puts to sea

to existence; it is a navy of the most efficient type and is so fortunately constituted that it is able to concentrate almost the whole of its fleet at its home ports.' So wrote Britain's new First Sea Lord, Admiral Sir John ('Jacky') Fisher in 1904. Three years later he was expressing himself in even more forceful terms: 'The only thing in the world that England has to fear is Germany', and that same year he was quoted as recommending to King Edward VII that the Royal Navy should 'Copenhagen the German Fleet *à la* Nelson' (to which the

Tirpitz: German naval master-mind

Monarch replied, 'Fisher, you must be mad.') But Winston Churchill's verdict on Fisher's obsession with Germany's new navy was accurate: after more than a century of Britain's post-Trafalgar complacency over her mastery of the seas, it was Fisher who, as Churchill wrote, 'hoisted the storm signal and beat all hands to quarters'.

'Our future lies on the water,' Kaiser Wilhelm II had stated with typical flamboyance in 1892; 'the trident must be in our hands.' The 'Second Reich' of which he became Emperor in 1888 had only come into existence in 1871, welded together out of the disparate German states by the diplomatic art of the 'Iron Chancellor', Bismarck, and by the prowess of the Prussian Army. To begin with, hegemony in Europe was Germany's sole aim, but when she began to participate in the scramble for empire which dominated the closing decades of the 19th Century, her reliance on the strength of the army was no longer enough. Germany acquired colonies in West, South, and East Africa; she flew her flag over Pacific islands and Chinese treaty-ports. A navy was needed, and a leader who could master-mind its building. In Alfred von Tirpitz, Germany got both.

Tirpitz had vision, energy, and the support of a monarch who was also Supreme War Lord. These were the three ingredients which dominated the building of the German High Seas Fleet in the 1900s, which in turn galvanised Fisher into countering its threat by bringing in the Dreadnought Age and launching the battleship building 'Naval Race'. Tirpitz had first-hand experience of how obsolete was the traditional Prussian reliance upon a vestigial, coast-defence navy his ship had been ignominiously blockaded in Schillig Roads during the Franco-Prussian War by a far stronger enemy blockading squadron. He urged the building of a rival to the British navy, and the Kaiser appointed him Secretary of State for the German navy in 1897. He lost no time in launching an intensive campaign to get his policies put into action. In 1900 the Reichstag passed Tirpitz's German Navy Act, and the High Seas Fleet was in business, its basic principles announced in the Act's preamble.

'Germany must have a battle fleet so strong that even for the strongest sea power a war against it would involve such dangers as to imperil its position in the world. For this purpose it is not absolutely necessary that the German battle fleet should be as strong as that of the greatest naval power; for such a power will not, as a rule, be in a position to concentrate all its fighting forces against us. But even if it should succeed in meeting us with considerable superiority of strength, the defeat of a strong German fleet would so substantially weaken the enemy that, in spite of the victory he might obtain, his own position in the world would be no longer secured by an adequate fleet.' These words alone announced the inevitability of the battleship building race which began with the launching of Britain's revolutionary, 'all-big-gun' HMS *Dreadnought* in 1906.

It is hardly an exaggeration to say that in 1914 the world was going war-

Fisher: sounded the alarm for Britain

ship-crazy. The Dreadnought battleship was the direct historical predecessor of the nuclear bomb, the ultimate military status-symbol, the most powerful instrument of mobile hitting-power the world had ever known. Every state in the world with pretensions to an international reputation that counted for something was clamouring for Dreadnoughts or for heavy armoured cruisers. Japan's navy had annihilated the bigger but dilapidated Russian Baltic Fleet at Tsushima in 1905, showing the power of a modern battle fleet for all the world to see. The United States was building Dreadnoughts. Brazil wanted Dreadnoughts because Chile and Argentina wanted Dreadnoughts, and vice-versa. Even the Ottoman Empire, shaken up by the vigorous 'Young Turk' revolution of 1908, was planning a modern navy to use against the Greeks.

To turn the advertising pages of the 1914 edition of *Jane's Fighting Ships* is to scent the warship frenzy in earnest. Every major shipyard, steel foundry, and instrument factory in the civilised world is there, peddling their warships, big guns, turret mountings, engines, rangefinders, and so on. Only the slogan 'Everything for the modern battle-fleet' seems to be missing, and that only by the barest of margins...

When war came in August 1914, Britain had apparently won the 'Naval Race' hands down. She had twenty Dreadnoughts and twelve lighter battle-cruisers, with twelve Dreadnoughts and one battle-cruiser still building. In addition, she had thirty-nine elderly 'pre-Dreadnoughts'. Germany, on the other hand, had thirteen Dreadnoughts and six battle-cruisers (including the hybrid *Blücher*, an armoured cruiser with twelve 8.2-inch guns). She had seven more Dreadnoughts and three battle-cruisers building, and a force of twenty-two pre-Dreadnoughts. Tipping the scale still further, Britain seized the three 'super-Dreadnoughts' she was building for foreign customers – two for Turkey and one for Chile – when war broke out; and this move led to the first episode in the war at sea.

Britain's superiority in the Dreadnought stakes was essential if she was to keep watch on her opposite numbers in foreign waters without weakening the vital 'Grand Fleet' covering the North Sea, where the main strength of the German High Seas Fleet was concentrated. In the Mediterranean, for example, the German battle-cruiser *Goeben* and the light cruiser *Breslau* had been engaging in a flag-showing contest with the three British battle-cruisers *Indomitable*, *Indefatigable*, and *Inflexible* since 1913. When war became imminent and the British seized the two Turkish super-dreadnoughts, the Kaiser promptly offered *Goeben* to the Turkish navy as a counterweight to British perfidy – a move which proved instrumental in bringing Turkey into the war as an ally of Germany. In a tense chase, *Goeben* and *Breslau* gave the slip to the far stronger British squadron and escaped to Constantinople, where they entered service with the Turkish navy. In the 1970s, *Goeben* (*Yavuz*, as she is known) is the last surviving relic of the Dreadnought age.

One German officer on the *Breslau*

Above: After their breakthrough, *Goeben* and *Breslau* arrive in the Dardanelles
Below: On the other side of the world: Spee's squadron forges across the Pacific

deserves mention. He was Karl Dönitz, who later transferred to the German U-boat arm, master-minded the building of Nazi Germany's U-boat fleet in the 1930s and its tactics in the Battle of the Atlantic in the Second World War, became Grand Admiral of the German navy – and eventually replaced Adolf Hitler as Führer of the Greater German Reich in 1945.

Out in the Far East, based on Tsingtau in China, was the German East Asiatic Squadron commanded by Vice-Admiral Graf von Spee. This force comprised the two burly, 8-inch gun armoured cruisers *Scharnhorst* and *Gneisenau* (named after the two great Prussian officials who had remodelled the Prussian administration and army to join the European alliance against Napoleon). Spee also had the light cruisers *Leipzig*, *Nürnberg*, and *Emden*, all armed with 4.1-inch guns. This was the crack gunnery squadron of the High Seas Fleet, *Scharnhorst* holding the Kaiser's special prize for naval gunnery. After detaching the *Emden* (Captain Karl von Müller) for independent commerce-raiding, Spee led his squadron across the Pacific into South American waters. Heading west from the Atlantic, *Dresden* had joined his flag by 18th October. In the Battle of Coronel off Chile (1st November, 1914), Spee won the greatest victory attained by the High Seas Fleet in the First World War. The lumbering elderly cruisers *Good Hope* and *Monmouth* of Rear-Admiral Sir Christopher Cradock's squadron were sunk, and the British light cruiser *Glasgow* and the armed liner *Otranto* were forced to flee.

Rounding Cape Horn, Spee planned a strike against the British-held Falkland Islands – but the British Admiralty had forestalled him. On 8th December 1914, as the German warships headed in for what Spee had expected to be an unopposed session of target practice, they sighted – too late – the tripod masts of the battle-cruisers *Inflexible* and *Invincible*, rush-

After Coronel: Spee at Valparaiso

ed to the South Atlantic after the news of the disaster of Coronel. In a running fight against hopeless odds, Spee and his entire force were overwhelmed and sunk, fighting gallantly to the last. Only *Dresden* escaped, to be hunted down and then to scuttle herself in Chilean waters on 14th December.

Meanwhile, Müller in *Emden* had made a three-month cruise in the Indian Ocean in which he had steamed 30,000 miles, sunk or captured twenty-three Allied merchantmen, inflicted £15,000,000 worth of damage on the Allied war effort, and won the unfeigned admiration of friend and foe alike. *Emden* had, moreover, kept over fourteen important Allied warships tied down looking for her – a fine achievement for a solitary light cruiser. *Emden*'s luck ran out on 9th November, 1914, when she was trapped by the stronger cruiser HMAS *Sydney*, and, after being battered defenceless, beached herself on North Keeling Island.

Müller of the *Emden* was one of the few commanders in the High Seas Fleet to become an international celebrity because of his prowess (Spee was another: the Royal Navy always had the highest regard for him). He generated the romance of the lone

13

wolf – a chivalrous and daring individualist in a bewildering war which seemed to be abandoning most of the traditional values in warfare. Britain's *Daily Telegraph*, for example, wrote in typical vein: 'It is almost in our hearts to regret that the *Emden* has been captured or destroyed . . . There is not a survivor who does not speak well of this young German, the officers under him and the crew obedient to his orders. The war on the sea will lose some of its piquancy, its humour and its interest now that the *Emden* has gone'.

Before the first twelve months of the war were over, the high seas had been cleared of virtually every German ship that had been at large in August 1914. On 13th September, 1914, there was an epic slogging-match in mid-Atlantic between a British armed merchantman, the *Carmania*, and a similar German vessel, the *Cap Trafalgar*. The two ships crippled each other and *Cap Trafalgar* sank, leaving *Carmania* to put out her raging fires and make a perilous voyage to Gibraltar. The German cruiser *Karlsruhe*, which had been raiding north of Pernambuco and had sunk eleven ships with a total of 76,000 tons, sank after an internal explosion on 4th November. Germany's base at Tsingtau, starting-point of Spee's fateful war cruise, had also fallen to an Anglo-Japanese force, and the occupation of Germany's other Pacific territories was speedily accomplished by Japan, Australia, and New Zealand. Meanwhile, the cruiser *Königsberg*, sole menace in African waters, was bottled up in the delta of the Rufiji river, south of Dar-es-Salaam, and was finally sunk on 11th July 1915. The high seas had been cleared, and German hopes that the British would send heavy naval forces to patrol their Empire in the Pacific, thus lowering the strength of the Grand Fleet to a level which the High Seas Fleet might hope to tackle, had come to nothing. All attention now turned to home waters, where the rival battle squadrons of the High Seas Fleet and the Grand Fleet watched each other from the Jade Bay and Scapa Flow.

It soon became obvious that the last thing the High Seas Fleet wanted was a deliberate, head-on clash with the far stronger Grand Fleet. The best the Germans could hope for was that a portion of the Grand Fleet might be cut off and annihilated. To accomplish this, the energetic Vice-Admiral Reinhard Scheer, who became commander of the High Seas Fleet in January 1916, planned a series of hit-and-run sorties, which culminated in the Battle of Jutland – a major encounter, which was the last thing he had wanted.

Yet the High Seas Fleet – or rather,

Left: *Scharnhorst* **takes on supplies at Valparaiso.** *Right:* **Brilliant tactician— Müller of the** *Emden,* **detached by Spee for independent raiding before Coronel.** *Below:* **The wreck of the** *Emden*

Scheer, C-in-C High Seas Fleet

Hipper, battle-cruiser pundit

its battle-cruiser scouting force – had already been in action. Rear-Admiral Franz von Hipper's battle-cruisers had bombarded towns on England's east coast, hoping to entice British warships to speed south to their own destruction under the German guns (they did not, and the German navy achieved little more than the British propaganda smear of being 'the baby-killers of Scarborough'). In the Battle of Dogger Bank (24th January 1915), Hipper's force had engaged in a running fight with Vice-Admiral Sir David Beatty's battle-cruisers, in which the British, due to misunderstood signals, contented themselves with overwhelming the lumbering armoured cruiser *Blücher* while Hipper's main force escaped.

In late May 1916, Scheer planned a bombardment raid on Sunderland, in which the battleships of the High Seas Fleet would follow the battle cruisers and engage any force the British sent south to counter them. What Scheer did not know was that British radio Intelligence was fully aware of the strength of this sortie, and that the whole of Admiral Sir John Jellicoe's Grand Fleet was speeding south to meet him head-on.

The resulting clash in the Skagerrak off Jutland on 31st May was a bitter disappointment for the Royal Navy and a merciful escape for the High Seas Fleet. Scheer twice extricated his fleet from the skilful manoeuvres of Jellicoe ('Silent Jack', as he was known in his fleet), and during the night steamed right through the fringe of the intercepting Grand Fleet to reach home in safety and break open the champagne as he anchored in the Jade on the morning of 1st June. He had lost one battle-cruiser (*Lützow*), one pre-Dreadnought battleship (*Pommern*), four cruisers, and five destroyers and torpedo-boats. The British, on the other hand, lost three battle-cruisers (*Queen Mary*, *Invincible*, and *Indefatigable*), three armoured cruisers, and eight destroyers and torpedo-boats. It was, on paper, a clear-cut tactical victory: Germany rejoiced, and the legend of the 'victory in the Skagerrak' was destined to outlive the High Seas Fleet itself.

Yet Jutland remained a strategic defeat for the German navy. Scheer had not achieved his object: to mutilate the Grand Fleet. The British blockade remained unbroken. 'The German Fleet has assaulted its jailer', wrote an American newspaper; 'but it is still in jail.' This was a neat summary of the facts. Scheer's fleet made further sorties during the war, but all of them were fruitless. Meanwhile the strength of the Grand Fleet grew from year to year, widening the gap between the power of the two fleets; and disillusionment and disaffection – reinforced by vivid memories of a horizon filled with belching enemy guns at Jutland – began to taint the fighting spirit of the men as the war dragged on.

In the months after Jutland, the German U-boat arm far surpassed the High Seas Fleet in importance. Surface raiders, however, had not been abandoned, and three of them made successful cruises. *Möwe* was out between 22nd November 1916, and 20th March 1917. She sank 122,000 tons of shipping in her four-months' cruise and had about twenty-four British cruisers combing the Atlantic in a fruitless search for her. *Wolf* (30th November 1916 – 19th February 1918) made a fifteen-month epic cruise, concentrating on the Indian Ocean trade routes and eliminating 120,000 tons of Allied shipping due to minelaying and capture. Last came the full-rigged sailing ship *Seeadler*, commanded by the dashing Count Felix von Luckner, who won himself a reputation like that of Müller of the *Emden* through his chivalrous depredations. Cruising from 21st December 1916, until 2nd August 1917, when she was wrecked on a South Pacific coral reef, *Seeadler* accounted for sixteen ships of nearly 18,000 tons. Noteworthy as these exploits were, they were dwarfed by the importance of the U-boat campaign; even so, they did a hundred per cent more damage than the battle squadrons of the High Seas Fleet, swinging round their anchors month in, month out.

A month after *Wolf*'s triumphant return to Germany, the last great gamble began for Germany: Ludendorff launched his *Kaiserschlacht*, the 'Kaiser's Battle', on the Western Front, and tore the British line wide open. After three fruitless years, the deadlock of trench warfare had been broken, and German armies were once more streaming towards Paris. But Allied manpower told. By midsummer the Germans had been held. By autumn they were in retreat. Exhausted and impoverished, Germany had nothing more to give, and nothing to expect except a relentless Allied advance into the heart of the Reich. The Kaiser's Germany had reached its breaking point – and then, in the early days of November, came the electrifying news: the men of the High Seas Fleet had mutinied.

They knew the war was over in all but name. They knew, too, that Scheer was planning another sortie for them, and they were not prepared to be sacrificed without cause. Months of demoralisation now bore their fruit as the mastheads of the High Seas Fleet blossomed with red flags, the decks rang with cheers for peace and for America's President Wilson, and armed gangs of sailors roamed the streets of Kiel and Wilhelmshaven. Here was the catalyst of the revolution which caused the Kaiser to abdicate and seek asylum in Holland. The inferiority complex of the German navy, it seemed, had reached its logical conclusion.

Yet the depths of humiliation had still to be plumbed by the High Seas Fleet. Under the terms of the naval armistice, the fleet was expected to steam into British waters and hand itself over to the Royal Navy. On board the US battleship *New York*, serving with the Grand Fleet, a young American lieutenant vividly recalled the sight of the High Seas Fleet coming in to surrender on the morning of 21st November 1918:

'The tiny light cruiser *Cardiff*, towing a kite balloon, leads the great German battle-cruiser *Seydlitz*, at the head of her column, between our lines. On they pass – *Derfflinger, Von der Tann, Hindenburg, Moltke* – as if in review. The low sun glances from their

17

Hipper's battle-cruiser squadron makes a foray in the North Sea

'Plain-clothes' raiders for the high seas included the *Möwe* (above) . . . and the *Wolf*, which carried a spotter seaplane to widen horizons

shabby sides. Their huge guns, motionless, are trained fore and aft. It is the sight of our dreams, a sight for kings! Those long, low, sleek-looking monsters, which we had pictured ablaze with spouting flame and fury, steaming like peaceful merchantmen on a calm sea. The long line of battleships, led by *Friedrich der Grosse*, flying the flag of Admiral von Reuter, commanding the whole force, *König Albert*, *Kaiser*, *Kronprinz Wilhelm*, *Kaiserin*, *Bayern*, *Markgraf*, *Prinz Regent Luitpold*, and *Grosser Kurfürst* followed in formation – powerful to look at, dangerous in battle, pitiful in surrender...'

Pity there was – but also embarrassment, shame, and contempt for any navy that could so humiliate itself. Indeed, many officers in the Grand Fleet had secretly hoped that the High Seas Fleet would arrive at the rendezvous with blazing guns. Beatty, who had replaced Jellicoe as C-in-C, Grand Fleet, in November 1916, blended genuine disappointment with professional contempt when he stated: 'We never expected that the last time we should see them as a great force would be when they were being shepherded, like a flock of sheep, by the Grand Fleet. It was a pitiable sight; in fact I should say it was a horrible sight...'

The British naval officers who boarded the German warships in Scapa Flow were appalled at what they saw: the ships filthy, the crews dirty, dejected, sulky, discipline virtually non-existent. Many officers were seen to have torn the Imperial insignia from their uniforms. And out of this scene of complete depression one British officer gleaned a significant reason: 'According to a man from the *Seydlitz* it was the appalling casualties she suffered [at Jutland] which decided them that they would mutiny rather than fight again.'

Yet this was a transient phase, not a final picture of total, abject collapse. As the weeks passed in Scapa Flow, the mood of the Germans could be seen to change. On 31st May 1919, they celebrated the third anniversary of Jutland with red and white Very lights and hoisted the German ensign along with the red flag. Admiral Fremantle, British gaoler of the High Seas Fleet, noted 'they appeared to be accepting their lot with submissive equanimity, but towards the end in some spirit of discontent' – if for no other reason than they were becoming sick of being gaped at like animals in a zoo by swarms of sightseers in small boats. As the deadline approached for the expiry of the Armistice and the ratification of the naval terms of the Treaty of Versailles, Admiral von Reuter, consulting with Berlin, was preparing for the one course of 'offensive action' left to his disarmed, immobile fleet: suicide by scuttling.

Completely unaware that Reuter was contemplating such a desperate move, Fremantle sailed on the morning of 21st June, 1919, to complete a series of exercise manoeuvres at sea. He had told Reuter unofficially that the Armistice had been prolonged from noon on the 21st until 1900 hours on the 23rd. But Reuter had already laid his plans for a mass scuttling to coincide with the expiry of the Armistice, and the news that Fremantle would be at sea on the 21st must have clinched his decision.

At 1020 hours on the 21st Reuter's flagship hoisted the signal 'Paragraph II – acknowledge' – the pre-arranged signal for 'Prepare to scuttle'. Then, at 1120: 'Condition Z – scuttle!' German ensigns soared to the mastheads as the sea-cocks and condenser intake valves were wrenched open and the sea came flooding in. Within an hour it was all over. Fremantle's ships, notified of the scuttling at 1220 when the first ships had disappeared, came pounding back to Scapa, far too late to intervene. Fifteen out of the sixteen German capital ships had gone (*Baden* was beached and subsequently refloated). The furious British patrols in the Flow ranged from ship to ship, shooting whenever they thought fit:

Left: The Imperial High Seas Fleet had Zeppelins under its control, but never had the chance to use them to the full. *Above and below left:* The shame of surrender. Reuter (*below right*) leads the Fleet into captivity

Above: The menace caged. *Baden, König Albert, Derfflinger,* and *Kaiserin* in Scapa Flow. *Left:* The end – *Hindenburg,* after the scuttling

ten Germans were killed (among them the captain of the *Markgraf*) and about sixteen were wounded. 'It was a marvellous sight,' wrote a German destroyer officer. 'All over the vast bay ships were in various stages of sinking . . .' After all the disgrace of surrender, the High Seas Fleet lay dead by its own hand. Its crews had won their last battle after all. Its ships would not be parcelled out among the victorious Allies.

The British reaction, naturally, was one of vicious sarcasm and contempt for what could justifiably be described as German perfidy in breaking the terms of the Armistice. But for the German navy, Scapa Flow became a symbol of defiance, of hopes for the future, cancelling if not wiping out the ignominy of surrender. The debate would rage for many years, but in the mind of Admiral Rheinhard Scheer there was no doubt that Scapa Flow marked, not the end, but a rebirth; 'I rejoice over the sinking of the German fleet in Scapa Flow . . . the stain of surrender has been wiped out from the escutcheon of the German Fleet. The sinking of the ships has proved that the spirit of the Fleet is not dead. This last act is true of the best traditions of the German navy.' For the German army, the period of rebuilding in the years to come would proceed to the tune of the legend of invulnerability in the field, of defeat by the 'stab in the back'. For the German navy, there would be memories of Spee and *Scharnhorst* and *Gneisenau,* Müller and the *Emden,* the 'death ride' of Hipper's battle-cruisers at Jutland – and, looming above all, the last tremendous symbol of defiance in Scapa Flow.

Rebirth

After the Scapa Flow sinkings and the share-out of the lighter German warships among the victorious Allies, nothing remained of the High Seas Fleet for which Tirpitz had striven. All that was left to the German navy were the elements of a thoroughly antiquated coast-defence force: eight ancient pre-Dreadnought battleships (some of them already scheduled for de-commission), no battle-cruisers, no heavy cruisers, eight old light cruisers, and thirty-two destroyers and torpedo-boats. In short, Germany had been cut back to a naval strength which was typical of the pre-Dreadnought era.

Even that strength was too much, the Allies thought. By the terms of the Treaty of Versailles, the German

navy must be further restricted to six old battleships, six light cruisers, and twelve destroyers. Now Germany's navy was diminutive indeed, and the Allies planned to keep it that way. The battleships and cruisers could be replaced when they were twenty years old – but under strict conditions. The replacement battleships must not be bigger than 10,000 tons; nor must they have a heavier main armament than 11-inch guns. That would make them, according to the orthodox conditions of warship design, virtually the size of heavy cruisers. As for the replacement cruisers, they were to be no bigger than 6,000 tons, with 6-inch main armament. Other replacement specifications set limits of 800 tons on destroyers and 200 tons on torpedo-boats. The other sanctions stood; no aircraft, no aircraft-carriers – and above all, no submarines.

The first C-in-C of the new German navy, Admiral Paul Behncke, was therefore faced with the severest limitations on his duty of remodelling the navy. Another restriction immediately made itself felt: money. The Allies, determined to 'make Germany pay' for the Great War, imposed enormous war reparations on the German state, which were never to be repaid in full and which did little to create post-war harmony in Europe. In the 1920s, Germany was a bankrupt power, and the social misery, cynicism, corruption, and all the other corrosive characteristics of the Weimar Republic would in time generate a snowball support for the well-organised hoodlums of the Nazi political machine.

Forced, therefore, to cut his coat according to a cloth of severely limited dimensions, Admiral Behncke selected modest targets for the first stage in the German navy's rebirth. His first duty was to give his threadbare fleet tasks which it could actually achieve in the defence of the Fatherland. Hence the setting up of two squadrons, North Sea and Baltic whose primary strategic aim was to prevent the French and Polish navies from ever joining up, thereby establishing command of the entrances to the Baltic.

As for new ships, Behncke could only make the most rudimentary beginnings, shackled as he was by the limitations of Versailles and the straightened circumstances of the Weimar Republic; but in 1921 the first light cruiser, *Emden* (named significantly after Müller's famous raider of 1914) was laid down. She kept the rules: 5,600 tons displacement, eight 5.9-inch guns. Finally launched in January 1925, she entered service with

Dressed overall: gleaming new units of the reborn German surface fleet

Admiral Behncke

Admiral Zenker

the navy the following year and made several foreign cruises, 'showing the flag' and acting as a training ship. In 1924 work began on a new torpedo-boat flotilla when the first boats of the *Möwe* class were laid down – but with these ships came the first evasion of the Versailles limitations. They were virtually destroyers: three 4.1-inch guns, six torpedo-tubes, displacing 924 tons. *Möwe* was launched in 1926, the year that the second group of new torpedo-boats, the *Wolf* class, was approved. *Emden, Möwe* and *Wolf* were all named after successful raiders of the Imperial Navy – proof that the achievement of the first High Seas Fleet had set a living tradition.

Behncke was replaced by Admiral Hans Zenker, under whose régime (1924–28) two more light cruisers, *Karlsruhe* and *Köln*, were laid down. And also in this period there appeared a remarkable and prophetic book; *Strategy of the World War*, written by Vice-Admiral Wolfgang Wegener and published in 1926. Wegener's thesis was built round the idea that if Germany ever became a great power again she would inevitably be challenged by Great Britain. The Reich therefore had two choices. Germany must build a large, balanced fleet, and make sure that it could operate from bases in France and Norway which could outflank a British blockade such as had been imposed in the First World War. Failing that, Germany must weave a pattern of alliances for herself which could neutralise Britain's domination of European trade routes.

Wegener was one of the 20th Century's classic 'prophets without honour'. His views were largely rejected as impractical: they were to be shatteringly vindicated by the march of events. Yet his advocacy of an ocean-going navy was followed in the last year of Zenker's leadership. The time had come for the first of the old pre-Dreadnought battleships to be replaced, and it was a straight choice between an ocean-going heavy cruiser or a sluggish, coast-defence monitor. The turning-point had come for the new German navy, not ten years after Scapa Flow. Would it aim, once again, for Tirpitz's goal? Or would it accept the defensive, insignificant rôle which the Allies had planned for it at Versailles?

The warship which finally appeared was a revolutionary weapon: *Deutschland*, first of the famous 'pocket-battleships'. The official classification

The first light cruiser launched for the new fleet: *Emden* takes the water

of these vessels was *Panzerschiff*, or 'armoured ship'. They were later re classified as *schwere kreuzer* ('heavy cruisers'), but it seems likely that 'pocket-battleship' will always be the most familiar term for them and they will be referred to as such in following chapters.

The idea of putting battleship-sized guns aboard a heavy cruiser was not, as is often thought, the sole product of German naval design. Towards the close of the First World War, the British had experimented with 'light battle-cruisers' – *Glorious* and *Courageous*, each with four 15-inch guns. *Furious*, third of these white elephants, was even more of a hybrid: from bridge to bow she was an aircraft-carrier, and she carried a single 18-inch gun (which had a shattering effect on so light a hull) mounted aft. *Glorious*, *Courageous*, and *Furious* (lampooned in the Grand Fleet as '*Uproarious*', '*Outrageous*', and '*Spurious*') were frail and short of range; they were all later disarmed and completely rebuilt as aircraft-carriers. But the *Deutschland*, based on the same principle as the light battle-cruisers, achieved a near-perfect combination of medium size and heavy hitting-power.

Deutschland packed six 11-inch guns in an electrically-welded hull which was 609 feet long and which displaced 11,700 tons (although for the sake of appearances, it was solemnly announced that she did not exceed the official 10,000 tons). She had a cruising radius of 19,000 miles at nineteen knots, and her 2-shaft diesel engines gave her a top speed of 26 knots. *Deutschland* was cast in the rôle of long-range raider. It was calculated that she would be able to out-run or out-gun any hostile cruisers she might be liable to encounter on the trade routes of the world, and that she need only fear destruction from faster battle-cruisers, such as Britain's *Hood*, *Repulse*, and *Renown*. When *Deutschland* was finally launched in 1931, she gave the German navy command of the Baltic; and two sister-ships soon followed, *Admiral Scheer* and *Admiral Graf Spee*.

Before *Deutschland* took to the water, however, the German navy had received a new C-in-C: Grand Admiral Erich Raeder, who replaced Zenker in the autumn of 1928. Raeder had been Franz von Hipper's Chief of Staff in the First World War, and had held his last seagoing command in 1923 as Flag Officer, North Sea Light Forces, before his appointment

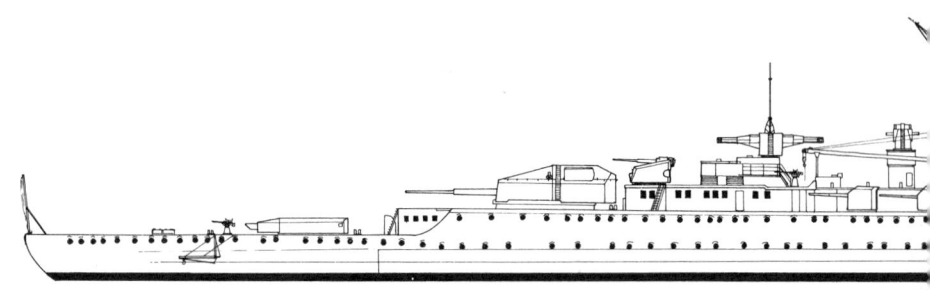

Deutschland, prototype for an entirely new breed of surface raider. She represented a near-perfect blend of battleship-sized hitting-power with cruiser-sized economy. Basic features included light armour, all-welded hull construction, all-diesel drive, and 11-inch guns. *Deutschland* was one of the earliest hard facts to make a mockery of the Versailles Treaty, and when war came she and her sister-ships soon put an end

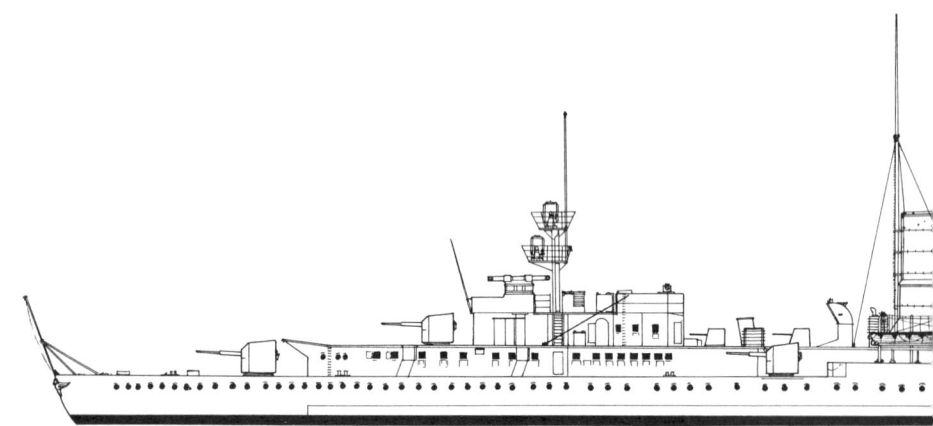

Emden, the first new light cruiser built for the German navy after the First World War. The old-fashioned arrangements of her main armament is very marked – single 5.9-inch turrets, with only four of them on the centre-line. Later German light cruisers had three triple 5.9-inch turrets, all on the centre-line. Originally coal-fired, *Emden* was converted to oil in 1934. Largely designed for foreign service,

as Flag Officer, Baltic, in 1925. A sober-minded professional with a strict moral code and a strong sense of duty, Raeder impressed the ageing Field-Marshal von Hindenburg, President of the Weimar Republic, who appointed him head of the navy in 1928. Raeder's ideal was to keep the navy out of political involvements and create an institution which would be an inspiration to the whole country. He certainly achieved the former objective. Raeder was no firebrand – he rejected Wegener's ideas on the ground that after her collapse in 1918 Germany would obviously never go to war with Great Britain again. And he flung himself into the immediate task of building up the new fleet.

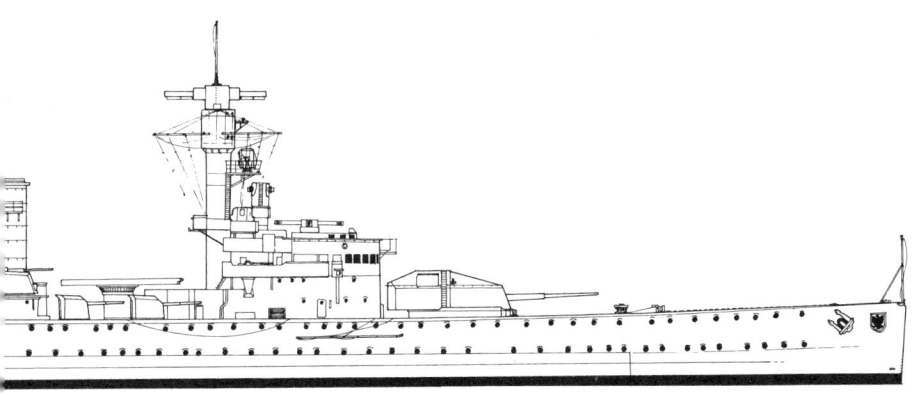

to the derision behind the label of 'pocket-battleship'. *Displacement:* 11,700 tons. *Length overall:* 609 feet. *Beam:* 67½ feet. *Draught:* 21¼ feet. *Max speed:* 26 knots. *Radius:* 19,000 miles at 19 knots. *Armour:* Side 4 inch; turrets 2-5½ inch, deck 1½-3 inch. *Armament:* Six 11-inch, eight 5.9-inch, six 4.1-inch AA, eight 37-mm AA, ten (later 28) 20-mm AA; eight 21-inch torpedo-tubes; two aircraft. *Complement:* 1,150

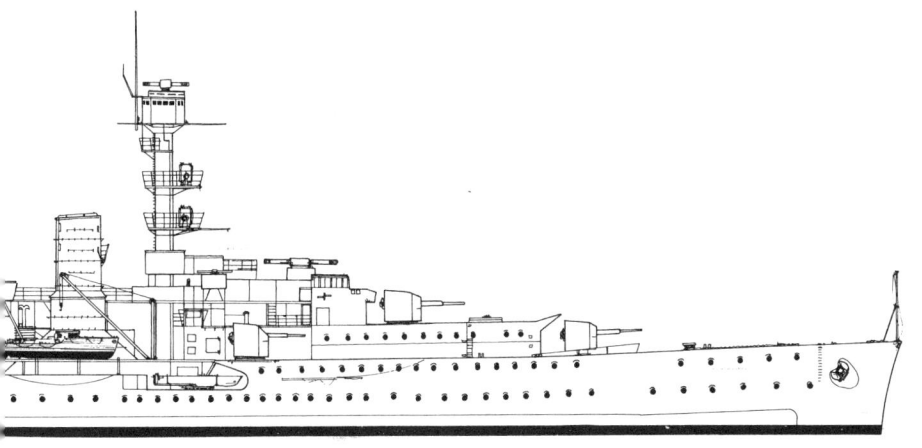

she made nine flag-showing cruises before 1939. *Displacement:* 5,600 tons. *Length overall:* 508 feet. *Beam:* 47 feet. *Draught:* 17½ feet. *Max speed:* 29 knots. *Radius:* 5,300 miles at 18 knots. *Armour:* Side 3-4 inch, gun housings 2-inch. *Armament:* Eight 5.9-inch, three 3.5-inch AA, four 37-mm AA; four 21-inch torpedo-tubes. *Complement:* 630

In doing this, Raeder gave cautious approval to the deceptive techniques which the German armed forces were adopting to side-step the restrictions of Versailles. Thus the German navy continued to experiment with submarines via a Dutch company in The Hague. It planned the use of converted freighters as auxiliary cruisers, of trawlers as minesweepers; civilian pilot-training schemes were laid on for potential officers of a naval air force. Raeder was a very good planner, and his goal was the construction of a balanced fleet – of the kind demanded by the Wegener thesis whose logical, deeper implications he rejected.

So it was that long before Adolf Hitler came to power the German

29

Left: Trainees aboard the square-rigger *Gorch Fock* take to the rigging. *Above:* The Führer and his Grand Admiral – Hitler and Raeder

navy was preparing for an eventual breach with the conditions laid down by the Treaty of Versailles. When Hitler became Reich Chancellor in January 1933, his accession was welcomed by Raeder. Hitler, typically, made every effort to impress the Grand Admiral, and soon won his confidence – especially with his assurances that while rearmament was essential, war with Great Britain was unthinkable. True to form, Raeder kept the navy aloof from the brutal politics behind the Reichstag fire and the Röhm 'Blood Purge' of 1933–34, which made Hitler effective dictator of Germany. The new régime rewarded Raeder's adherence by promising support for a naval building programme up to and beyond the limits of Versailles. And the first major milestone on Germany's road to rearmament was taken in March 1935 when Hitler denounced the Treaty of Versailles and proclaimed the re-establishment of the Luftwaffe, the German Air Force.

Now the weakness of Raeder's position began to show. He had decided to keep the navy out of politics but this did not apply to Hermann Göring, ex-First World War fighter ace, key Nazi leader, and C-in-C of the Reich's new Luftwaffe. It was Göring whose management of the Air Ministry and the Luftwaffe ruined the chances of a unified command system for all three branches of the German Armed Forces – the Wehrmacht, a title which, used correctly, covers the army (*Heer*), the navy (*Kriegsmarine*), and the air force (*Luftwaffe*). General von Blomberg, chief of the *Oberkommando der Wehrmacht* (OKW), the Armed Forces High Command, could not overcome Göring's superior position in the Nazi hierarchy.

Nor could Raeder. All the secret

Above: Detail of the battle-cruiser *Gneisenau*, with her crew manning ship
Below: First of the big new battleships: the launch of *Bismarck* in 1938

plans for the new German Fleet Air Arm were immediately blocked by Göring's monopoly of Nazi Germany's military aircraft programme. Göring's one concession, which sounded generous enough, was to agree to the establishment of a Naval Aviation Branch which the navy would control in time of war. By 1942, Göring promised, this branch would be supplied with sixty-two squadrons of 700 aircraft - a more than reasonable (if intangible) offer which Raeder accepted. He was soon to discover the unsavoury reality behind most of Göring's promises.

Also in 1935 came the Anglo-German Naval Treaty, signed in June. Having renounced the Versailles limitations in March, Germany now gained the right to build up her navy to 35% of the strength of the Royal Navy. The rebirth of the U-boat arm, too, was agreed on. The Treaty was a masterpiece of propaganda which piously announced to the world that Nazi Germany had no intention of challenging Great Britain to another naval race. But only eleven days after the signing of the Treaty, U-1 was commissioned at Kiel. By January 1936, eleven more U-boats were in commission - every single one of which had been under construction for months before the Treaty.

Now the building of the battle fleet proper began. First came two enlarged *Deutschlands:* small battleships in essence, mounting three triple 11-inch gun turrets instead of the two triple 11-inch turrets in the pocket-battleships. They also had a heavy secondary armament of 5.9-inch guns, and were designed for a top speed of thirty-two knots. Their displacement was announced as 26,000 tons; in fact, both ships displaced 32,000 tons, much of which was due to heavy armoured protection. They were, in fact, battle-cruisers, with comparatively light guns but ample armour. Their names echoed Admiral Graf von Spee's cruisers and their triumph at Coronel in 1914: *Scharnhorst* and *Gneisenau.*

In 1936, work began on two of the most powerful battleships ever built until the Imperial Japanese Navy came up with the super-battleships of the *Yamato* class: *Bismarck* and *Tirpitz,* armed with eight 15-inch guns. Again, the German authorities understated their tonnage: 35,000 tons instead of 41,700 tons for *Bismarck* and 42,900 tons for *Tirpitz.* Meanwhile, the navy's manpower was being increased, and many more shore installations planned and built. Two more light cruisers, *Leipzig* and *Nürnberg,* had already joined the fleet, and a sixth, *Königsberg,* was launched in 1937, together with the first two heavy cruisers, *Admiral Hipper* and *Blücher,* armed with eight 8-inch guns. It was a mushroom growth; and 1937 also saw the curious Anglo-German Naval Agreement, a postscript to the 1935 Treaty. This reaffirmed the 35,000-ton limit for battleships, which the 1935 Treaty had agreed and which the Germans had already broken. As if to symbolise the renaissance of German sea power, Hitler's new High Seas Fleet was represented at the British 1937 Coronation Naval Review in Spithead by the latest of the pocket-battleships, *Admiral Graf Spee* - whose armoured fighting-top sported as a battle honour one of the saddest words in the history of the British navy: 'Coronel'.

Another significant event occurred in 1937. On 5th November, Hitler summoned his military leaders and abruptly informed them that armed force would be needed to solve the Reich's 'problems' in Europe: Austria, Czechoslovakia, and Poland. Raeder was still confident that there would be no war - but the army generals thought otherwise. So did Admiral Dönitz, head of the U-boat arm since 1935, who could not believe that Britain and France would not act. Raeder, however, had been impressed by the accuracy of Hitler's forecast that the Western powers would not march to prevent Germany's reoccupation of the Rhineland in March 1936.

33

He still believed that, despite inevitable crises in the months to come, the Führer's tactics would indeed win time for the rebuilding of the Fleet.

On Monday, 14th March 1938, the Austrian *Anschluss* was clinched when Hitler entered a swastika-bedecked Vienna in triumph. Austria was *Osterreich* no more, but the *Ostmark* of the Greater German Reich – and still the Western powers did not act. Czechoslovakia's time had come – and yet again Britain and France capitulated to a 'final territorial request' and 'proposal for a lasting peace' from Hitler in the form of the Munich Agreement on September 30 1938.

That same month – September 1938 – planning at last began for a naval war against Great Britain. After a winter of intense activity, there emerged the famous naval 'Z-plan', accepted by Hitler in January 1939 and given priority over every other armament programme in the Reich. The Z-Plan was basically a six-year programme of accelerated warship construction with the Royal Navy considered the chief competitor. Its basic provisions were:

War with Britain inevitable by 1945; the German fleet to have been raised to a strength of

(a) Six battleships of 56,000 tons;
(b) Two battleships (*Bismarck* and *Tirpitz*) of 42,000 tons;
(c) Three battle-cruisers of 31,000 tons, mounting 15-inch guns, with *Scharnhorst* and *Gneisenau* converted from 11-inch to 15-inch;
(d) Three pocket-battleships (*Deutschland, Admiral Scheer, Graf Spee*);
(e) Two aircraft-carriers (*Graf Zeppelin*, launched in 1938, plus one other);
(f) Five heavy cruisers (*Hipper, Blücher, Prinz Eugen, Seydlitz, Lützow*);
(g) Forty-four light cruisers (of which six were already completed);
(h) Sixty-eight destroyers and ninety torpedo-boats;
(i) Some 249 U-boats – coastal, seagoing, and ocean-going.

The Z-Plan reflects, as nothing else

can, the complete contempt for the reaction of France and Great Britain which had set in by the New Year of 1939. It assumed that the German navy would emerge in 1945 with a strength equal to that of the Royal Navy. It overruled the contention of Dönitz and his sympathisers that the real equalisers in a war with Britain would be the U-boats, and that U-boat production should be given top priority. And it practically ignored the rapidly-deteriorating relationships between Raeder's navy and Göring's Luftwaffe, which in 1939 made any sort of early completion of units of the German Fleet Air Arm highly unlikely.

The summer of 1939 produced one last illusory triumph for Hitler's sledgehammer diplomacy: the Russo-Germany Non-aggression Pact. And in the last week of August the German fleet was brought to operational readiness – as it had been so often since the re-occupation of the Rhineland in 1936 – while the German armies moved into position for the invasion of Poland. When the invasion went in on 1st September 1939, Raeder was confident that despite the tougher attitude shown by the British during the summer, the result would be the

Above: Scouts for the fleet – light cruisers *Nürnberg, Leipzig,* and *Köln. Right:* Blueprint for the future – Hitler views models of planned additions to the fleet

same as before and the Western powers would climb down. The Z-Plan was still forging ahead, and Raeder could measure the present strength of his surface fleet as two battle-cruisers, three pocket-battleships, one heavy cruiser, five light cruisers, and some fifty destroyers and torpedo-boats (with, as a bonus, the old pre-Dreadnought battleships *Schlesien* and *Schleswig-Holstein*). Raeder was sure that after an alert of about a week the fleet would be able to stand down yet again.

But on 3rd September the British ultimatum that Germany must withdraw from Poland or consider herself at war with Britain expired. Raeder's plans collapsed around him as the two countries went to war; his reaction might well have been that of Hitler, who was seen to glare at his Foreign Minister, Ribbentrop, and bark 'What now?'

And that of Göring, who commented, 'If we lose this war, then God have mercy on us!'

From Graf Spee to Narvik

Hitler's attack on Poland on 1st September 1939, and the refusal of the western Allies to allow him to get away with it, spelled the death of the Z-plan and the ruin of Raeder's plans for a balanced High Seas Fleet. Germany could never hope to match the ship-building capacity of Britain and her Allies, and the British lead in capital-ship superiority could never be overtaken. It was a bitter blow to the hopes of the Reich navy; but Raeder's often-quoted lament of 3rd September 1939, 'the surface forces can do no more than to show that they know how to die gallantly', certainly did not represent the war plans of the German navy in 1939. From the start they were offensive, and from the start they achieved their aim: the dislocation of the Allies'

plans to use their naval strength against Germany in the way they had planned.

When the Luftwaffe and the army launched their one-sided campaign against Poland, the German navy had its part to play, too. The last of the old pre-dreadnoughts, *Schleswig-Holstein* and *Schlesien*, may have been so obsolete that their division was given a rear echelon even in the Battle of Jutland in 1916, but they still had 11-inch guns; and in 1939 they used them with deadly effect against the Polish coastal forts at Hela and Westerplatte. In fact these two old war-horses were demonstrating one of the most useful rôles of the battleship in the aircraft age; and the Allies, too, later in the war, would use battleship gun-power time and again to soften up Axis shore defences. In September 1939, however, the modern units of the German fleet were based in western ports, free from Baltic duties, awaiting their turn to strike.

As far as the surface fleet was concerned, the pocket-battleships would be the first in action. Raeder had already despatched them to their 'waiting areas' in mid-Atlantic, *Graf Spee* sailing from Wilhelmshaven on 21st August and *Deutschland* three days later. Two supply-tankers were told off for their maintenance on the high seas, *Altmark* for *Graf Spee* and *Westerwald* for *Deutschland*. The third of the pocket-battleships, *Admiral Scheer*, was kept in home waters for nominal service with Naval Group West, based in Wilhelmshaven: an extensive refit was planned for her. The pocket-battleships at sea had a clear brief. Actual commerce destruction was only regarded as a desirable by-product of their main function: to keep the Allied fleets off-balance. As long as the raiders kept the seas, avoiding action with Allied warships, staying out of trouble, striking where least expected, heavy surface forces would have to accompany every Allied convoy that sailed, thus dissipating the hitting-power of the British Home Fleet and making it easier for further German naval strikes to be sent out.

Graf Spee's operational zone was to be south of the Equator, while *Deutschland* was to hunt in the North Atlantic – but for three weeks Hitler refused to allow the commerce-raiding programme to begin. He hoped for a rapid knock-out against Poland and for a peace settlement with the western Allies; and not until 23rd September did he yield to Raeder's requests for action. The pocket-battleships were unleashed, and it was not before time. The British had taken the offensive from the outset.

***Graf Spee* under way, with after 11-inch turret at full elevation**

On the first two days of the war, the cruiser *Ajax* of the British South American Division had sunk the German merchantmen *Olinda* and *Carl Fritzen* in the South Atlantic, on 3rd and 4th September respectively. Now it was the Germans' turn; and on 30th September Captain Hans Langsdorff of the *Graf Spee* opened his war cruise by sinking the merchantman *Clement* off Pernambuco.

From the outset the Allied dispositions were hampered by uncertainty as to how many raiders were out, and what they were. This uncertainty was enthusiastically fostered by the German captains, who used every possible trick of disguise: false gun turrets to make their ships look like battleships, false nameplates to upset the Allied plotting of the German ships already known to be out – even false 'enemy surface raider' signals. The time-factor, too, worked in the Germans' favour. The crews of captured Allied ships, if not retained as prisoners of war, often took days to reach ports or embassies which could relay accurate news of the German raiders to the Allied admiralties. Thus on 5th October the very day the Allies formed five hunting-groups to comb the Atlantic from every point of the compass, the pocket-battleships put them off-balance, *Graf Spee* capturing the *Newton Beech* some 400 miles northeast of St Helena, and *Deutschland* sinking the *Stonegate* 500 miles east of Bermuda. It was not until 8th November when the masters of the *Clement* and *Stonegate* were released, that the Allies could put the pieces together and deduce that *two* pocket-battleships were out for certain – and even then they thought one of them was *Admiral Scheer*.

By this time – 8th November – *Graf Spee* had sunk the *Huntsman* and *Trevanion* and was heading east to spread alarm and despondency for the Allies in the Indian Ocean. *Deutschland* had sunk the *Lorentz W Hansen* on 14th October – the same day Günther Prien's U-47 got into Scapa Flow and sank the British battleship *Royal Oak* – 400 miles east of Newfoundland, and was recalled to Germany on 1st November. She made the breakthrough into the North Sea without any trouble from the British blockade, and arrived in Kiel on 15th November. Thus the Allied search continued for two German raiders at large in the Atlantic, while one of them was actually heading for home and the other was in the Indian Ocean.

Graf Spee's success in the Indian Ocean was limited to the sinking of the small tanker *Africa Shell* off Lourenço Marques on 15th November – but *Africa Shell*'s crew, allowed to row for the shore, reached land the same day, and the prompt warning that a pocket battleship was loose in the Indian Ocean coincided almost exactly with *Graf Spee*'s change of course to her original hunting-ground near St Helena, sinking the *Doric Star* on 2nd December and the *Tairoa* on the following day. Langsdorff then decided to quit the St Helena area and strike at Allied shipping on the other side of the Atlantic; and on 6th December *Graf Spee* and *Altmark* made their last rendezvous, the warship taking on provisions and fuel, and the supply-ship prisoners from *Tairoa* and *Doric Star*. *Graf Spee* then headed west – towards the River Plate.

Meanwhile the German home fleet had not been idle. On 8th October the battle-cruiser *Gneisenau*, the light cruiser *Köln*, and nine destroyers embarked on a 48-hour sortie off southern Norway. This was an operation very reminiscent of the High Seas Fleet's sorties in the First World War: a sweep to scoop up any Allied merchantmen in the area and destroy any British light units patrolling there – and on no account to get into action with heavier forces. But no forces, heavy or light, were

High seas raider *par excellence*: *Graf Spee* seen from the air

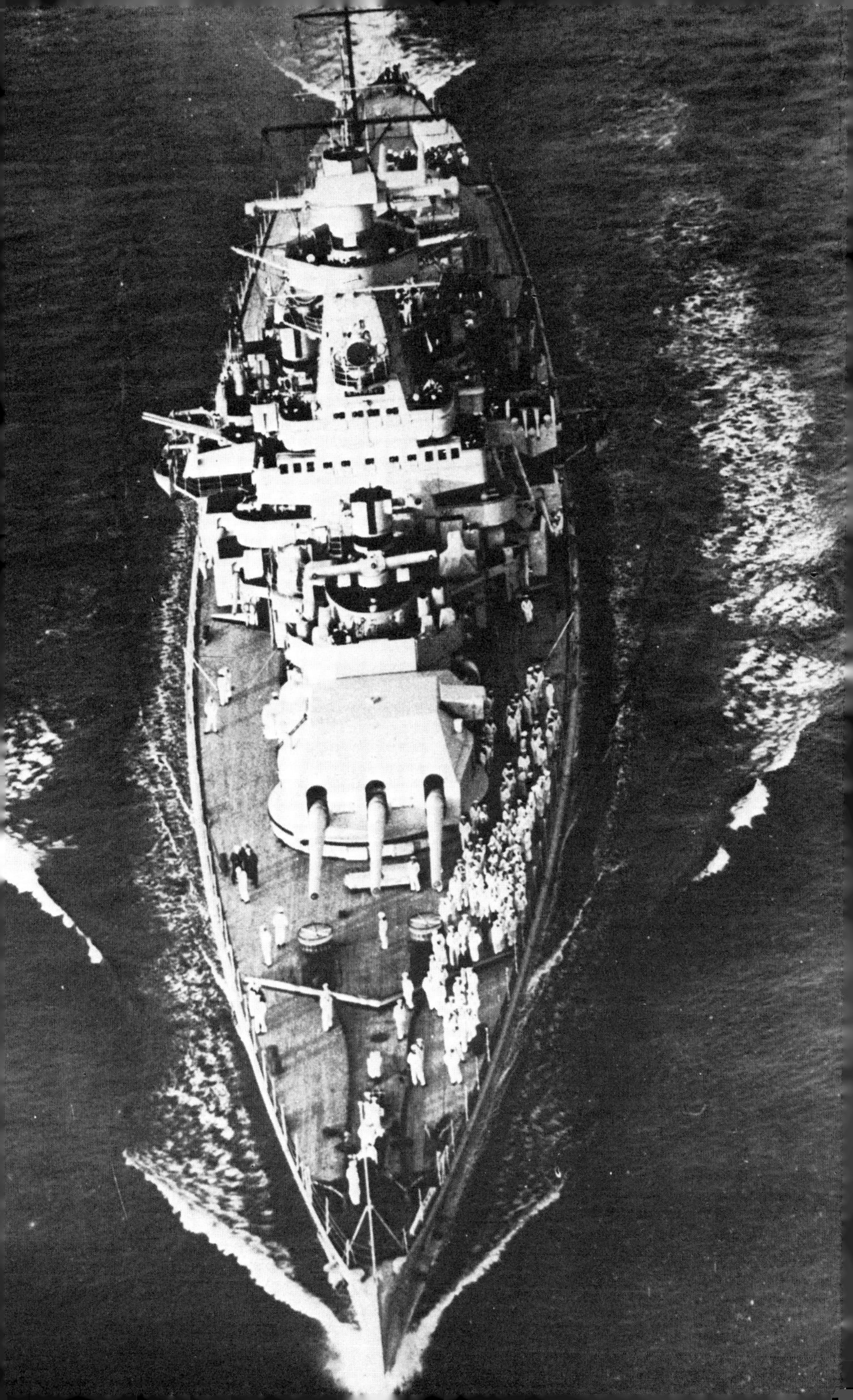

to be found, and the German squadron returned to Kiel on 10th October. The German home fleet's next move was a much more energetic affair, planned after *Deutschland*'s return to take pressure off *Graf Spee*. Vice-Admiral Wilhelm Marschall, Commander of the Fleet, sailed with the battle-cruisers *Scharnhorst* and *Gneisenau* on 21st November to disrupt the pattern of the British dispositions in the North Atlantic. Aided by foul weather – which worked to the advantage of the German navy time and again during the Second World War – the battle-cruisers were still undetected on 23rd November as they headed for their chosen entrance to the Atlantic: the Iceland-Faeroes passage.

As evening came down on the 23rd, *Scharnhorst* sighted a ship which turned out to be the British auxiliary cruiser *Rawalpindi* – hopelessly outclassed by the well-armoured, hard-hitting battle-cruisers with their 11-inch guns, forced to run for her life, but still ready to put up a fight. It was a brief, brutal affair, completely one-sided (though *Rawalpindi* managed to land one hit on *Scharnhorst*, which did little or no damage), lasting fourteen minutes – and followed by two hours of rescue work in which the crews of *Scharnhorst* and *Gneisenau* hunted for survivors in the waters around the *Rawalpindi*'s blazing hulk. *Rawalpindi*'s gallantry was superb, but her defeat was made the sadder because her 'enemy in sight,' signal, originally mentioning a battle-cruiser, was corrected by a second signal identifying her assailant as the *Deutschland* – still thought to be in the North Atlantic. (Such was the state of British Naval Intelligence that as late as June 1941 the British air-crews being briefed for a torpedo strike against *Lützow*, as *Deutschland* had been renamed, were told 'This is the ship that sank the *Rawalpindi*.')

Next on the scene was the British light cruiser *Newcastle*, and Marschall decided it was time to go before the full power of the British Home Fleet could be concentrated against him. He broke away at high speed under cover of smoke, waited for two days in northern waters, and headed south for home down the Norwegian coast, arriving at Wilhelmshaven on 27th November.

Down in the South Atlantic, *Graf Spee* headed west after her rendezvous with *Altmark* on 6th December and took her last victim, the *Streonshalh*, on the 7th. But Langsdorff's luck had run out. Commodore H H Harwood of the British South American Division had reckoned for some time that no pocket-battleship raider could resist the temptation of the dense merchant shipping around the trade-focus of the River Plate. There he patrolled with his lightly-armoured cruiser force *Ajax* and *Achilles* (6-inch guns), and *Exeter* (8-inch guns). He had been forced to detach his fourth cruiser, the 8-inch gun *Cumberland*, to refit in the Falkland Islands – but he held firm to his hunch that after its last successes to the east the German raider would come west, either to the Plate, or to raid the Falklands (as the original Admiral Graf von Spee had tried to do in 1914, after his victory over the British at Coronel). And it was off the River Plate, at dawn on 13th December 1939, that Harwood's three cruisers sighted *Graf Spee*.

It now seems clear that Langsdorff interpreted the cluster of masts spotted by his lookouts as belonging to the escorts of a convoy of merchantmen, headed in to engage, and realised his mistake too late when the distinctive silhouette of *Exeter* – *York* class cruiser, one funnel bigger than the other – materialised over the horizon. Whatever his motives, he decided on battle even when it was clear that he would have no merchantmen as a reward of victory – for three cruisers, however lightly-armed, were not the sort of odds the pocket-battleships had been designed to face. As for Harwood, the question of tactics against such a heavily armed foe as a pocket-battleship was never in doubt. On 12th December he had given his battle orders. 'My policy with three cruisers in company versus one pocket-battleship. Attack at once by day or night. By day act as two units. 1st Division (*Achilles* and *Ajax*) and *Exeter* diverged to permit flank marking. 1st Division will concentrate gunfire . . .' At 0609 hours on the 13th, smoke was sighted; *Exeter* was detached to investigate, and in minutes the signal came back to Harwood, commanding in *Ajax*: '*I think it is a pocket-battleship.*' At 0617 *Graf Spee* opened fire on *Exeter*, who replied at 0620 while *Ajax* and *Achilles* crammed on speed to take the pocket-battleship in flank. The Battle of the River Plate had begun.

There are many excellent detailed accounts of the battle, describing how *Graf Spee*'s 11-inch guns pounded the gallant *Exeter* into a blazing shambles; how the ruined cruiser struggled to stay in the battle, launching torpedoes, firing her last turret by local control until flooding cut off its power; how Langsdorff was never able to concentrate his full broadside against *Exeter* and eliminate her because of the destroyer-like tenacity of the attacks of *Ajax* and *Achilles*; how, at the moment when Harwood was forced to disengage because of the grievous damage to *Ajax*, *Graf Spee* failed to pursue, swung west under cover of smoke, and headed out of the action. The battle died away, became a stern chase; and as the day wore on it became clearer and clearer that Langsdorff was running for port. During the long chase, *Graf Spee* lashed out several times with her 11-inch guns, but *Ajax* and *Achilles* would not withdraw, continuing to herd their opponent towards the Plate; and when the pocket-battleship anchored in Montevideo Roads at 0050 hours on 14th December, they immediately took up patrol stations off the mouth of the roadstead.

Now it was the turn of the diplomats, for Montevideo was a neutral port, and international law demanded that no warship belonging to a belligerent power could stay in a neutral port for over twenty-four hours without being interned. On the British side, a tragi-comic situation came into being, for the first reaction of British Naval attaché, Captain Henry McCall, and the British minister, Mr E Millington-Drake, was that *Graf Spee* must have been severely damaged to have run into port, and that obviously she must be diplomatically chivvied out to sea again before her crew could have the chance to make repairs and render her battle-worthy. But Harwood soon gave them the facts of the matter: that the lion's share of the damage had been suffered by the British ships, and that until *Cumberland*, pounding north from the Falklands at her top speed, could join *Ajax* and *Achilles*, there was every chance of *Graf Spee* slipping out under cover of darkness and escaping.

So now Millington-Drake was forced to change his tune. He ordered the British merchantman *Ashworth* to sail immediately from Montevideo, enabling him to demand the statutory twenty-four hour period before *Graf Spee* might be allowed to sail in pursuit. And the BBC began to spin an immense web of propaganda, describing the mighty fleet of capital ships hastening towards the Plate to annihilate the wretched *Graf Spee* as soon as she came out. By 15th December, *Cumberland* had at last joined hands with *Ajax* and *Achilles* off the roadstead. And the Germans had won an extended time period of seventy-two hours' stay in Montevideo for repairs commencing with the inspection made of her condition by Uruguayan naval authorities, and thus amounting to some ninety hours after first dropping anchor. Also on the 15th, Harwood refuelled his battered cruisers – and Langsdorff presided at the funeral of the *Graf Spee* dead, causing considerable embarrassment to the Nazi propagandists

41

Above: Battle-scarred *Graf Spee* in Montevideo (note shell hole on port bow)
Below: An unspoken comment on Nazi pageantry at the funeral of the *Graf Spee* dead in Montevideo: Langsdorff gives the correct naval salute

by being photographed with his hand in the traditional naval salute, while all around him were giving the Nazi salute (including the priests).

Langsdorff, consulting the Naval High Command in Berlin, was given one positive order: no internment in Uruguay. He could move his ship to the more friendly port of Buenos Aires (risking the chance of clogging her engines' cooling system or of running aground in the narrow, muddy channel), or he could try to break through for home. But British propaganda, for once, was doing its work superbly. Langsdorff was becoming convinced that it had substance, that even if he did break past Harwood's force he could not evade the capital ships which would be covering his route home. The decision was his, and his alone – and at 1700 on the 16th the British gave the decisive twist to his dilemma. They sent another merchantman, the *Dunster Grange*, out of Montevideo, thus ensuring that, with the twenty-four hour rule complicating Langsdorff's seventy-two hour deadline, *Graf Spee* would be compelled to leave in daylight on 17th December.

With, presumably, the armada of British battleships twenty-four hours closer to Montevideo...

It was later calculated that a crowd of three-quarters of a million watched the pocket-battleship creep slowly towards the open sea in the late afternoon of the 17th, with the German merchantman *Tacoma* in company. Harwood had already been told of the transfer of 700 German crewmen and their baggage to the *Tacoma*; he was sure that this indicated that Langsdorff would scuttle his ship. He ordered his cruisers to head inshore, hoping to board the pocket-battleship and dismantle the charges before she could be scuttled – but this was not to be. Langsdorff headed his ship out of the main channel, took off her demolition crew – and stood at the salute when at 2054 hours, exactly at sunset, successive fierce explosions tore the bottom out of the *Graf Spee*, made a flaming wreck of her, and sank her in the mud fringing the harbour channel. Three days later, on 20th December, the German captain wrapped himself in the flag of the Imperial German Navy under which he had fought in the First World War, and shot himself

An excellent campaign, an unexpected battle, a fatal decision to run for shelter – that was the tragedy of Langsdorff, and of the *Graf Spee*. No British merchant seamen had lost their lives during the *Graf Spee*'s war cruise, in which nine ships totalling some 50,000 tons had been sunk. Langsdorff had set the pattern for high seas raiding which would be followed with greater success but no greater honour in later forays. He had chosen to enter a battle which, on paper, he could have won – but he was out-fought, forced off balance by the gallantry and determination of Harwood's flimsy cruisers, and shaken by the loss of thirty-seven of his beloved crew in the action off the Plate. As for material damage, *Graf Spee* had been hit twenty times. Her galleys were wrecked, her bridge badly damaged, and there were several holes in the deck and side-plating, the largest of them six feet square. He knew that he had insufficient ammunition to fight a breakthrough battle off the Plate, and – if the worst came to the worst – scuttle his ship. Given his fears about the opposition waiting for him outside the Plate, one can see why he believed that *Graf Spee* could never have fought another action and then tackle the stormy North Atlantic in winter in a damaged state with a weakened (and demoralised) crew. For the Allies, the destruction of the *Graf Spee* was a brilliant opening to the war at sea, more than compensating for the ignominious loss of the *Royal Oak* in Scapa Flow; for the German High Command, it was a sobering reminder of the strength of British sea-power.

On the very eve of the Battle of the

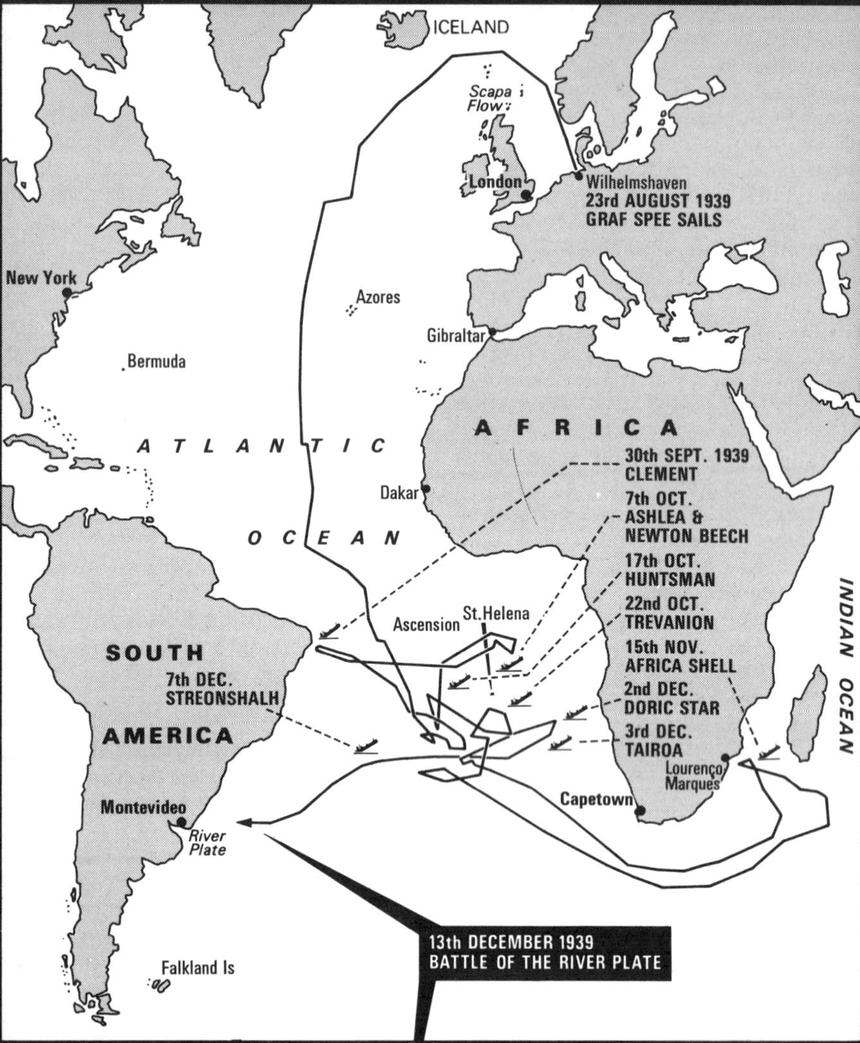
ICELAND
Scapa Flow
London
Wilhelmshaven
23rd AUGUST 1939
GRAF SPEE SAILS
New York
Azores
Gibraltar
Bermuda
AFRICA
ATLANTIC
OCEAN
Dakar
30th SEPT. 1939
CLEMENT
7th OCT.
ASHLEA & NEWTON BEECH
17th OCT.
HUNTSMAN
22nd OCT.
TREVANION
15th NOV.
AFRICA SHELL
2nd DEC.
DORIC STAR
3rd DEC.
TAIROA
Ascension
St. Helena
SOUTH
AMERICA
7th DEC.
STREONSHALH
INDIAN OCEAN
Lourenço Marques
Capetown
Montevideo
River Plate
Falkland Is
13th DECEMBER 1939
BATTLE OF THE RIVER PLATE

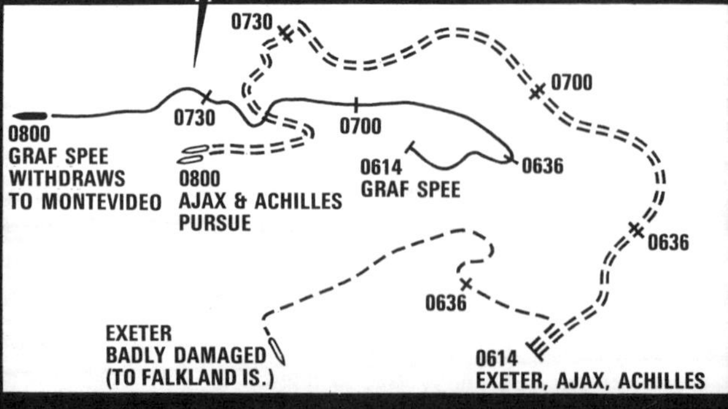
0730
0700
0800
GRAF SPEE
WITHDRAWS
TO MONTEVIDEO
0730
0700
0800
AJAX & ACHILLES
PURSUE
0614
GRAF SPEE
0636
0636
0636
EXETER
BADLY DAMAGED
(TO FALKLAND IS.)
0614
EXETER, AJAX, ACHILLES

River Plate, with the *Graf Spee* saga moving to its climax in the South Atlantic, the German fleet suffered a severe setback in home waters. On the night of 12th December, five German destroyers, escorted by the light cruisers *Köln*, *Leipzig*, and *Nürnberg*, headed across the North Sea to lay a large field of contact mines off the Tyne. At dawn on the 13th the British submarine, *Salmon*, patrolling in the Heligoland Bight, sighted the returning German squadron and attacked. Nine days before, *Salmon* had achieved the rare feat of sinking a U-boat – U-36 – with torpedoes. Now she added to her laurels by hitting both *Nürnberg* and *Leipzig*. Both cruisers struggled back to port, but *Nürnberg* was unserviceable until May 1940 and *Leipzig* until the following December. Thus the German fleet was deprived of two valuable units on the eve of its most daring venture: the assault on Denmark and Norway in the spring of 1940, in which the German fleet played a vital and dramatic rôle.

'Norway is the zone of destiny in this war', Hitler was to pronounce in later years, and while this was a definite over-statement of the priorities of the Third Reich in the Second World War, it was certainly accurate as far as the German navy was concerned. Since the days of Tirpitz and the first High Seas Fleet, the importance of Norway in Germany's maritime strategy had always been obvious. Germany's imports of iron ore were utterly dependent on the sea route down the Norwegian coast from the port of Narvik. In the First World War, the extension of the British blockade into Norwegian territorial waters had been an essential part of Britain's stranglehold on the Reich; and Raeder had always considered the best possible method of circumventing this danger in the event of another war.

Raeder wanted Norway. He wanted bases there – bases which would give him advantages which could enable the Reich navy to outflank the British blockade; bases which would provide admirable sally-ports for Germany's U-boat fleet. Given bases in Norway, Raeder's fleet could ruin the sort of war the British wanted to fight, according to the pattern of the First World War – and it was only to be expected that Raeder was the earliest and most persistent advocate among the German High Command for the seizure of ports in Scandinavia.

To begin with, Hitler favoured Norwegian neutrality. It had an obvious advantage: the German freighters could continue to steam down the Norwegian coast inside Norwegian territorial waters. But as 1939 drew to its close it became evident that an end to this convenient state of affairs was only a matter of time. On 30th November Soviet Russia invaded Finland. Against all expectations, the Finns fought the Red Army to a humiliating standstill, and the Free World rang with applause and proposals for military aid for Finland. This could only be furnished in one way: through Narvik, the Norwegian port at which the German ore freighters took on their cargoes before setting their illicit course for Germany down the Norwegian coast, with the co-operation of Norway and Sweden. An uneasy waiting period began . . .

Churchill, First Lord of the Admiralty in London, had always favoured the laying of minefields in Norwegian waters. To him it was intolerable that enemy shipping should exploit international law to escape the Royal Navy. But his Government thought otherwise. The war, after all, was still in the stage when plans to bomb targets in the Black Forest were rejected because of the threat to private property there, and when both sides were scrupulously – and ostentatiously – ordering their aircrews not to drop bombs on non-military targets. Respect for neutrals – especially small neutrals – was one of the keenest scruples which kept the

45

'Phoney War' phoney. Churchill, however, continued to press for the mining plan, and schemes were in preparation for its implementation, and for parrying the furious German countermoves which could be expected. Unfortunately for the British, Raeder's plans, although similarly hampered, were progressing with a slight lead over those of Churchill, and would come to fruition first.

Raeder found the most unlikely ally in the muddle-headed, pro-Nazi Norwegian, Vidkun Quisling, whose views in the 1930s had won him an unqualified record of failure in Norwegian politics. But Quisling's contact with Alfred Rosenberg, chief ideologist of the Nazi Party, gave him a flying start. Quisling's ludicrous claims for pro-Nazi sympathies in the Norwegian army 'on which he could call' precipitated one of the more extraordinary patterns of intrigue of the Second World War. Raeder welcomed the extremely dubious lever offered by Quisling for the furtherance of the Reich's interests in Scandinavia; he encouraged an audience with the Führer for Quisling, which took place on 14th December; and the original German plan for the seizure of Scandinavia was backed by the full authority of Raeder, despite the misgivings of his staff.

Only the practicalities and the pretext remained, and their resolution deserves some attention here. The resounding success of the Norwegian campaign was so unlikely, given the circumstances of its planning . . .

'I have a reactionary army, an Imperial navy, and a National Socialist air force', Hitler was fond of saying; and the first plans for Norway were framed without the C-in-C of the army (Brauchitsch) being told that soldiers were going to fight in Norway, or the C-in-C of the Luftwaffe (Göring) being told that aircraft were going to be needed to protect, supply, and support the whole affair. Both were kept in the dark for as long as possible while the misgivings of the 'Imperial' (sometimes the Führer would substitute 'Christian') navy were being overborne by Hitler. On 27th January Hitler ordered more detailed plans for the operation, now dubbed *Weserübung* – 'Exercise Weser'. But it was not until the middle of February that the German plans really got going, and the catalyst was in fact the tailpiece to the *Graf Spee*'s cruise: the *Altmark* affair.

Since the *Graf Spee*'s foray had ended so dramatically on 17th December, Captain Dau of the *Altmark*, now without a warship to support, and with 299 British merchant seamen prisoners on board, had been engaged in outwitting the Royal Navy while shaping his course for home. A sound seaman and a wily tactician, he had kept clear of the British until he was sighted on 14th February as he headed into Norwegian territorial waters on the last leg of his voyage home. Churchill's order went out: neutrality or no neutrality, *Altmark* was to be intercepted and her prisoners freed. Captain Philip Vian of the destroyer *Cossack* found *Altmark* lying-up in Jössing Fjord on the night of 16th February. The Norwegians had made the most perfunctory inspection of *Altmark* at Bergen; they told Vian that she carried no weapons and contained no prisoners, but Vian headed into the fjord, boarded her, and discovered that she had both. The prisoners were freed to the historic cry of 'The Navy's here!' and Vian headed for home, while the British Press celebrated, the Norwegian government protested, and Hitler fumed.

He was now absolutely convinced that Norway would not use force to prevent the British from doing what they pleased in Norwegian waters. *Weserübung* must therefore be pressed forward. First, however, as General Jodl pointed out to him on 19th February, it was high time that a Commander-in-Chief for the operation was selected and briefed. Hitler chose

The scorched, twisted wreck of *Graf Spee*, scuttled in the Plate estuary

Above: Trapped *Graf Spee*'s supply-ship *Altmark*, grounded in Jössing Fjord
Below: Captain Dau of the *Altmark* denounces British 'piracy' to neutral pressmen

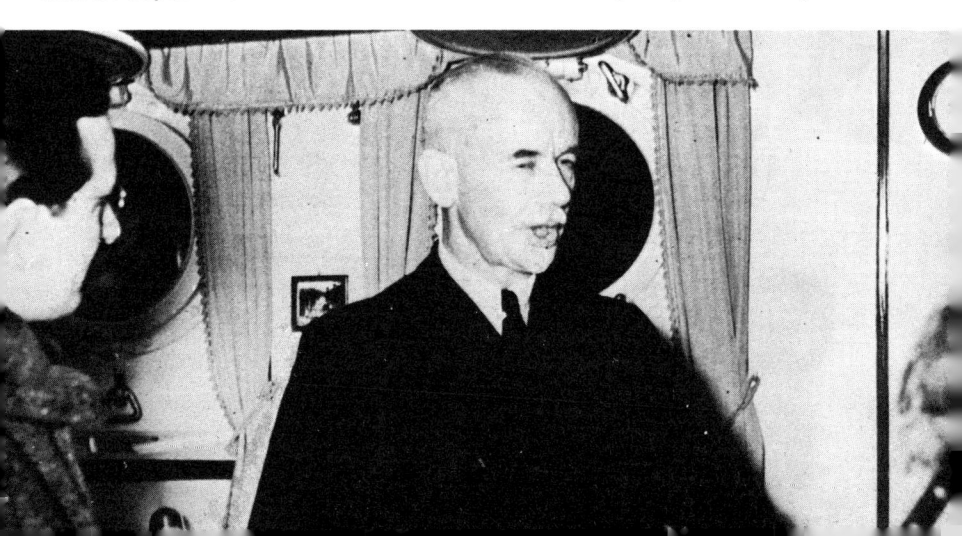

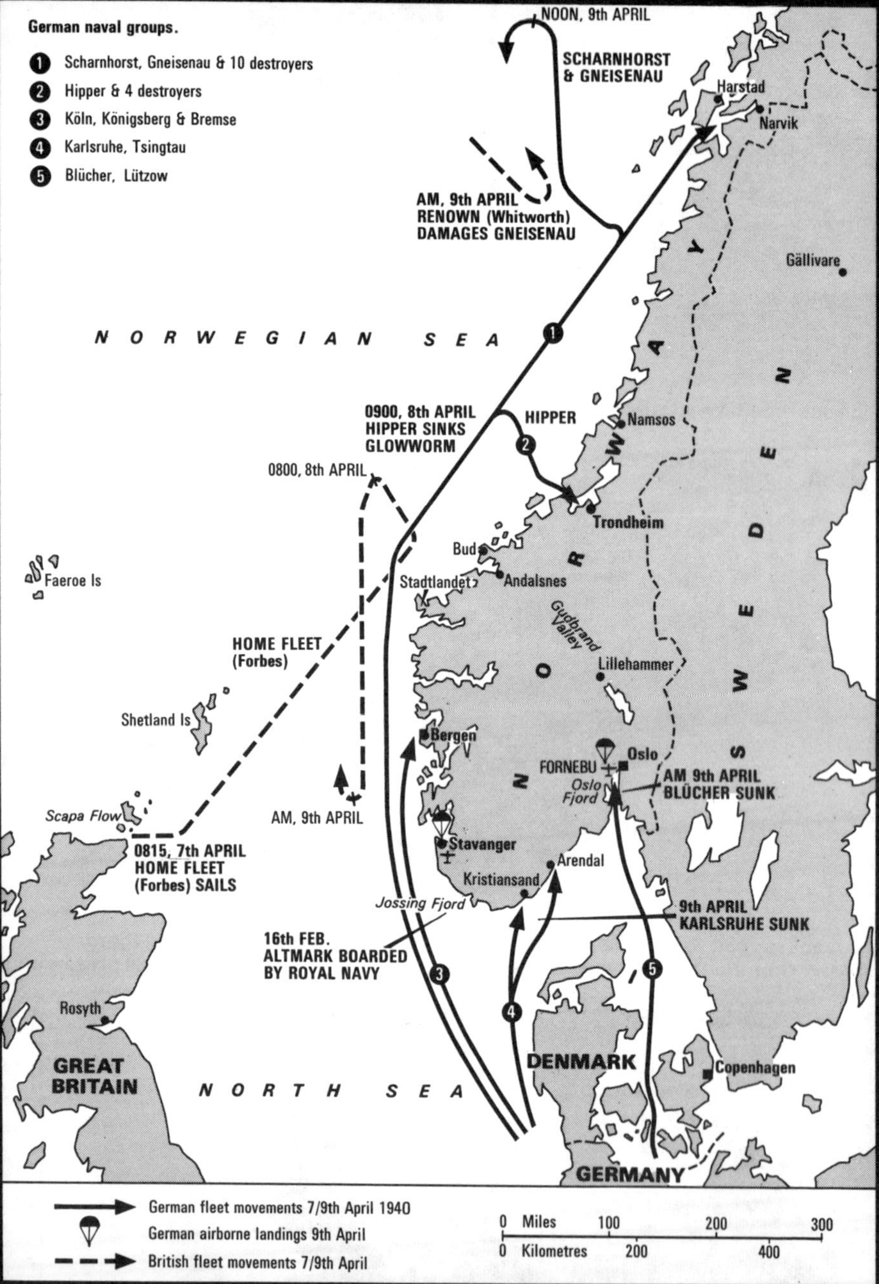
German naval groups.
1 Scharnhorst, Gneisenau & 10 destroyers
2 Hipper & 4 destroyers
3 Köln, Königsberg & Bremse
4 Karlsruhe, Tsingtau
5 Blücher, Lützow
NOON, 9th APRIL
SCHARNHORST & GNEISENAU
Harstad
Narvik
AM, 9th APRIL RENOWN (Whitworth) DAMAGES GNEISENAU
Gällivare
NORWEGIAN SEA
0900, 8th APRIL HIPPER SINKS GLOWWORM
HIPPER
Namsos
0800, 8th APRIL
Trondheim
Bud
Stadtlandet
Andalsnes
Faeroe Is
Gudbrand Valley
HOME FLEET (Forbes)
Lillehammer
NORWAY
SWEDEN
Shetland Is
Bergen
Oslo
FORNEBU
Oslo Fjord
AM 9th APRIL BLÜCHER SUNK
Scapa Flow
AM, 9th APRIL
Stavanger
0815, 7th APRIL HOME FLEET (Forbes) SAILS
Arendal
Kristiansand
Jossing Fjord
9th APRIL KARLSRUHE SUNK
16th FEB. ALTMARK BOARDED BY ROYAL NAVY
Rosyth
DENMARK
Copenhagen
GREAT BRITAIN
NORTH SEA
GERMANY
German fleet movements 7/9th April 1940
German airborne landings 9th April
British fleet movements 7/9th April
0 Miles 100 200 300
0 Kilometres 200 400

General Nikolaus von Falkenhorst, a nominee of Keitel, Chief of the Armed Forces High Command, who had fought in Finland in the First World War and was now commanding an army corps on the Western Front. It was a very surprised Falkenhorst who left the presence on 21st February, having been given five hours to prepare 'plans' for the invasion of a country about which he knew precisely nothing. His reaction, as told at Nuremberg after the war, was simple, if somewhat unmilitary: 'I went out and bought a Baedeker travel guide'. When his five hours were up, he presented himself to the Führer again. His solution was equally straightforward: given the five divisions mentioned by Hitler as a working start, with the navy guaranteeing transport and protection, he proposed to take the five major ports of Norway: Oslo, Stavanger, Bergen, Trondheim, and, of course, the all-important Narvik.

Meanwhile, Generals Brauchitsch and Halder of the Army High Command were busily preparing for the spring offensive on the Western Front in blissful ignorance of these doings. They were astounded, then furious, when Falkenhorst arrived at the Army Chief of Staff's office on 26th February asking for troops – especially mountain units – to tackle Norway. But all recriminations and heart-burning were in vain. Falkenhorst's plans were enthusiastically backed by Hitler, who now stated that Denmark must be taken *en passant* and that troops would be needed for that operation as well. On 1st March, Hitler issued the Directive which put *Weserübung* in business: 'The situation in Scandinavia makes it necessary to prepare for the occupation of Denmark and Norway . . . the crossing of the Danish frontier and the landing in Norway will take place simultaneously.'

The German plans now raced ahead, and the reason was mainly the plight of the Finns, now fighting desperately to stem the relentless Soviet offensive launched by Marshal Timoshenko on 1st February. On 3rd March Hitler laid down that *Weserübung* would take precedence over the Western Front offensive planned for the spring. On the 4th orders went out that after 10th March *Weserübung* should be ready to be put into operation on four days' notice. On 5th March the heads of the three armed services were summoned for final talks with Göring ranting and raging because of his omission from the previous planning. But on 12th March the Finns finally capitulated before the massive Soviet attacks. The 'Winter War' was over – and so, for the time being, was the pressure on *Weserübung*, whose planning was by now four-fifths complete.

But although both for the Allies and for Germany a pretext for intervention in Norway had been cut away by the Finnish armistice, the urgency of the German iron ore traffic remained as keen as ever. On 26th and 29th March Raeder urged Hitler to decide on an early invasion date for Norway. Bad weather was essential to screen the planned German naval movements; on the other hand, the severe winter of 1939–40 meant that the Great Belt, between Denmark's offshore islands, would not be free of ice until the end of the first week in April. On 2nd April the die was cast: *Weserübung* would go in on 9th April, with the first supply-merchantmen setting out along the Norwegian coast for northern waters on the 3rd.

Meanwhile, in the Allied camp, events were running a course which could only result in direct collision with the German plans. On 2nd March the French Premier Daladier had forced the Allies' arm by pledging 50,000 French troops for Finland's aid. Ten days later – the very day of the Finnish armistice – the British Cabinet decided to revive their sketchy plans for military landings in Norway, first at Narvik and Trondheim, then at Stavanger and Bergen, plans which were naturally shelved

49

when the news of the Finnish armistice came in. But the failure to help Finland in time proved fatal to Daladier. On 21st March a new French government was formed under Reynaud. He and Churchill thought the same way. The war had reached a deadlock. The result: Germany's trade must be hit, hard and fast. The sequel: Churchill's long dreamed-of mining plan, 'Wilfred', two British naval groups which would mine Norwegian territorial waters off Bud and Stadtlandet. The date for this was set for 5th April, later postponed until the 8th. And it was on the 8th that the Norwegian campaign opened with the first clash between the British and German navies.

The German heavy forces had sailed on 2nd April. *Scharnhorst* and *Gneisenau*, the most powerful German warships available, were to be the bait which would keep the British Home Fleet away from the Norwegian coast while the landings were going in. Ten destroyers would put 2,000 troops ashore at Narvik; the heavy cruiser *Hipper*, with four destroyers, would land 1,700 more at Trondheim. The light cruisers *Köln* and *Königsberg*, with the gunnery training-ship *Bremse*, would cope with Bergen, landing 900 men. The light cruiser *Karlsruhe* and the depôt-ship *Tsingtau* would land 1,100 troops at Kristiansand and Arendal. And Oslo, the capital, would be tackled by a landing force of 2,000, covered by the *Hipper*'s sister-ship *Blücher* and the pocket-battleship *Lützow* (as *Deutschland* had by now been renamed, due to Hitler's obsession that no warship named after the Fatherland should be lost). The Luftwaffe would cope with Stavanger with a paratroop drop, and airborne troops would also go in to clinch matters at Oslo. The key ports and airfields thus in German hands, army columns would then probe inland, mop up any resistance from the Norwegian army, and join hands to complete the 'peaceful' occupation of the country.

Meanwhile, the British plan for 'Wilfred' was also under way. (It involved a supplementary plan – 'R4' – under which Stavanger, Bergen, Trondheim, and Narvik would be seized if the Germans reacted to the mining operation by moving against Norway). Like the Germans, the British had provided capital-ship protection for the main operation: the elderly battle-cruiser *Renown* (Admiral Whitworth, responsible to the C-in-C Home Fleet, Admiral Forbes), screened by four destroyers: *Hyperion*, *Hero*, *Greyhound*, and *Glowworm*. And it was the latter ship which made first contact with *Weserübung*'s shielding warships.

Glowworm had parted company from the main force to search for a man overboard, and failed to rejoin because of thick weather. Early on 8th April she ran straight into the *Hipper* off Trondheim. Her captain, Lieutenant-Commander Roope, failed to shake off the German cruiser and soon found himself under heavy fire. Battered by 8-inch shells, *Glowworm* was soon ablaze; and Commander Roope earned a posthumous VC by ramming his ship into *Hipper*. *Glowworm* was lost, but *Hipper* was winged – 528 tons of water flooded in through a 120-foot gash in her side, and she took on a four-degree list to starboard. Yet *Hipper*'s vitals were unharmed, and she was able to carry out her mission at Trondheim. The same day, the Polish submarine, *Orzel*, torpedoed and sank the German troop-carrier *Rio de Janeiro*. Surviving German troops taken ashore made no bones about the fact that they were on their way to Bergen to 'protect' Norway from British aggression – but, incredibly, no immediate alert was ordered by the Norwegian government.

All this was unknown to Admiral Whitworth in *Renown* when, on the morning of 9th April, he suddenly sighted *Scharnhorst* and *Gneisenau*, fifty miles off Narvik, in wild weather. The British were determined to pre-

50

Above: Pygmy and giant – *Glowworm* trails a pall of smoke as she closes on *Hipper*
Below: Gallant defiance – *Glowworm*'s blazing hull sinks after ramming *Hipper*

Strike in the north: German destroyers head up Narvik Fjord in line-ahead

vent heavy German warships from getting out into the Atlantic; the German commander (Vice-Admiral Günther Lütjens, who had temporarily replaced Marschall as Fleet Commander while the latter was on sick leave) was under orders to lure British battle units away from the Norwegian coast. He ran; *Renown* gave chase. There was a brief gunnery duel, in which *Renown* landed three 15-inch shells on *Gneisenau*, ruining her fire-control system and knocking out her forward 11-inch turret. In the foul weather repeated squalls screened the ships from each other; the Germans worked up to full speed and *Renown* soon lost contact. German strategy had triumphed over British tactics: for the price of one damaged battle-cruiser the Germans had prevented *Renown* from closing the Norwegian coast and savaging the German invasion forces. For this was D-Day for *Weserübung* – and Narvik had already fallen to Commodore Paul Bonte's ten destroyers, which had smashed the Norwegian coast-defence ships *Eidsvold* and *Norge* and landed their troops, who took the port and town without trouble.

Down at Trondheim, *Hipper* and her four destroyers had also done their job. They used vague Morse-blinker signals in English to keep the coast batteries guessing, and it worked. Only one battery opened fire, but *Hipper*'s gunfire soon silenced it, and the German troops swarmed ashore, took the town, and overran the batteries. There was stiffer resistance at Bergen, where *Bremse* and *Königsberg* were both damaged by gunfire from the shore. *Königsberg* was stopped dead, and aircraft of the British Fleet Air Arm attacked and sank her the next morning as she lay alongside Bergen pier. Stavanger fell without difficulty to the German paratroops, and the Luftwaffe was soon operating from this vital airfield. With Luftwaffe help, the naval attack on Kristiansand succeeded at the third attempt, and by noon both Kristiansand and Arendal were in German hands.

But at Oslo there was near disaster. All the approaches to Norwegian ports involved a considerable amount of bluff by the German warships, and at Oslo the bluff was called. As the heavy cruiser *Blücher* and the pocket-battleship *Lützow* steamed into the Drøbak Narrows in Oslo Fjord, the alert Norwegian gunners opened up at point-blank range, crippling *Blücher*. Two torpedoes from a shore battery finished her off, and she sank with heavy loss of life to her crew and to the German troops she was carrying. The Oslo invasion force, now under command of the captain of *Lützow*, withdrew from the Narrows and landed its remaining troops ten miles down the fjord. Thanks to brilliant work by the Luftwaffe, Oslo and the neighbouring Fornebu airfield fell later on the 9th, but the delay enabled the Norwegian Royal Family and Government to escape inland, taking the country's gold reserves with them.

Despite the loss of *Blücher* and the immobilisation of *Königsberg*, the first day of *Weserübung* had been a brilliant success. Denmark had been overrun without resistance. The Danish government had accepted subjugation; its opposite numbers in Norway were determined to fight on, but they were fugitives up-country. All the major Norwegian ports had fallen. And with the vital airfields in German hands, the invasion could proceed under the broad umbrella of Luftwaffe air cover, which the British, with their distant bases and outmoded aircraft, could not hope to challenge. The only serious counter-offensive the British could mount must lie with the Royal Navy – and it soon came.

By noon on the 10th the British Home Fleet was concentrating fast. Admiral Forbes, the C-in-C, had with him three battleships, *Rodney*, *Warspite*, and *Valiant*, the aircraft-carrier *Furious*, and the heavy cruisers *York*, *Devonshire*, and *Berwick*. To the north,

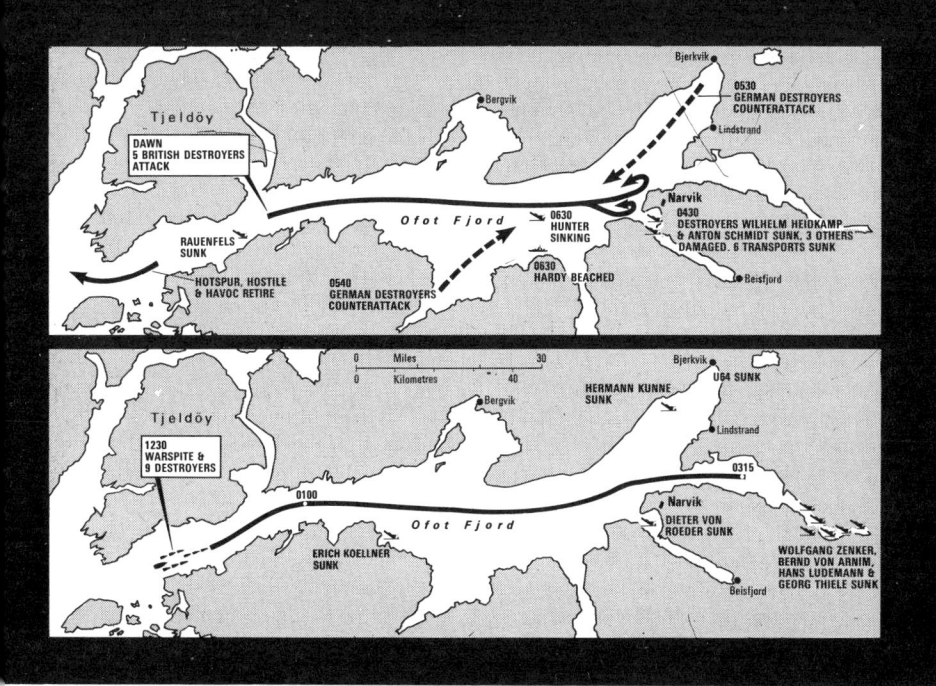

Admiral Whitworth in *Renown* had been joined by her sister battle-cruiser *Repulse*, and he also had Captain Bickford's 20th Destroyer Flotilla and Captain Warburton-Lee's 2nd Destroyer Flotilla. Whitworth's eye was already on Narvik, and so was that of Forbes. On the morning of the 9th, Forbes ordered Warburton-Lee to go to Narvik 'to make certain that no enemy troops land'. At noon, however, the British Admiralty intervened, breaking in with the news of the fall of Narvik and ordering Warburton-Lee direct to take his destroyers into Narvik's Ofot Fjord and attack any warships and merchantmen he found there. By 1751 hours on the 9th Warburton-Lee had sounded out the German strength at Narvik (which was sadly underestimated) from the Norwegian pilot station at Tranöy before entering the fjord, and he signalled back to Whitworth and Forbes: '*Intend attacking at dawn high water*'.

And at dawn on the 10th attack he did. The destroyers *Hardy*, *Hunter*, and *Havock* sailed up the fjord and sank Bonte's flagship *Wilhelm Heidkamp*, and the *Anton Schmidt*, damaging three other destroyers in the same attack. *Hotspur* and *Hostile* weighed in for a second attack, which sank six transports. But the other five German destroyers were well deployed up the branching side-fjords and came in for a savage counterattack, trapping Warburton-Lee's gallant force. Warburton-Lee was killed (earning the Royal Navy's second posthumous VC of the Norwegian campaign), his flagship *Hardy* was knocked out, and *Hotspur* badly damaged. Luckily for the British the victorious German destroyers did not press home their attacks, and by 0630 the First Battle of Narvik was over. The British retreated down Ofot Fjord and sank the cargo ship *Rauenfels* (carrying most of the German landing-force's ammunition) on their way out. Both sides had lost two destroyers, but the Germans had three more damaged against the damaged *Hotspur*, and had lost six valuable supply vessels as well, quite apart from the ammunition-ship. Admiral Forbes,

Success for *Weserübung*: *Gneisenau*, *Hipper*, and German seaplanes keep watch in Trondheim harbour

with such abundant proof of the German strength in Narvik, prepared for a second attack – this time with battleship support.

10th April saw other successes for the British, as the German warships, their tasks accomplished at their targets in Norway, headed for home. The submarine *Truant* caught the light cruiser *Karlsruhe* on her way back to Germany from Kristiansand and damaged her so badly that she had to be sunk by her escorts. *Lützow*, heading for Kiel from Oslo, was torpedoed by the submarine *Spearfish*. Seriously hurt, she was towed back to Germany but was out of action for twelve months. Elsewhere, however, the story for the British was not so good. Admiral Forbes' air strikes from the carrier *Furious* against Trondheim did no damage, and his ships failed to prevent *Hipper* from escaping by the narrowest of margins and joining hands with the returning *Scharnhorst* and *Gneisenau* at 0830 on the 11th. They evaded the massive air strike force (totalling ninety-two aircraft) sent against them – aided by foul weather – and reached Wilhelmshaven on the evening of the 12th.

That same day, 12th April, saw the preparations for the Second Battle of Narvik, which took place on the 13th. Admiral Whitworth took the *Warspite* up Ofot Fjord with nine destroyers and completed the job which Warburton-Lee had begun with such gallantry. The German destroyers were hunted down and smashed, one by one. By nightfall on the 13th none of the original ten German destroyers sent to Narvik was left, and U-64 had been sunk as well. The U-boats sent by Dönitz to fend off such a British naval counterblow failed completely, due to inefficient torpedoes (which provoked Günther Prien, ace commander of U-47, to make his famous complaint to Dönitz that he could not be expected to fight 'with a dummy rifle'). On 10th April the Germans in Narvik had lost the bulk of their ammunition; on the 11th their motor transport went, sunk in the transport *Alster;* on the 13th their warship screen was annihilated. Had the British been able to land the troops originally earmarked for

Narvik by Plan 'R4', their job would have been straightforward. As it was, the Germans were given a reprieve.

Until now, Admiral Forbes's task had been offensive: to contain and wherever possible destroy the German spearheads in Norway. From now on he was to be distracted by the needs of defence – defence for the Allied land counterattack now being belatedly prepared.

The first Allied landings in Norway went in on 14th April. There were two objectives: Trondheim and Narvik, and despite the British run of success at Narvik it was the Trondheim attack which got under way first. The idea was to attack from bases at Namsos and Andalsnes, on either side of Trondheim. The Namsos force got nowhere; the Andalsnes force pushed down the Gudbrandsdal valley to Lillehammer, met the advancing Germans head-on, and fell back on Andalsnes after a twenty-four-hour battle. Complete German air superiority and the Allied lack of light tanks, even of artillery, made retirement from Namsos and Andalsnes inevitable by 27th April. Both bases had been evacuated by 1st May. As for Narvik, the Anglo-French force, increasingly paralysed by mounting German air attacks, was finally influenced by the Allied failures at Namsos and Andalsnes, which accelerated the Germans' northward advance, and by the new urgency created by the German offensive in the West, which opened on 10th May. Narvik finally fell on 28th May, but the Allies could do little but wreck the port as thoroughly as possible. Their evacuation of Narvik on 8th June followed the 'deliverance of Dunkirk' by exactly four days.

Churchill has summed up the dismal story of the land campaign in typical style. 'At Narvik a mixed and improvised German force barely six thousand strong held at bay for six weeks some twenty thousand Allied troops, and, though driven from the town, lived to see them depart . . . We divided our resources between Narvik and Trondheim and injured both our plans. At Namsos there was a muddy waddle forward and back. Only in an expedition to Andalsnes did we bite. The Germans, although they had to cover some hundreds of miles of rugged, snow-clogged country, drove us back in spite of gallant episodes.

55

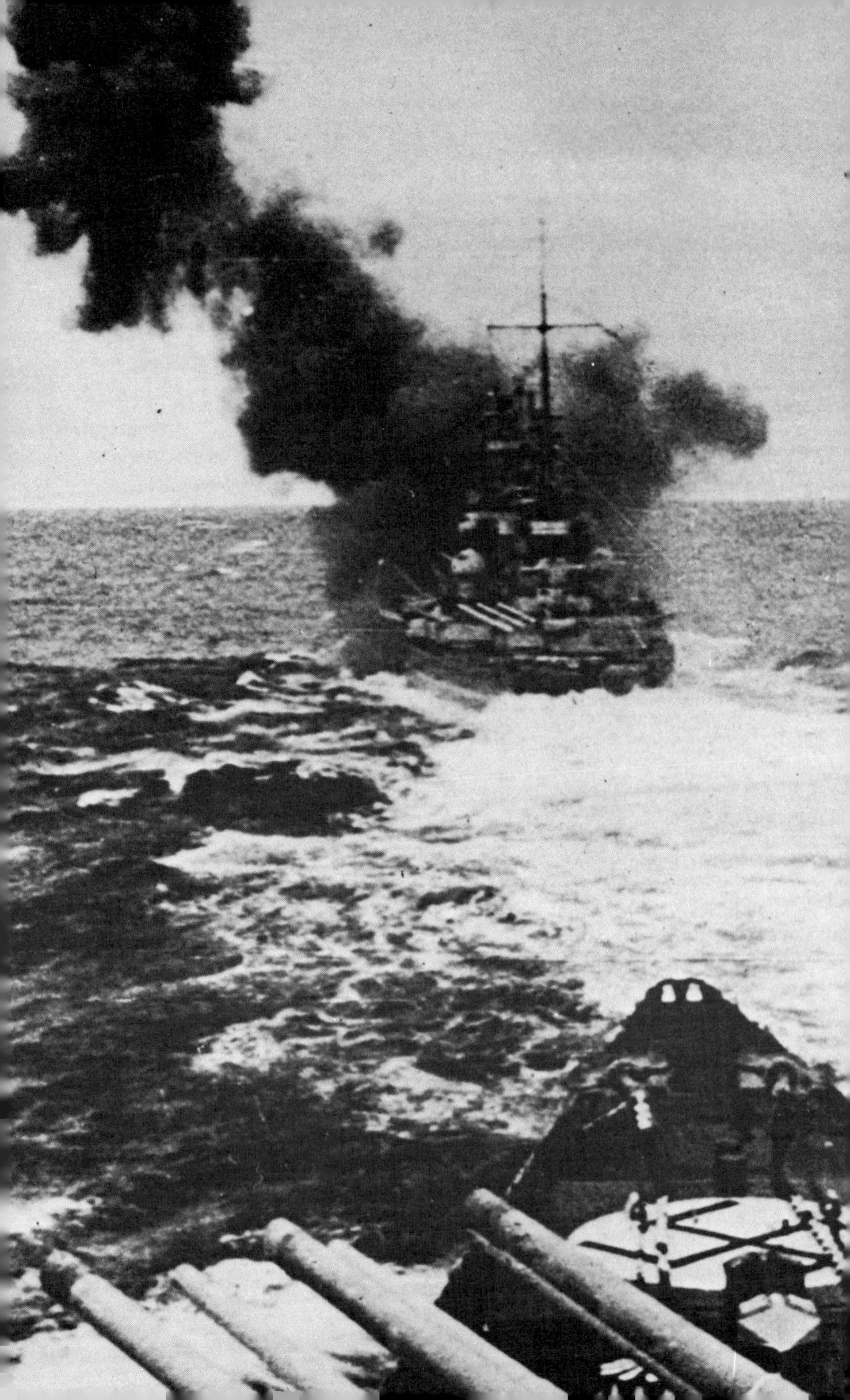

We, who had the command of the sea and could pounce anywhere on an undefended coast, were out-paced by the enemy moving by land across very large distances in the face of every obstacle.'

The German navy had done its job in landing the army in Norway; the army completed its task superbly; and the Germans clinched their triumph in Norway with a final victory at sea. By late May the heavy ships had been patched up sufficiently to admit another sortie in force, and on 4th June Admiral Marschall, back in command of the fleet, sailed from Kiel with *Scharnhorst, Gneisenau, Hipper*, and four destroyers, under orders to bombard the British base at Harstad, near Narvik. On the 7th, Marschall received Luftwaffe reports of two groups of ships, and he decided on his own initiative to tackle the southernmost one. On the morning of the 8th he was rewarded by sinking the tanker *Oil Pioneer*, the empty troopship *Orama*, and the escort trawler *Juniper* – scrupulously sparing the hospital ship *Atlantis*, which was in company. The same day he sent *Hipper* and the destroyers into Trondheim because of fuelling difficulties, and pressed on with his cruise.

The German battle-cruisers then scored the greatest victory by German surface warships since Admiral Graf von Spee's victory at Coronel in 1914. At 1600 hours on the 8th *Scharnhorst* sighted the aircraft-carrier *Glorious* and attacked. Two British destroyers, *Acasta* and *Ardent*, were with *Glorious*; all three ships were sunk, but *Acasta* scored a torpedo hit on *Scharnhorst* which damaged her badly seconds before she herself was overwhelmed by the German battle-cruiser's shells. *Scharnhorst* and *Gneisenau* headed back to Trondheim, where they survived a Fleet Air Arm bombing attack on 13th June. On the 20th *Gneisenau* and *Hipper* sortied from Trondheim, feinting towards Iceland to cover *Scharnhorst*'s limping retreat home to Germany – but *Gneisenau* was hit yet again, this time by a torpedo from the British submarine *Clyde*. Both ships eventually followed *Scharnhorst* back to Germany, via Trondheim. The Norwegian campaign was over.

It did not end, however, without a flurry of recriminations in Berlin and a change of Fleet Commanders. Raeder severely criticised Marschall for using his initiative and not sticking to the letter of his orders, forgetting that this sin is a prime ingredient in the 'Nelson touch'. Convinced that the Fleet Commander should have full tactical initiative, Marschall resigned. He was replaced as Fleet Commander by Günther Lütjens, who had so successfully drawn *Renown* away from Narvik on the first day of *Weserübung*.

Weserübung had succeeded. Hitler's High Seas Fleet had got its Norwegian bases – most of them badly damaged but repairable – and Germany's iron ore trade had been saved while Allied trade with Scandinavia was now decisively severed. But the price was high: one heavy cruiser (*Blücher*), two light cruisers (*Königsberg* and *Karlsruhe*); ten new destroyers ('sunk at Narvik' is the epitaph of the *Von Roeder* and *Leberecht Maass* class destroyers, which lost five apiece), and four U-boats had been sunk. *Scharnhorst, Gneisenau, Lützow*, and *Hipper* were all dockyard cases. After *Weserübung*, Raeder's navy was thoroughly mauled, much in the same way as the German capture of Crete mauled the Luftwaffe's paratroop arm in May 1941.

Yet Norway was no Pyrrhic victory for the German fleet. The months of 1940–41 would see the greatest successes of the surface ships, winning unheard-of triumphs on the high seas – and ending in one of the greatest dramas in the history of ocean warfare.

Triumphant tailpiece: *Gneisenau*, seen from *Scharnhorst*, fires an 11-inch salvo against the *Glorious*

The surface raiders strike

The fall of Norway gave Germany naval bases as far as the North Cape; the fall of France gave her the great Biscay ports – Brest, St Nazaire, Lorient. With this revolutionary state of affairs – of which few German naval strategists had ever dared to dream – the opportunities for ocean-going surface raids on commerce by the German Fleet were transformed. The blockade on Germany could now be punctured to the north and south of the British Isles. In the summer of 1940, the long-term prospects of the German navy – both for the surface Fleet and for the U-boat arm – had never looked better.

Between July and September 1940, however, all eyes were focussed on the English Channel. The great gamble of invading Britain – Operation 'Sea Lion' – dominated German planning. For the German navy, it was a comparatively simple matter. The losses and damage suffered during the Norwegian campaign meant that the navy's rôle would be limited to that of providing light flotilla escorts and tugs for the troop-carriers and invasion barges. The onus was placed fairly and squarely on Göring's Luftwaffe. If German air power could break the Royal Air Force, dominate the Channel, and guarantee immunity for the invasion fleet from British air *and* naval attacks, 'Sea Lion' might be considered. If not, it would never stand a chance. Hence the Battle of Britain. By mid-September it was evident that British air power was unbroken; with autumn approaching, and the inevitability of boisterous weather in the Channel which would complicate the shipping of troops still further, the deadline was drawn. On 17th September 1940, Hitler postponed 'Sea Lion' indefinitely. For Raeder, it was an unparalleled relief. Now he could concentrate on how best to exploit the strategical prizes won by Germany's victories in Scandinavia and France.

Orama, victim of the *Hipper*

When the Z-Plan was ruined by the outbreak of war, the German navy immediately issued orders for the conversion of light merchantmen into armed commerce raiders, and work on several of these vessels had continued throughout the winter of 1939–40. By the spring of 1940 the first of them were ready for sea, and Raeder hoped that they would be as effective in keeping the Royal Navy off-balance as the big ships had already shown they could be. His hopes were soon to be abundantly fulfilled.

The disguised merchant raiders were extraordinary ships, each one of them a floating Pandora's box of tricks. They were chosen primarily not for their speed, but for their endurance. Secondly, they were invariably nondescript in appearance – the more nondescript the better. Thirdly, they had to be masters of disguise – not merely relying on false nationality-flags and quick-change nameplates, but using telescopic funnels and masts, dummy deck-cargoes and superstructure – even, on occasion, women's dress for some of the crew to add to the appearance of a peaceful passenger-carrying merchantman.

Fourthly, and most important, every one of them was as deadly as a cruiser. In a way, they used the tactics of the 'Q-ships' in the First World War; but whereas the 'Q-ships' looked innocent to lure unsuspecting U-boats within range of their guns, the disguised merchant raiders looked innocent to get within range of their unsuspecting victims. They were built for the unobtrusive offensive. They carried between six to eight 5.9-inch guns, not to mention light and heavy machine guns, torpedo-tubes, mines, and either one or two aircraft for reconnaissance. All in all, they were a far more worrying prospect to the British Admiralty than orthodox warships. They were harder to identify, harder to track down, and they did much more damage on aggregate. They were maintained and supplied

59

Disguised merchant raiders. *Above: Komet* (sank 42,959 tons)
Below: Atlantis, most successful of them all (sank 145,697 tons)

Above: Thor, victor over three Allied merchant cruisers (sank 83,000 tons)
Below: Pinguin, which savaged the Antarctic whaling fleets (sank 136,551 tons)

from Germany with very great efficiency, with the result that they could make cruises of well over a year; to take two examples, *Orion* ('Raider A', as the British Admiralty designated her) was out for 510 days, while *Komet* ('Raider B') was at sea for fifteen months. Nine of these ocean-going pests eventually reached the high seas; and six of them sailed between March and December 1940.

The most famous of them all, *Atlantis*, sailed on 31st March 1940. *Orion* was next out, on 6th April; her departure was part of the *Weserübung* venture, and her first task was to help distract the British during the fight for Norway by making a kill in the North Atlantic and sending out a false 'attacked by pocket-battleship' distress signal. Then came *Widder* (5th May), *Thor* and *Pinguin* (mid-June), and then, on 9th July, *Komet*, which made the most remarkable début of all. Assisted by three ice-breakers provided by Soviet Russia, *Komet* made the North-East Passage along the Siberian coast, reaching the Pacific via the Bering Strait after a two-month voyage. These six marauders the Germans called the 'first wave'; a 'second wave' was planned, of which the first, *Kormoran*, broke out into the North Atlantic in mid-December 1940.

Atlantis (Captain Bernhard Rogge) was under orders to keep on the move, making unexpected appearances at widely-separated points. After ten days in the North Atlantic she headed south to try her luck on the Freetown-Cape Town shipping lane. There, disguised as a Japanese freighter, she sank the British *Scientist* on 3rd May before heading into the Indian Ocean, now arrayed as a Dutch cargo steamer. Thus disguised, she sank the Norwegian tanker *Tirrana* on 10th June, and then settled down to work the Australian trade routes and the Indian Ocean. By 20th September, when Rogge decided to head east, *Atlantis* had been at sea for six months and had beaten *Graf Spee*'s tonnage

Bernhard Rogge of *Atlantis*

score, having sunk nine ships of about 66,000 tons. By the end of 1940 the score of *Atlantis* had risen to thirteen ships of nearly 94,000 tons, and she was lying-up at the island of Kerguelen, refitting herself, her cruise still far from over.

After securing her first victim – the British *Haxby* – in the North Atlantic on 24th April, *Orion* headed for the Pacific via Cape Horn. There her first operation, on the night of 13th June, was to lay 228 mines off Auckland, New Zealand, one of which sank the bullion-ship *Niagara* with about £2,500,000 in gold ingots (subsequently recovered in a brilliant salvage operation). *Orion* then moved to the Australia-Panama shipping route, capturing the Norwegian *Tropic Star* on 19th June, which she sent off as a prize to France. But *Tropic Star* was intercepted by a British submarine, and as she had prisoners from *Haxby* on board, the British Admiralty – four months late – got its first definite information about *Orion*'s cruise. *Orion* sank the *Tukarina* on 20th August after a stiff fight in the Coral Sea; the cruiser *Achilles*, veteran of the Battle of the River Plate, was sent off to hunt for the raider, but without success, for *Orion* was now off the coast of southern Australia.

In October *Orion* moved to the Japanese-held Marshall Islands and joined forces with the *Komet*. Together they sank the liner *Rangitane* (27th November), attacked the phosphate-producing island of Nauru (7th–8th December), and sank four phosphate ships of about 21,000 tons. Both raiders returned to the Marshalls for supplies, and then parted company. By the New Year, *Orion* had been 268 days at sea and moved to the Marianas on 12th January 1941, to refit from two supply ships, which took four weeks. *Komet* meanwhile attacked Nauru again on 27th December, destroying the phosphate plant and oil tanks, before heading south round New Zealand to meet *Pinguin* and a supply-ship at Kerguelen in March 1941. Unsuccessful as a solo operator, *Komet* could claim half-shares in seven ships of about 43,000 tons as a partner of *Orion*.

Widder, third raider in the German 'first wave', limited her operations to the Atlantic. Between 19th May, when she broke out into the North Atlantic via the Denmark Strait, and 31st October, when she ended her cruise by returning to Brest, *Widder* ran up the score of ten ships totalling 58,645 tons. But her cruise was marred by the ruthlessness of her Captain, Helmuth von Rückteschell. He tended to open fire after stopping his victims and was not over-zealous in picking up survivors from ships he had sunk far from shore. Rückteschell's conduct tarnished the otherwise high reputation of the German navy – and it was not forgotten. Rückteschell found himself on trial as a war criminal in 1947, and he died in prison.

Like *Widder*, *Thor*'s cruise covered the Atlantic only. It was on this cruise that the formidable strength of the German disguised merchant raiders was convincingly shown. After accounting for six victims in her

Helmuth von Rückteschell of *Widder*

first month at sea, *Thor* was brought to action by the Armed Merchant Cruiser *Alcantara* (detached by Harwood, victor of the River Plate, an admiral now, but still commanding the South American Division). In a short, violent battle on 28th July, 600 miles from the coast of Brazil near the small island of Trinidade, *Thor* outfought and out-gunned the *Alcantara* and mauled her badly. The German raider suffered minimal damage and proved that she could fire extremely rapid and accurate broadsides. Captain Otto Kähler then took his ship out into the South Atlantic for repairs and replenishment from a supply ship. By early September *Thor* was ready for action again, and scored two more victims by the end of October.

Thor now had to repeat her performance during the *Alcantara* action. On 5th December, she met another Armed Merchant Cruiser, the *Carnarvon Castle*. She missed the British ship with a couple of torpedoes, but slammed her repeatedly with gunnery salvoes sometimes only six seconds apart. After an hour's battering, the *Carnarvon Castle* retreated, badly damaged, and the battle was over. *Thor*'s cruise continued, though she

63

Otto Kähler of *Thor*

drew no more blood in 1940. She had proved herself definitely superior to the British merchant cruisers, and was in fact the only disguised German raider to fight them.

Fifth ship of the German 'first wave', *Pinguin* followed *Thor* through the Denmark Strait on 30th June. She too, began operations in the Atlantic, sinking her first victim near Ascension on 31st July, then moving to the southern Indian Ocean. There the hunting was good. Between 26th August *Pinguin* accounted for six valuable ships, four of them being tankers. One of them, the Norwegian tanker *Storstad*, was taken into service. Captain Felix Krüder decided to convert her into an auxiliary minelayer, renaming her *Passat*. The two ships laid many mines in the waters off Australian and Tasmanian ports, and the Bass Strait was also mined. Early in November, *Pinguin* and *Passat* came west again, returning to the area where the early captures of the cruise had been made. Four more ships were accounted for – three of them being British refrigerator-merchantmen. As 1940 drew to a close, *Pinguin* was heading south towards the Antarctic Circle, bent on hunting down Allied whaling ships.

Distracted by the fall of France, the danger of invasion, and Italy's entry into the war, on 10th June, which pinned down vital ships in the Mediterranean, the British could do little to counter the German raiders in 1940. The first nine months' cruising by these 'plain-clothes' units of the German fleet was a resounding success. In October 1940 there were six of them at sea – and now the turn of the regular fleet warships had come. *Hipper* and *Admiral Scheer* would be the first to join in the commerce war; as soon as the damage suffered in the Norwegian campaign had been made good, *Scharnhorst* and *Gneisenau* would follow. Meanwhile, two more valuable warships were almost ready for the fray: *Prinz Eugen*, third of the *Hipper*-class heavy cruisers, and the battleship *Bismarck*. The second battleship, *Tirpitz*, was still completing. Such were the successes of 1940 that work on the aircraft-carrier *Graf Zeppelin*, suspended at Raeder's suggestion in April 1940, was resumed. With luck, Raeder hoped, he would in time be able to assemble a battle squadron which could annihilate any convoy it attacked, while being strong enough to cope with any battleship screen the British could provide. Meanwhile, the warships would go out as they became available, and the disguised merchant raiders would continue cruising, snapping up prizes, mining coastal waters, keeping the British naval dispositions at full stretch.

The heavy cruiser *Hipper*, her damage from the Norwegian campaign repaired, would be the first to move. It was intended to base her on the French port of St Nazaire, and she sailed for the north Atlantic late in September 1940, but it was a false start. Her engines began to fail badly while she was still off the Norwegian coast, and although the British Home Fleet, briefed by wireless Intelligence on 28th September that she was at sea, made a North Sea sweep, *Hipper* managed to struggle home to put matters right. No such difficulties, however, hampered the pocket-battle-

Admiral Scheer, Graf Spee's sister-ship, as she looked before refit

ship *Admiral Scheer*. Her major refit – giving her a marked face-lift by removing the heavy armoured fighting mast with which she (and *Graf Spee*) had originally been equipped – was now complete. And on 27th October Captain Theodor Krancke took her out of Brunsbüttel, embarking on what was destined to become one of the classic cruises in the history of maritime raiding.

Once again, British air reconnaissance failed badly. *Scheer* headed undetected up the Norwegian coast, and, aided by violent weather, broke safely into the North Atlantic on the last day of October – just as the merchant raider *Widder*, her first cruise complete, was entering Brest. Krancke spotted his first victim on 5th November. She was an independently-routed British merchantman, the *Mopan*, and she was soon overwhelmed. Luckily for the Germans, she failed to transmit a surface raider warning; had she done so, Krancke would probably have been baulked of his greatest single success of the cruise: the harrying of Convoy HX-84, just over the horizon, and unprotected except for a solitary armed merchantman. The latter was the *Jervis Bay*.

On the evening of the 5th, *Scheer*'s lookouts sighted the first of HX-84's thirty-seven merchantmen. Krancke raced in to engage before daylight went and the convoy could scatter – and promptly found himself being challenged by the puny *Jervis Bay*, whose commander, Captain E S F Fegen, trailed a smokescreen to shield his convoy and courted a futile battle to try to give the merchantmen time to scatter. It was *Rawalpindi*'s sad story all over again, a one-sided pounding-match; Krancke had no intention of risking damage even from an armed merchantman's popguns, and he kept to a range where only the *Scheer*'s six 11-inch guns mattered. The gallant Fegen (posthumously awarded the VC), 200 of his crew, and *Jervis Bay* were eliminated in just twenty-two minutes, but those twenty-two minutes were

The raiders' objective: an Allied convoy at the moment of zig-zag

enough. The convoy had scattered, and Krancke was only able to sink five ships and damage three others before darkness closed down to end the hunt. One of those damaged ships provided an epic of her own. She was the British tanker *San Demetrio*, whose crew abandoned ship, only to find her next day, burning but still afloat. They boarded her again, put out the fires, and somehow struggled home with the greater part of her precious cargo of oil still intact.

Krancke's work on 5th November threw the entire British convoy system out of gear, and for a week no convoy arrived in a British port. From now on, every major convoy would be given battleship protection, which was exactly what the German surface raiders were trying to do: make the British fritter away the might of their combined battle squadrons on independent convoy-escort missions. It was a brilliant opening to *Scheer*'s cruise, and it did far more damage to the British war effort than merely depriving it of the cargoes of five merchantmen.

Aided by a competent supply-system, *Scheer* headed south. By 14th December she had sunk two more victims – *Port Hobart* on 24th November and *Tribesman* on 1st December – and was refuelling from the supply-tanker *Nordmark* just north of the Equator. On the 18th *Scheer* captured a rich prize – the British *Duquesa*, loaded with food – and deliberately allowed her to send out a surface-raider warning before capturing her intact in order to take pressure off the *Hipper*, which had finally succeeded in reaching the Atlantic after her earlier setbacks. And Christmas Day, 1940, saw the *Scheer*, her prize the *Duquesa*, the merchant-raider *Thor*, and two German supply-ships exchanging seasonal greetings for supplies and ammunition at 24° South 13° West in the South Atlantic, while far to the north the *Hipper* was attacking a British convoy.

Hipper had sailed from Brunsbüttel on 30th November, dodged undetected up the Norwegian coast, waited for weather which would ground British air patrols, and had broken through the Denmark Strait on the night of 6th December. Unlike *Scheer*, she was under orders to attack convoys, not independently-routed ships. After getting nowhere in the western Atlantic, she headed east to try the West African shipping lanes, and on Christmas Eve fell in with troop convoy WS-5A, twenty ships *en route* for the Middle East.

After shadowing the convoy through the night, *Hipper* attacked at dawn on Christmas Day, only to run into a strong cruiser escort – *Berwick*, *Bonaventure*, and *Dunedin*. (Also in company was the aircraft carrier *Furious*, bound for Takoradi with cased aircraft which would be assembled there and flown across Africa to join Wavell's Middle East Command). There was a brisk gun action in which both sides suffered slight damage – but any damage was too much for *Hipper*, now suffering engine trouble again. She broke away, headed north, and surprised the British blockade by slipping into Brest on 27th December, instead of breaking north through the Denmark Strait. *Hipper* had had a disappointing cruise. Her endurance was low in comparison to that of the pocket-battleships with their diesel engines (the three heavy cruisers had 3-shaft turbines), and this, compounded with the faults of unreliable engines, helped place *Hipper* at the bottom of the list of successful German surface raiders for 1940.

By late December, then, *Admiral Scheer* was the only heavy regular German warship at sea – but also still at large were the *Thor*, the *Atlantis*, the *Komet*, the *Orion*, the *Pinguin*, and the *Kormoran*, first of the 'second wave' of merchant raiders, which had slipped out through the Denmark

A disappointing raider: *Admiral Hipper* in dry dock at Brest

66

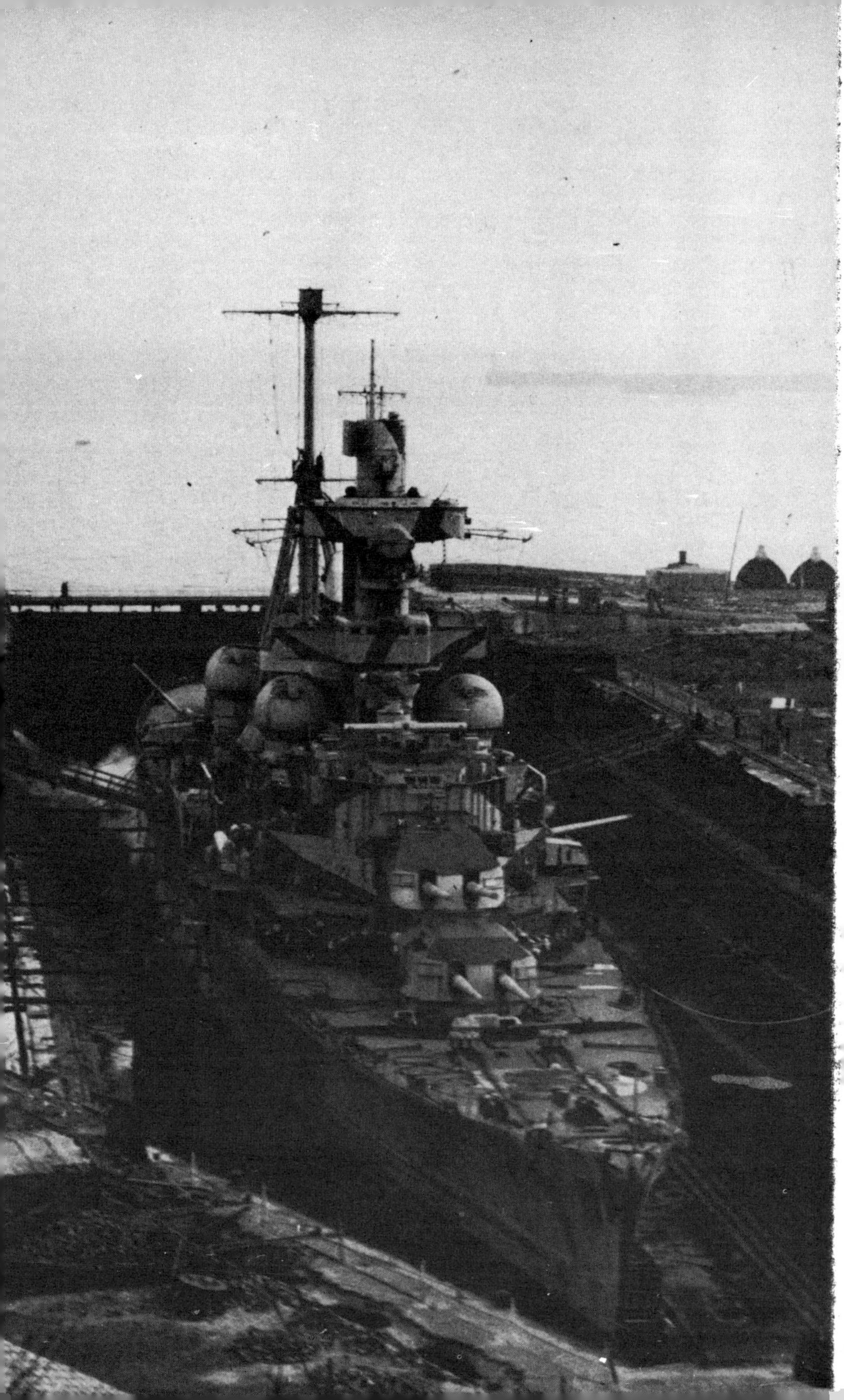

Strait a few days after *Hipper*. Here was a very different story to that of the original High Seas Fleet in the First World War: seven German warships at large after over fifteen months of war. And for the first time in history, ships of the German battle fleet were preparing for a Atlantic war cruise: the battle-cruisers *Scharnhorst* and *Gneisenau*, led by Fleet Commander Admiral Günther Lütjens.

Six months had now passed since the fall of Norway, and the damage suffered by the two battle-cruisers during the Norwegian campaign had been repaired. On 27th December they duly sortied from Kiel – but *Gneisenau* suffered storm damage off the Norwegian coast, and the battle-cruisers retreated to base. This was just as well for the British, who were concentrating on finding the *Hipper* (by now safe in Brest, though she was not sighted there until 4th January) because again their air patrols had failed to spot the sortie. The time taken to locate the *Hipper* only rubbed in the lesson.

On 23rd January 1941, the battle-cruisers sortied again, after five supply-ships had been sent out to await their needs – but this time the British were ready. Admiral Sir John Tovey, who had replaced Admiral Forbes as C-in-C, Home Fleet on 2nd December, was warned by the Admiralty on 20th January that another surface raider break-out seemed to be in preparation. Tovey promptly sent two cruisers to cover the Iceland/Faeroes passage between the North Sea and the Atlantic. On the 23rd the Admiralty received definite news that the battle-cruisers had been seen passing the Great Belt. Tovey was at sea with the Home Fleet by the 26th – and early on the 28th the cruiser *Naiad* sighted the battle-cruisers as they headed into the Iceland/Faeroes passage. It seemed that *Scharnhorst* and *Gneisenau* were going to be brought to action by the main battle squadron under Tovey – the battleships *Nelson* and *Rodney*, with the battle-cruiser *Repulse*, sister-ship to the *Renown* which had damaged *Gneisenau* off Norway back in April 1940. But German radar, for once, stole a march on that of the British. Lütjens had located two of Tovey's cruisers at least six minutes before *Naiad* spotted the German ships, and he turned and ran, outpacing *Naiad*, who lost contact and failed to regain it.

During the Norwegian campaign, Lütjens had shown that he had a flair for disengaging from the enemy at high speed and leaving him on the wrong foot. This he did again, running far to the north. After refuelling in Arctic waters, Lütjen's ships tried again to make the breakthrough into the Atlantic, this time attempting the Denmark Strait, which they passed on the night of 3rd February. The battle-cruisers refuelled again the following night, off southern Greenland, then turned south and at once began to hunt, concentrating on the Halifax convoy route in the western Atlantic where *Scheer* had caused so much panic in the previous November.

Within a few days, *Scharnhorst* and *Gneisenau* were patrolling *Scheer*'s former hunting ground, and on 8th February the outlying masts of Convoy HX-106 were sighted from *Scharnhorst*. Lütjens split his force to take the convoy from north to south – but he got a rude shock at 0947 hours when *Scharnhorst* sighted the fighting-top of a battleship. This was the *Ramillies*, 15-inch gun veteran of the First World War, sent to protect the convoy after the lessons so painfully learned the previous year. Taking on a battleship was no part of Lütjens's plan and he broke away at once, while *Ramillies*, whose lookouts had only sighted *Scharnhorst*, and at very long range, signalled the sighting of what seemed to be a *Hipper*-class cruiser. This was what the British Admiralty were expecting to hear, for they believed that either *Hipper* or the

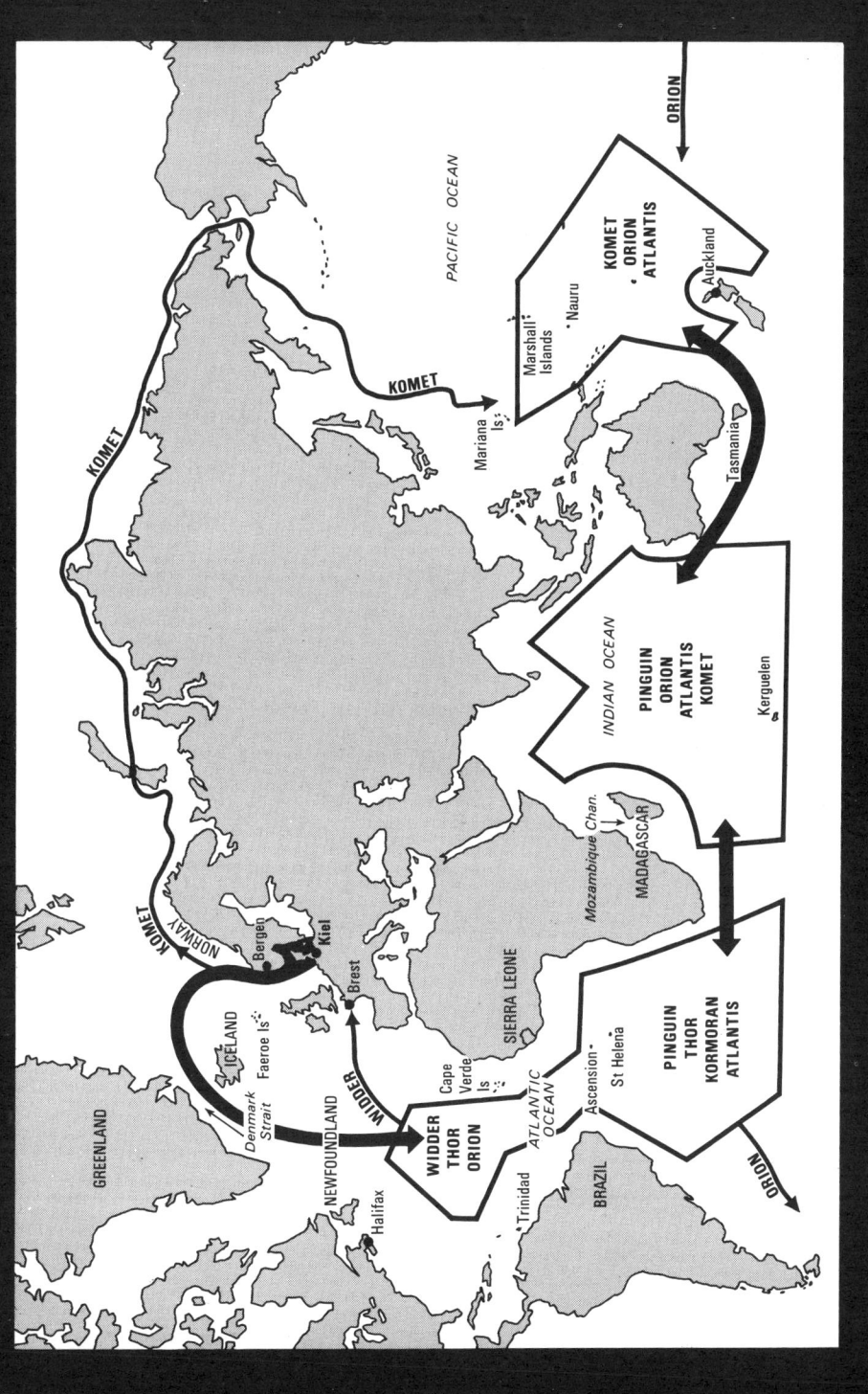

Break-out routes and hunting grounds used by disguised merchant raiders, 1940-1941

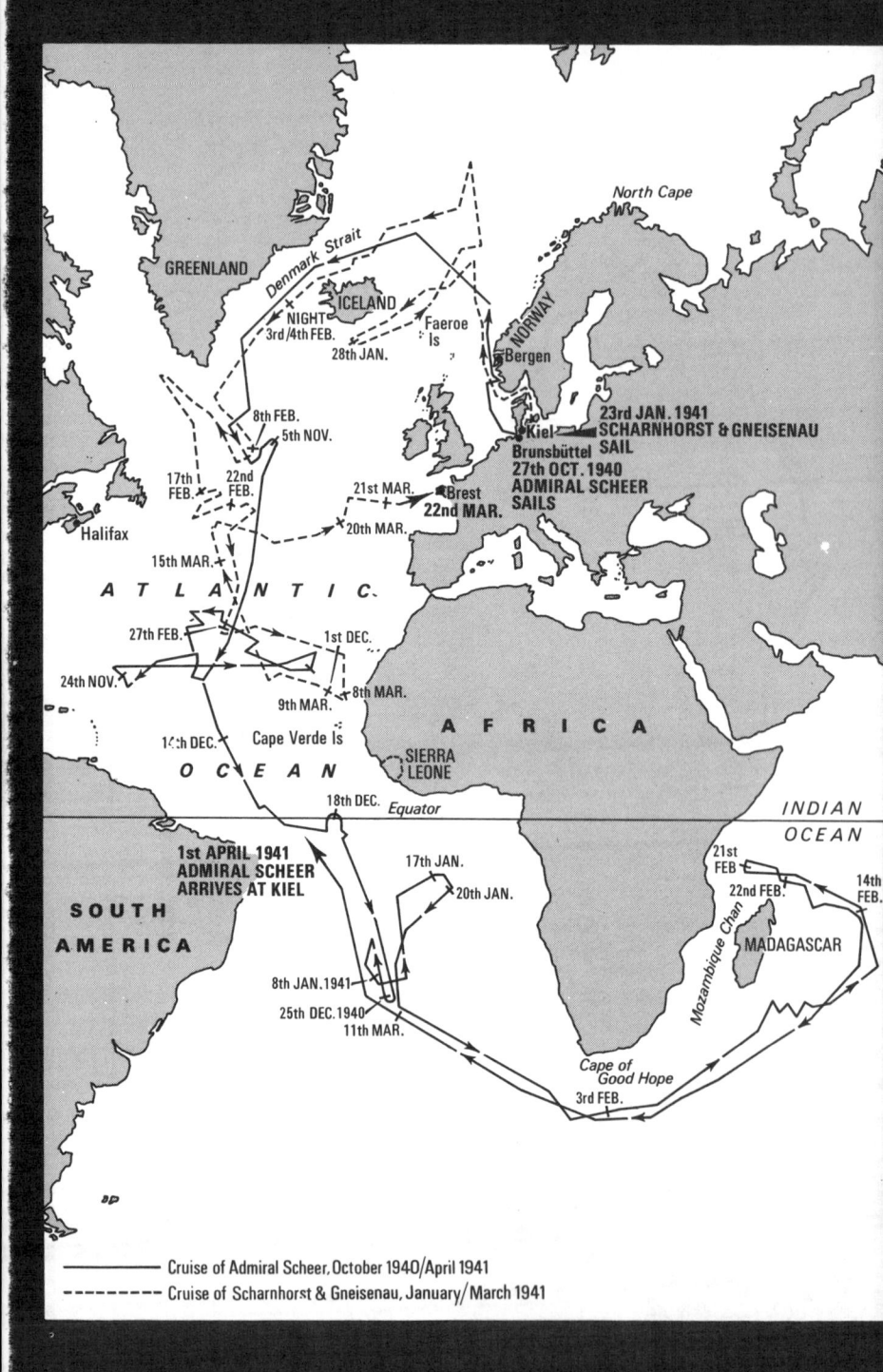

Glory days: *Scheer's* brilliant solo cruise, and the *Scharnhorst/Gneisenau* foray

Scheer would be attempting to break through for home waters about this time. And Tovey, who had by now concluded that *Naiad*'s sighting-report of 28th January must have been a mistake, took up position to cover the most likely routes that a homeward-bound raider would take. Lütjens lay low, however, until 17th February, then returned to the Halifax route. He was soon rewarded. On the 22nd, 500 miles east of Newfoundland, he sighted the smoke of several merchantmen which had just dispersed from an outward-bound convoy. *Scharnhorst* and *Gneisenau* went into action and scored five ships with a total of 25,784 tons. The German radio-jammers could not prevent one raider warning from getting through, and within minutes the British Admiralty knew that heavy surface raiders were operating in the western Atlantic. This helped them little, however, for Lütjens had no intention of staying where he was until the Home Fleet came down on him. He fuelled in mid-Atlantic between 26th and 28th February, then headed east to work the West African trade route.

Here he had a chance to attack Convoy SL-67 – but this convoy, too, was protected by a battleship, the *Malaya*, whose aircraft spotted the German battle-cruisers on 8th March, 350 miles north of the Cape Verdes. Lütjens was no more prepared to tackle the *Malaya* than he had been to tackle the *Ramillies*; after picking up the British sighting-report he swung west again, sank one independently-routed merchantman on the 9th, refuelled again in mid-Atlantic, and headed back to search for further prey on the Halifax route.

While the British heavy surface forces – including *Rodney*, *Nelson*, and *King George V* – tensely waited for the German battle-cruisers either to try to break through for home or to renew their attacks on the homeward-bound convoys, Lütjens was preparing to see if he could repeat his success against outward-bound convoys, many miles to the south of the British patrols. This time, however, he kept a couple of his supply-ships with him, using them as scouts to widen his horizon. It worked superbly. In the space of forty-eight hours – between 15th and 16th March – *Scharnhorst* and *Gneisenau* destroyed sixteen merchantmen from recently dispersed outward-bound convoys, totalling 82,000 tons. The ether rang with raider reports and appeals for help; *King George V* headed for the dangerzone to reinforce *Rodney*, which had caught a brief glimpse of the battlecruisers; and Tovey strengthened the guard on the entrances to the North Sea. For Lütjens it was the triumphant climax to a brilliant cruise – but the last success of the sortie. From Berlin the order reached him: he must retreat from the North Atlantic to take pressure off the returning *Scheer*, and also off the *Hipper*, which had just completed another cruise.

Lütjens therefore shaped his course for Brest, and he ended his cruise with another skilful display of evasive tactics. Sighted on 20th March by one of the aircraft from *Ark Royal*, belonging to the Gibraltar-based 'Force H', Lütjens ostentatiously changed his course to the northward, waited until the aircraft had vanished, then stood on towards the French coast. All might still have ended well for the British if the aircraft had reported the change of course, but only the northerly course was mentioned in the sighting-report. Not until evening on the 21st were the battle-cruisers sighted again, this time by RAF Coastal Command: under 200 miles from the French coast and safety, with no hope now for a British interception. Jubilant, Lütjens brought *Scharnhorst* and *Gneisenau* into Brest on the morning of 22nd March. He had made history for the German navy, and had proved himself the most skilful battle-fleet commander that that navy had produced since its rebirth after Scapa Flow.

Above: Enter the battle fleet: *Scharnhorst*, seen at full speed
Below: A salvo from the forward 11-inch turrets of the *Scharnhorst*

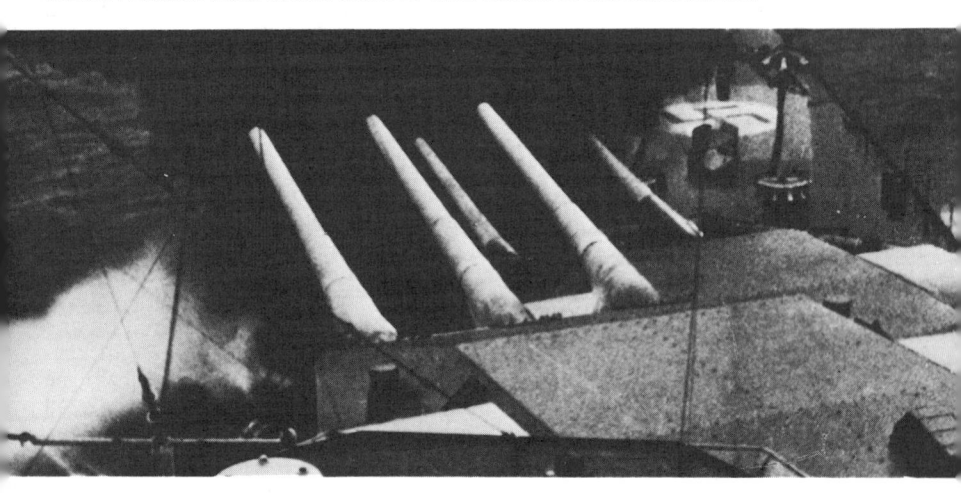

Success at last for *Hipper:* one of the victims of Convoy SLS-64

There remains to be told the successful close of the cruise of the *Scheer*, and the second sortie of the *Hipper*. Krancke left his South Atlantic Christmas and New Year rendezvous on 8th January 1941, hoping to fall in with the convoy *Hipper* had so abortively attacked on Christmas Day. He failed to find the convoy, but captured a Norwegian tanker on 17th January and sent her off to Bordeaux as a prize. Krancke now decided to adopt new deceptive tactics. Wearing British-style warpaint, *Scheer* began to close in on likely-looking victims like an investigating British cruiser – a sight to which merchant captains were becoming accustomed by January 1941. Bows-on wherever possible, *Scheer* would close the range at top speed, disguising her distinctive three-gun turrets in an ingenious way: two barrels up and one depressed, to give the effect of the standard British two-barrel armament. It worked well right from the start. Using this trick, *Scheer* made a left-and-right bag of two merchantmen within a few hours on 20th January; neither vessel managed to get off a raider report, and for months the British Admiralty wondered what had happened to them . . .

Krancke then decided, like Langsdorff of the *Graf Spee* before him, that a change of hunting-ground was essential, and, like Langsdorff, he decided on the Indian Ocean. After another mid-ocean fuelling rendezvous with the raider *Thor* and the tanker *Nordmark*, *Scheer* rounded the Cape of Good Hope early in February. A week passed without any further victims being sighted, but on 14th February *Scheer* met the raider *Atlantis* with two prizes in company, and Rogge of the *Atlantis* advised Krancke to try to the north of the Mozambique Channel between Madagascar and the African mainland. *Scheer* found rapid success here with her new tactics – three victims fell between 20th and 21st February – but the third of these victims got out a raider report, and the British East Indies Division reacted sharply. On 22nd February the pocket-battleship was spotted by the aircraft of the cruiser *Glasgow*, and retreat became essential. Swinging far to the east and south – again like Langsdorff in November 1939 – Krancke headed back to the South Atlantic: homeward-bound, to receive the Knight's Cross awarded him by a grateful Führer and a replica of the decoration, knocked up in his ship's machine-shop, hanging round his neck.

On 11th March 1941, after a complete engine refit, radar overhaul, and waterline clean-up, *Admiral Scheer* steamed away from the last in a long series of mid-ocean rendezvous with the tanker *Nordmark*, which had served her so well. *Scheer* crossed the Equator in four days and on 22nd March, the day of Lütjens's triumphant return to Brest with *Scharnhorst* and *Gneisenau*, she entered the danger-zone of the Halifax sea-lane, which should have been like a disturbed hornet's nest after the havoc wrought by *Scharnhorst* and *Gneisenau* the week before. But Lütjens had done his work well. The British battleships were either tied down to escort duties or were still vainly hunting for the vanished battle-cruisers; and by the time a battle squadron with *King George V* as its core was sent to cover the North Atlantic approaches it was two days too late. Wily to the last, Krancke had waited for foul weather to relieve *Scheer* of the danger of being spotted by aircraft on the last leg home; like so many of his colleagues before (and after) him, he slipped through the over-stretched British cruiser net and entered Norwegian waters. On 30th March, safe in Bergen harbour, *Scheer* dropped anchor – about the only piece of her equipment completely unused in the last five months – then cruised south to reach Kiel on 1st April.

What Lütjens with *Scharnhorst* and *Gneisenau* had done for the German battle fleet, Krancke in *Admiral Scheer* had done for the pocket-battleships.

But the pride of the Fleet had yet to sail: the battleship *Bismarck*, seen completing her preparations for service on the high seas

He had proved what excellent raiders they were. He had made the most successful single-ship cruise by a regular warship of the modern German navy. In a five-month odyssey he had steamed 46,419 miles, sinking not only the *Jervis Bay* but sixteen ships totalling 99,059 tons, and had amply fulfilled his far more important rôle of dislocating British convoys and the disposition of their escorts. It was a superb achievement.

Meanwhile, *Hipper* had made a second cruise, and had put up a considerably better performance than on her first sortie. She had slipped out of Brest on 1st February, her first destination, in view of her depressingly low endurance, being a refuelling-point in mid-Atlantic. There she stayed until 9th February, when her cruise began in earnest. As before, *Hipper*'s hunting-ground was to be the Sierra Leone convoy route – and on 11th February she came upon Convoy SLS-64, an unescorted group of nineteen merchantmen. With absolutely no opposition, *Hipper* ran up an easy score of seven ships totalling 32,806 tons. But what with the inevitable raider reports from the survivors – not to mention rapidly-dropping fuel gauges in the engine-room – that was all that could be done. By 14th February *Hipper* was back in Brest, again the target of sustained but inaccurate bombing by the RAF.

Hipper obviously needed a complete engine overhaul, and for that she would have to return to Germany. This was far from easy, in view of the increasingly-congested state of naval strategic priorities in the North Atlantic by March 1941. The German Naval Staff finally decided to bring *Hipper* back through the Denmark Strait just before the *Scheer*'s home run, and laid on another efficient piece of organisation to do it. *Hipper* left Brest on 15th March, refuelled south of Greenland, made the now routine wait for thick weather, and ran the Denmark Strait on 23rd March. She reached Kiel (after another refuel) two days before *Scheer* reached Bergen: 28th March. Her return from Brest was yet another re-statement of the need for the British to tighten their grip on the northern entrances to the Atlantic. It was only to be expected that they would do so, and that the German fleet would not find it so easy in the months to come; but this was hard to see in the heady days of March 1941.

The successes of Hitler's High Seas Fleet had almost reached their zenith. The past twelve months had seen triumphant cruises by battle squadrons and by lone raiders, backed by the establishment of a beautifully-running supply-system. Churchill's comment on Admiral Graf von Spee's Pacific wanderings in 1914 – 'He was a cut flower in a vase, fair to see yet doomed to die' – did not apply to the German navy in 1940–41. It fed, equipped, and re-equipped its crews and warships on every ocean of the world. And this was not all. Germany's well-disguised fleet of merchant raiders was still at sea, steadily increasing its total of kills, with yet more raiders preparing to join their colleagues.

Almost the zenith, but not quite. There remained a decisive clash with the British battle fleet. By March 1941 Raeder was ready even for this gamble. He was preparing the greatest venture yet for the German surface fleet: *Rheinübung*, 'Exercise Rhine', which would send the pride of the German navy to join hands with *Scharnhorst* and *Gneisenau* on the high seas. After months of training and preparation, battleship *Bismarck* was ready for action.

75

Battleship Bismarck

Compared with the successes of the previous months, *Bismarck*'s story was both glorious and tragic, dominated by the eternal 'if'. *If* Germany had had a combined land, sea, and air high command, three leaders working together instead of being riven by court politics; *if* Göring's jealousy for Luftwaffe predominance had been overcome, allowing Raeder to build a German fleet air arm, with long-range bombers as well as an aircraft-carrier force; *if Scharnhorst* and *Gneisenau* had been able to make a simultaneous sortie from Brest; and lastly, *if* the British had not had so many lessons to learn – and learn fast – since September 1939 . . .

If all these things had happened, the *Bismarck* saga would have turned out very differently. *Bismarck* could have come out with the aircraft-carrier *Graf Zeppelin*, joined *Scharnhorst* and *Gneisenau* at sea, and won command of the North Atlantic. As it was, the huge battleship scored the biggest single triumph yet attained by Hitler's High Seas Fleet, sinking the proudest warship in the Royal Navy – but within seventy-two hours she had been hunted down by the greatest air-sea search in maritime history, crippled by the British Fleet Air Arm, pounded into a defenceless wreck by the guns of *Rodney* and *King George V*, and sunk. It was the clearest possible indication that in a mere two months the British had learned their lesson, and that from now on the German surface fleet would no longer have such freedom of action on the high seas as it had enjoyed since March 1940.

The original plan which eventually sent *Bismarck* to sea crystallised when Günther Lütjens brought *Scharnhorst* and *Gneisenau* into Brest on 22nd March. Here, potentially, was the southern claw of a decisive naval pincer-movement. If *Bismarck*, with the fleet's other new warship, the heavy cruiser *Prinz Eugen*, could reach the Atlantic from the north while *Scharnhorst* and *Gneisenau* came out from the south, Raeder knew that he could achieve a combination of strength which the British could not hope to match without stripping their convoys of their battleship escorts – which was exactly what Raeder wanted.

This was the essence of his *Rheinübung* plan. It was the logical outcome of the pattern of ocean warfare since the outbreak of hostilities. The successes of the German surface raiders had forced the British not merely to do all they could to concentrate their mercantile shipping in convoys, but to give these convoys heavy protection. The last three forays of the German Fleet – by *Admiral Scheer*, *Hipper*, and *Scharnhorst* and *Gneisenau* – had shown that, given the right conditions, convoys could be attacked with success. Battleship escorts, however, remained the stumbling-block. Raeder reckoned that *Rheinübung* was a natural winner whichever way the British reacted. If they held to their present strategy of defending their convoys with battleships, this would not worry a squadron as strong as *Bismarck*, *Scharnhorst*, and *Gneisenau*. If the British concentrated their battleships into a force strong enough

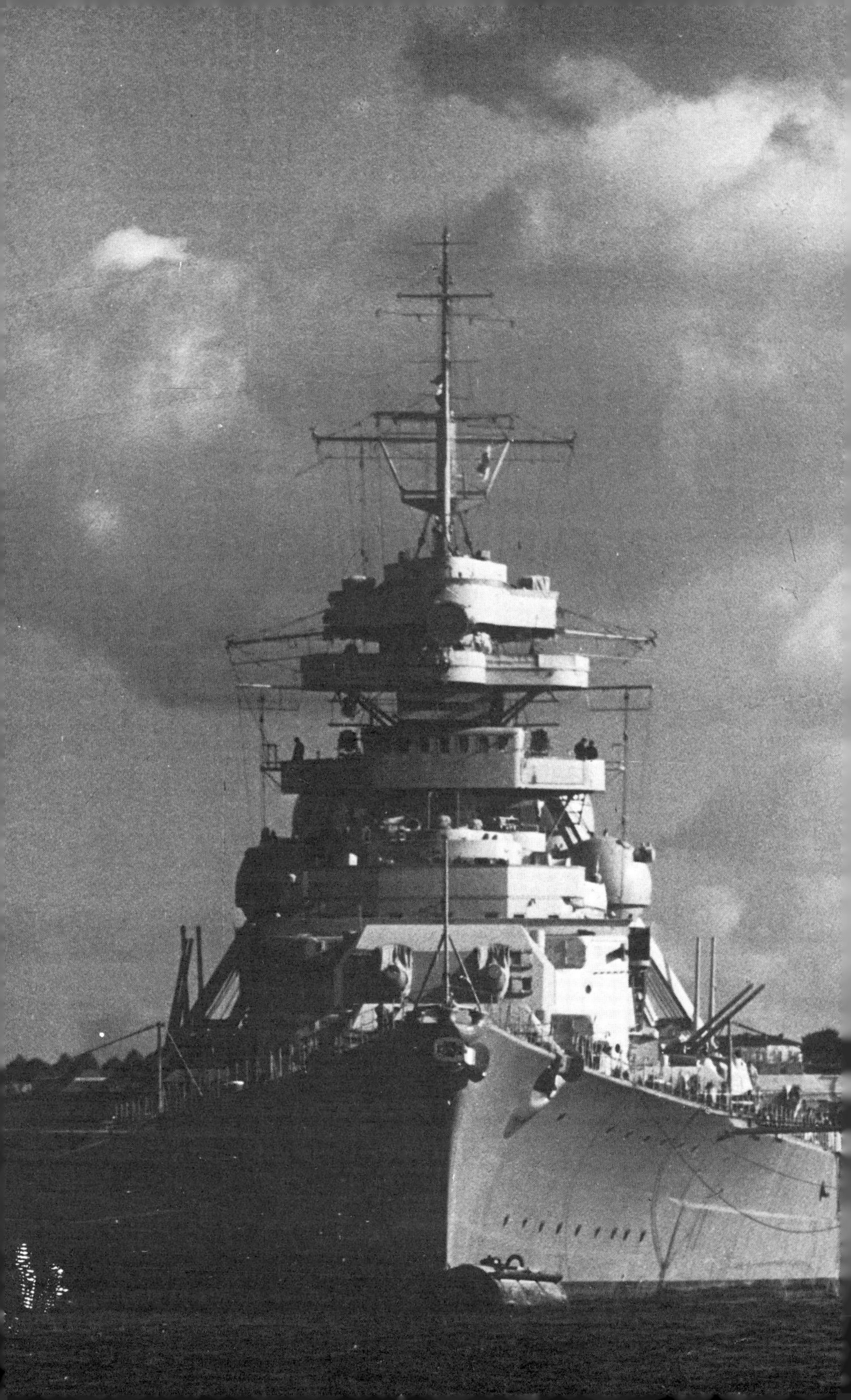

to overwhelm the German battle squadron, the convoys would have to be stripped of their battleship escorts; the Germans would still retain the initiative while the British hunted for them, and the convoys could offer little or no resistance. It all depended on whether or not *Scharnhorst* and *Gneisenau* could be brought to operational readiness and put to sea at the same time as *Bismarck* and *Prinz Eugen* – hopefully in the latter half of April.

Almost at once, however, the Naval High Command knew that this was not to be. *Scharnhorst* needed a major engine refit and would be a dockyard case until June, although *Gneisenau* would be available for *Rheinübung*. The only danger was that the British might immobilise *Gneisenau* before *Bismarck* and *Prinz Eugen* were ready for sea. Brest was a superb strategic base for ocean warfare, but it lay well within the striking range of the RAF. As soon as the battle-cruisers were located in Brest, they became a number-one target for RAF Bomber Command. True, they were not the easiest of targets, and Brest had a terrifying concentration of anti-aircraft guns. Even so, Churchill lamented the Air Ministry's 'neglect', and 'very grievous error', and complained of Bomber Command's 'very definite failure' to eliminate the battle-cruisers. Why, he asked, could trained bomber crews not hit these immobile targets?

'The answer is simple', Guy Gibson wrote in *Enemy Coast Ahead*, his superb testament to Bomber Command. 'The crews couldn't see them. Moreover, not only the glare of hundreds of searchlights, the many decoys, coupled with the thousands of flak shells filling the sky above the very small target area, made it virtually impossible even to hit the docks, let alone the ships. Even when our bomber formations had bombed Brest by day, the Germans would fill the whole area with thick yellow smoke, which completely hid everything from view. When I say that in order to get the bombs anywhere near the docks it was necessary to do a five-minute timed run from an island nearby, it will perhaps be realised why no serious damage was done.'

For all that, it was Bomber Command which was indirectly responsible for knocking *Gneisenau* out of *Rheinübung*. In the first fortnight after their arrival in Brest, the battle-cruisers were attacked by a total of some 200 RAF bombers, none of which scored direct hits. But one of them scored a near-miss which failed to explode, and until this unexploded bomb could be dealt with, *Gneisenau* was moved out into the open harbour away from the danger-zone. *Scharnhorst* had already quitted dry dock and was moored to the north quay, protected by a special anti-torpedo boom. And that was where they were when a reconnaissance Spitfire photographed Brest on 5th April, bringing home proof that there was a faint chance of making a torpedo attack on the battle-cruiser (thought to be *Scharnhorst*) in the open harbour.

'Every effort by the Navy and the Air Force should be made to destroy them,' ran Churchill's edict of 22nd March, 'and for this purpose serious risks and sacrifices must be made.' Only on these terms could the attack be considered, for the crews making it would have to fly deliberately into the fire of over a thousand flak guns, quite apart from those on the ships, as they made their runs. But the attack had to be made at once, before *Gneisenau* was moved back into dry dock; and it went in early on 6th April, with Flying Officer K Campbell of 22 Squadron, Coastal Command, earning a posthumous VC by putting a torpedo into *Gneisenau* seconds before he was shot down and killed with all his crew. It was not in vain. A huge gash was torn in her stern; eight months later, her starboard propeller-shaft was still being repaired. Meanwhile, bombing attacks on the two ships were continued by the

RAF, and the Royal Navy added to the Germans' problem by laying several minefields off Brest.

Rheinübung had received a major setback: both battle-cruisers would now have to stay in Brest when *Bismarck* and *Prinz Eugen* sailed. But this did not deter Raeder. He knew that the battleship and the heavy cruiser were a formidable pair, and he hoped to repeat the success of the *Scharnhorst/Gneisenau* cruise with them. He did not intend them to operate as a team, as the battle-cruisers had done, but expected that *Bismarck*'s presence in the Atlantic would act like a magnet on the British battleship dispositions, drawing them away from the convoys to search for *Bismarck* and leaving *Prinz Eugen* with a free hand.

Fleet Commander Günther Lütjens, who would lead the operation, was not so sanguine. He pleaded that *Rheinübung* should be postponed until the battle-cruisers were ready, but Raeder overruled him. *Rheinübung* was to be pressed forward. To wait until summer would mean losing the bad weather and the long periods of darkness in northern waters which helped the break-out of German surface raiders so much. And he had a far more urgent reason. June 1941 was the scheduled date for Nazi Germany's greatest gamble: 'Barbarossa': the invasion of Soviet Russia. Once the war with Russia had begun, Raeder knew that top priority would be given to the needs of the Army and the Luftwaffe. Only a smashing success at sea would keep Hitler's interest in the Navy active; and he already knew that Hitler would not listen to reason.

Back in 1940, on 26th September, Raeder had had a private interview with the Führer, unaware that Hitler was even contemplating tackling Soviet Russia. It was an historic meeting, for it was probably the only time that one of Hitler's military commanders suggested an independent strategy. Raeder wanted to end the Mediterranean problem before renewing plans for the invasion of Britain. He suggested an Italo-German offensive to clear the British out of Egypt and to take Suez. And, banking on the bitterness caused by the British attacks on the French fleet at Oran, Mers-el-Kébir, and Dakar in July and September, he wanted to offer big inducements to Vichy France to secure the French bases in West Africa for the German navy, extending its reach from the North Cape to Dakar. But Hitler did not understand: his face was set to the east, and all Raeder's attempts to dissuade him during the planning of 'Barbarossa' were ignored. On 6th April, while salvage crews fought to keep the crippled *Gneisenau* afloat after Campbell's torpedo attack at Brest, the Wehrmacht was invading Yugoslavia and Greece to subdue the Balkans and secure the southern flank before the Russian venture began.

On Raeder's insistence, therefore, the final plans for *Rheinübung* were also laid. Once again, a supply fleet was sent out to keep the German raiders at sea: five tankers and two supply-ships. At first it was intended to send *Bismarck* into Brest while *Prinz Eugen* continued to raid, but this idea was abandoned – unless some emergency should arise – after the damage suffered by *Gneisenau* in the attack of 6th April. There was another setback on 23rd April, when *Prinz Eugen* hit a mine and fourteen days of repairs were needed; and it was not until 18th May that Lütjens took *Bismarck* and *Prinz Eugen* out of Gdynia on the first leg of the cruise.

The British Admiralty knew that *Bismarck* was nearly ready for sea, and when the report came in via Sweden that the two warships had been seen passing the Great Belt on the 20th the British began an intense air search. On 21st May, *Bismarck* and *Prinz Eugen* were spotted in Grimstad Fjord, just south of Bergen, where they were topping up with fuel before the break-out into the Atlantic. To Admiral Tovey in Scapa Flow, too, the

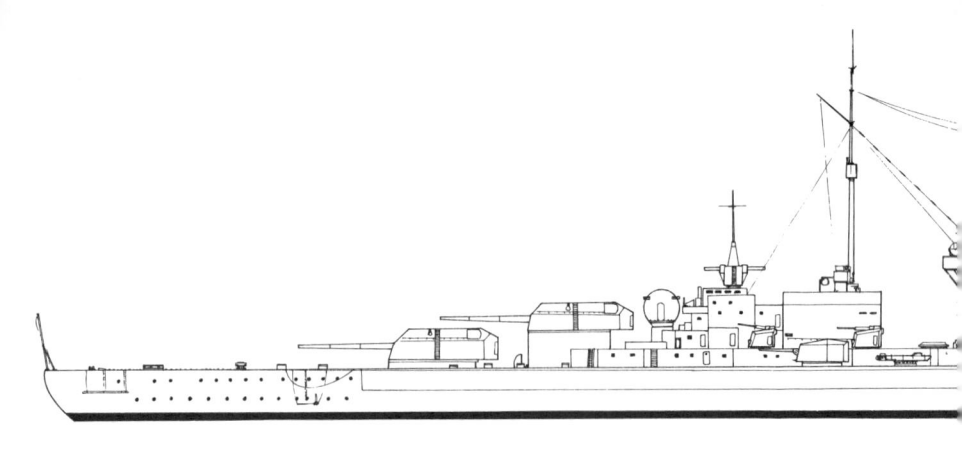

Bismarck, first of the Reich navy's heavy battleships. *Bismarck* and her sister-ship *Tirpitz* were the heaviest German battleships ever built, and until the advent of Japan's *Yamato*-class 'super-battleships' they were the most powerful warships in the world. Layout of the 15-inch main armament was orthodox; secondary and tertiary armaments were lavish and formidable. *Displacement:* 41,700 tons. *Length*

news was not unexpected. German air reconnaissance of Scapa Flow had been stepped up in the last ten days, and Tovey had warned Captain Ellis of the cruiser *Suffolk*, on patrol in the Denmark Strait, to keep a sharp watch on the waters along the edge of the Greenland ice pack (which flucuates with the seasons, and which at this period had narrowed the Strait to sixty miles). The same orders were given to *Norfolk* when she relieved *Suffolk*, due for refuelling, on the 19th.

When Tovey heard that *Bismarck* and *Prinz Eugen* were in Grimstad Fjord, he sent off a battle squadron to Hvalfjord in Iceland – the battle-cruiser *Hood*, flying the flag of Vice-Admiral Holland, the new battleship *Prince of Wales*, and six destroyers. He ordered the patrol of the Iceland-Faeroes passage to be maintained, and sent off *Suffolk* to help *Norfolk*'s patrol of the Denmark Strait. Tovey himself, in the battleship *King George V*, waited in Scapa Flow with five cruisers and five destroyers. He received an important bonus when the Admiralty cancelled the sailing of the new aircraft-carrier *Victorious* and the *Repulse*, which had been intended to escort a convoy, and put them at Tovey's disposal. He knew where the enemy was; he had made the best dispositions in his power; and now he waited, relying on the RAF to keep him posted as to *Bismarck*'s movements.

Rheinübung gets under way: *Bismarck* sets out for the Atlantic venture

overall: 792 feet. *Beam :* 118 feet. *Draught:* 26 feet. *Max speed:* 30 knots. *Radius:* 8,100 miles at 19 knots. *Armour:* Main belt 12½ inch, turrets 14 inch, deck 8 inch. *Armament:* Eight 15⅜-inch, twelve 5.9-inch, sixteen 4.1-inch AA, sixteen 37-mm AA, twelve 20-mm AA; eight 21-inch torpedo-tubes; six aircraft. *Complement:* 2,400

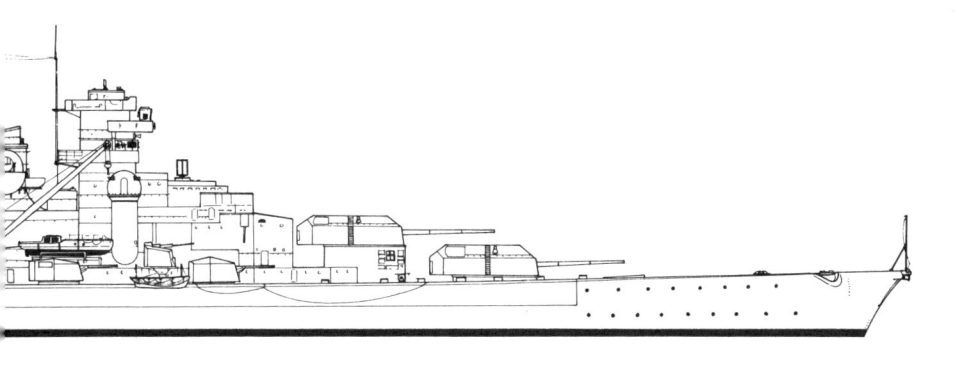

Then the worst happened. The weather closed down, and for nearly twenty-four hours the British were blind. Nothing could have given Lütjens a better chance, and he seized it with both hands. He put to sea at once, heading for the Denmark Strait. Ironically, in view of the events of the next forty-eight hours, he was acting on dangerously false Intelligence: the last Luftwaffe report on Scapa Flow had told him that all Tovey's battleships were still there, but *Hood* and *Prince of Wales* were in fact well on their way to Iceland. For the British, 22nd May was a day of tortured anxiety. Not until the evening did a Royal Navy reconnaissance plane from Hatston in the Orkneys, which had braved the foul conditions over the North Sea and forced home a close reconnaissance of the Norwegian coast, bring back the news that *Bismarck* and *Prinz Eugen* were neither in Grimstad Fjord nor in Bergen. The hunt was on.

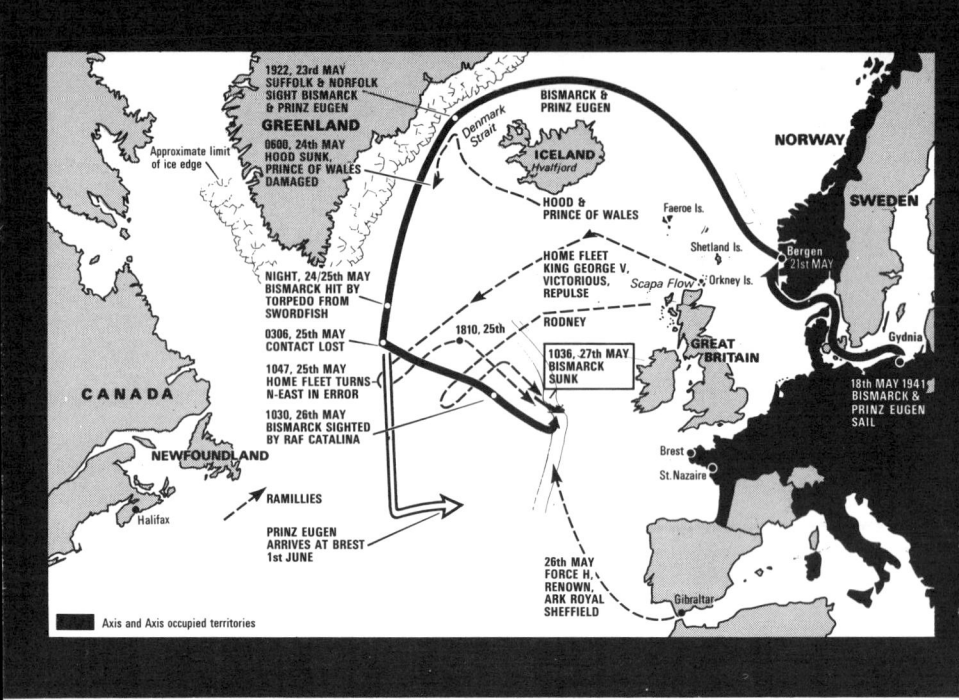

Within three hours of hearing that the German warships had sailed, Tovey was at sea with the Home Fleet, heading for the southern exit of the Denmark Strait. Throughout the night, while *Bismarck* and *Prinz Eugen* were preparing to swing west around the northern tip of Iceland, the British battle fleet was also heading west, picking up the *Repulse* (which had just escorted her last convoy to the Clyde) at 1710 hours on the morning of the 23rd. Meanwhile, further to the south, the battleship *Rodney*, with four destroyers, was escorting the *Britannic* out into the Atlantic on a parallel course. Thus by the late morning of the 23rd all the British battleships were heading in the right direction to intercept the German warships, whether the latter used the Iceland/Faeroes passage or the Denmark Strait. As soon as *Bismarck* and *Prinz Eugen* were pinpointed, the British battleships could be concentrated.

But meanwhile they were dispersed. And the battle squadron which was nearest to the Germans was Admiral Holland's: *Hood* and *Prince of Wales*. And of all Tovey's battleships, those two were the least ideal to put up against the *Bismarck*.

One simile sometimes used when matching *Hood* against *Bismarck* is to compare a biplane fighter of the early 1920s with a Messerschmitt 109. Although dangerously facile, this comparison goes a long way to establishing the type of odds facing the British vessel. But *Hood*'s main problem was not merely her age. It stemmed from the original concept which had brought her into being. She was a battle-cruiser, not a battleship. She had the same basic hitting-power as the *Bismarck* – eight 15-inch guns – but that was the only similarity between them. Nothing else mattered but the impressive difference in armoured protection which marked the two ships – and this was the result of the battle-cruiser concept, born of the Anglo-German 'Naval Race' in the years before the First World War.

Battle-cruisers, basically, were long-range super-cruisers which could smash any orthodox enemy cruiser – much as destroyers had come into being to smash enemy torpedo-boats. They were built to outpace battleships while carrying battleship-sized guns. 'Jacky' Fisher, founder of Britain's Dreadnought navy, referred to the British battle-cruisers he brought into being as his 'New Testament ships', because, he claimed, they 'fulfilled the promise of the "Old Testament ships" ' – the Dreadnought battleships. This sounded impressive but meant little in practice, for Fisher's battle-cruisers were handicapped by his fallacious claim that 'speed is armour'. With this idea in mind, he claimed that the battle-cruiser should be able to take its place in the battle fleet after completing its task of scouting ahead of the battleships – as indeed did the battle-cruisers of both the British and German navies at Jutland. But speed is not armour. No Dreadnought battleships were sunk at Jutland, but three British battle-cruisers blew up and one German battle-cruiser was battered into a sinking wreck and had to be abandoned. Yet the battle-cruiser concept survived; and *Hood*, launched three months before the High Seas Fleet steamed out to surrender in 1918, had been designed before the basic flaws of this hybrid breed of capital ship had been fully appreciated.

Writing *The World Crisis* after the First World War, ex-First Lord of the Admiralty Winston Churchill had put the problem succinctly: 'To put the value of a first-class battleship into a vessel which cannot stand the pounding of a heavy action is a false policy. It is far better to spend the extra money and have what you really want. The battle-cruiser, in other words, should be superseded by the fast battleship, ie fast strongest ship, in spite of her cost.' And in the 1930s the designers of Raeder's battle fleet had carried out this theory to the letter.

Scharnhorst, Gneisenau, Bismarck, and *Tirpitz* were all designed 'to stand the pounding of a heavy action'. Armoured protection came first, enabling the production of a new breed of battle-cruiser in which a lighter, 11-inch main armament was selected to give priority to armour. In the case of the battleships, *Bismarck* and *Tirpitz,* they got both. The contemporary battleships of the British *King George V* class were smaller and more lightly armed. They packed ten 14-inch guns, and they had a maximum deck armour of six inches; *Bismarck* had eight 15-inch guns and a maximum deck armour of eight inches, as compared to *Hood*'s eight 15-inch guns and maximum deck armour of 3¾ inches. *Prince of Wales, Hood*'s running-mate against the *Bismarck,* was one of these 'KGVs'. Her working-up period was barely over. Her main armament was not fully operational – one of her forward guns, in fact, would only be able to get off one round before becoming inoperative. She had to put to sea with civilian engineers still on board. Yet *Hood* and *Prince of Wales* were the two ships which would challenge the *Bismarck* first. Nothing could speak so eloquently of the urgency imposed on the British Home Fleet by *Bismarck*'s sortie.

As 23rd May wore on, that urgency increased with every hour. The weather was still on the Germans' side: rain and heavy mist, with visibility sometimes coming down to under 150 yards. The British air patrols were virtually all suspended. The Norwegian coast patrol was still grounded – Tovey had no way of knowing for sure that *Bismarck* and *Prinz Eugen* were not holed-up in some obscure Norwegian fjord, or even heading back to Germany. The Denmark Strait patrol was also grounded, and the Shetland/Faeroes patrol was abandoned after noon. Only the Iceland/Faeroes patrol could be con-

A practice oiling drill for *Bismarck*, astern of *Prinz Eugen*

tinued throughout the day. And at 1817 hours a report from Iceland added to the gloomy picture, warning that the most recent air reports of the Greenland ice indicated that heavy ships might find it possible to shoulder their way through the leads in the pack ice without having to use the open water of the Denmark Strait. Tovey was forced to rely on the vigilance of his widely-scattered cruiser force. He would not get the advanced warning that only air reconnaissance could provide.

But here he did have one advantage which would come as an unpleasant surprise to the Germans: radar. *Rheinübung* had been launched under the assumption that British seaborne radar was vastly inferior to that carried in the German warships. *Norfolk* and *Suffolk*, the British cruisers in the Denmark Strait, both had radar. It was not without its blind spots: *Suffolk*, which was fitted with the latest, improved set, could not use it when it was trained dead astern. But, given an early sighting and the chance to drop back and shadow on the enemy's quarter, the two cruisers were well equipped to track their quarry and report its movements to Tovey and the battle fleet.

By evening on the 23rd, the sharply-defined weather conditions in the Denmark Strait were being tackled by *Norfolk* and *Suffolk* as follows. *Suffolk* was working the clear, open waters up to the edge of the Greenland ice pack; *Norfolk* was patrolling in the heavy mist which extended as far as the coast of Iceland. At 1922 hours, right at the worst moment – when, on the south-western leg of her patrol, *Suffolk* could not train her radar on the waters behind her – she suddenly sighted *Bismarck* and *Prinz Eugen* coming right at her on the same course, at the dangerously close range of seven miles.

Reporting to *Norfolk*, *Suffolk* hastily

dodged into the fog banks to port and began to shadow, soon joined by *Norfolk*. At 1939 hours, Admiral Holland in the *Hood* picked up one of *Suffolk*'s reports. By this time he was about 300 miles due south of the German ships, and put on speed to intercept. But the cruisers' reports had not yet reached Tovey in *King George V*. Not until 2032, after *Norfolk* had raced out of a fog bank to find herself right under the *Bismarck*'s guns and retired precipitately, pursued by an accurate salvo of 15-inch shells, did *King George V* pick up a sighting report. Tovey was then 600 miles south-east of *Bismarck* and *Prinz Eugen*. He would have to rely on *Hood* and *Prince of Wales* to draw first blood: there was no chance to concentrate all available British battleships if the Germans were to be brought to action before they reached the open Atlantic.

Night closed down, and *Norfolk* and *Suffolk* continued to shadow. They were in great danger. They knew that *Bismarck* might well turn and try to destroy them, and that if she did they would get no help. But they did not lose the flickering radar contacts which kept the German warships pinpointed, and *Bismarck* and *Prinz Eugen* kept to their course. Unknown to them, next morning would bring battle. At 2256 hours on the 23rd, Tovey signalled 'I am hoping *Hood* may head them off and force them to turn back or to the southward.' Pounding north to intercept, Admiral Holland signalled '*Prepare for action*' to his squadron as early as 0015 on the 24th, and the broad battle ensigns were broken out on *Hood* and *Prince of Wales*.

About midnight *Norfolk* and *Suffolk* lost contact, due to heavy snowstorms which both ruined visibility for the lookouts and cluttered the radar screens. Holland reacted by detaching his six destroyers and sending them to sweep to the north. Not until 0247 did the two cruisers regain contact – and they held it. By 0400 the visibility from *Hood* was about ten miles, half her estimated distance from the *Bismarck*. *Norfolk* and *Suffolk* at last heard that British capital ships were in the area at 0445, and sighted their funnel smoke at 0515. Twenty minutes later, *Bismarck* and *Prinz Eugen* were sighted, *Prinz Eugen* leading, seventeen miles off *Hood*'s starboard bow. And at 0546 Holland swung his ships towards the Germans, racing in bows-on to shorten the range before opening fire.

Holland must have been acutely aware of the weaknesses of his two ships – *Hood* with the vulnerability of her deck armour under long-range plunging fire, and *Prince of Wales* with her defective guns and unseasoned crew. Hence his desire to get in close as soon as possible, and not to turn and open the full broadsides of *Hood* and *Prince of Wales* at long range. What was a fatal mistake was his decision to manoeuvre the two ships as a single unit, speeding into action only 800 yards apart, with *Prince of Wale*'s view of the enemy obscured by the *Hood*'s funnel-smoke and by the shell-splashes thrown up around the flagship. This only made things easier for the German gunners. And another serious mistake was his identification of the leading German ship as the *Bismarck*, which meant that during the opening salvoes *Hood* was firing at *Prinz Eugen*, *Prince of Wales* (disregarding Holland's original order) was firing at *Bismarck* – while both the German ships were concentrating on the *Hood*, who after her celebrated peacetime 'goodwill' cruises in the 1920s and 1930s was probably the most easily-recognisable warship in the world.

It was all over very quickly:
0549: *Hood* signals for concentration of fire on leading ship.
0552: Range 25,000 yards. *Hood* and *Bismarck* open fire, followed by *Prince of Wales*. *Hood* signals 'Shift target right' (onto *Bismarck*). *Bismarck*'s first salvo falls short of *Hood*, but close.
0555: *Bismarck*'s third salvo sets fire to

ready-use ammunition on *Hood*'s boat-deck. *Hood* signals for a turn to port to open full broadsides on *Bismarck*. Fourth salvo from *Bismarck* straddles *Hood*.
0600: Range 14,100 yards. *Hood* and *Prince of Wales* still turning. *Bismarck*'s fifth salvo penetrates *Hood*'s armour, reaches a magazine, and blows her up. *Prince of Wales* swerves to avoid *Hood* as she sinks.
0602: *Bismarck* and *Prinz Eugen* concentrate fire on *Prince of Wales*. She receives a bad hit on the compass platform, killing all personnel there except Captain Leach and a signalman.
0606-12: *Prince of Wales* hit four times by *Bismarck*, three times by *Prinz Eugen*.
0613: *Prince of Wales* breaks off and retires. *Suffolk* and *Norfolk* continue to shadow, soon joined by *Prince of Wales*.

Whatever the rights and wrongs of Admiral Holland's tactics may have been, the saddest point about their failure was that when *Hood* was blown up all dangers of the run-in were over and she was in the act of bringing her full broadside to bear. Her last salvo was still in the air when she received her death-blow. Her sickeningly rapid disappearance was the result of 42,000 tons of capital ship breaking its back at full speed; only three men out of her complement of 1,419 survived. What made her loss most tragic was that she had inflicted little or no damage in return. *Prinz Eugen*, on whom she had opened fire, was unscathed. And the three hits suffered by *Bismarck* were positively identified by the Germans as having come from the *Prince of Wales* after the *Hood* was sunk.

But these three hits, none of them vital in themselves, changed the course of the *Rheinübung* venture. A boiler-room was flooded, dropping *Bismarck*'s top speed to twenty-eight knots, and a forward oil tank had been pierced, causing the ship to trail an oil slick. *Bismarck* was still fully seaworthy and her fighting capacity was untouched; what was serious was that the hit on the oil tank had left 1,000 tons of fuel oil inaccessible, and that a long-range Atlantic cruise was no longer possible. At 0800 hours Lütjens signalled his intention of turning aside into St Nazaire – the only one of the Biscay ports with a dry dock big enough to hold a ship of the *Bismarck*'s tonnage. By the afternoon he had modified this plan. *Prinz Eugen* would stay at sea and begin the commerce-raiding programme of *Rheinübung*, while *Bismarck* lured the pursuing Home Fleet over a line of U-boats which he asked to be deployed before heading for France.

Why, after his triumph over the *Hood* and *Prince of Wales*, did Lütjens reject the idea of returning to Germany? One obvious reason is that he had just completed the most difficult part of the *Rheinübung* plan: getting out to the open Atlantic. He could certainly be excused for deciding not to repeat the tricky passage of the Denmark Strait, knowing that the alert British Home Fleet would expect him to do just that and would deploy accordingly to get between him and his base. He had given the British the slip by heading for France with *Scharnhorst* and *Gneisenau*; why not again? Events certainly proved his decision to be sound: the British began by searching everywhere but on the course he would have to take to get to France.

Another point is worth considering, too. Lütjens knew that he had just destroyed the most famous ship in the British Navy. He believed that he had driven off the flagship of the Home Fleet. (It was not until later the same night that Naval Group West informed him that he had beaten *Prince of Wales*, not *King George V*). In view of Günther Lütjens's past successes against the British, it is perfectly easy to understand why he headed out into the Atlantic instead of running for home.

What he did not know was that this time the British had an overwhelming advantage: aircraft-carriers. Lütjens had proved himself a master at eluding enemy battleships, but he had never had to cope with the long arm of naval air power on the high seas.

As evening closed in on 24th May, however, Lütjens's most urgent problem was not the British Fleet Air Arm but the persistent radar tracking of *Norfolk* and *Suffolk*. To enable *Prinz Eugen* to slip away, he made a mock attack on the British cruisers at about 1800 hours, and there was a brief exchange of harmless gunfire before *Bismarck* resumed her southerly course, on her own now, but still held by the British radar.

What of the British? The Home Fleet had no time to mourn the loss of the *Hood*, though perhaps its feelings were best summed up by the matter-of-fact Captain Philip Vian (liberator of the *Altmark's* prisoners, and now commander of the 4th Destroyer Flotilla) when he wrote, 'I believe I felt no stronger emotion at any time in the war.' When *Prince of Wales* retreated and the Battle of the Denmark Strait had ended at 0613 that morning, Tovey and the Home Fleet were 330 miles away to the southeast. The British Admiralty reacted with all the vigour displayed in 1914 after the British defeat by Admiral von Spee at Coronel. Admiral Somerville's Force H – the battle-cruiser *Renown*, aircraft-carrier *Ark Royal*, and cruiser *Sheffield*, ordered north from Gibraltar on the 23rd – was to stay in the Atlantic. The chase of the *Bismarck* was held to be far more important than the battle for Crete, now in its fifth day, and already putting grievous demands on the over-taxed British Mediterranean Fleet. The battleship *Ramillies*, escorting a Halifax convoy, was ordered to seal off *Bismarck*'s most probable route westwards, and the battleship *Revenge*, too was ordered to sail from Halifax and approach from the west.

Denmark Strait. *Bismarck*, seen from *Prinz Eugen*, opens fire on the *Hood*

But all this would take time; *Bismarck* was still making twenty-four knots, and Tovey knew that she must be slowed still further to allow his net time enough to tighten. He only had one weapon ready to his hand which could conceivably attempt this: the aircraft-carrier *Victorious*, a ship as new and untrained as *Prince of Wales*. But he had no alternative. At 2200 hours on the 24th, *Victorious*'s one and only strike force was on its way: nine torpedo-carrying Swordfish led by Lieutenant-Commander Eugene Esmonde. They were making history, for this was the first time that aircraft had left a carrier's deck to attack a German battleship at sea. Conditions were bad and the Swordfish had to be guided to their target by the radar reports of the shadowing cruisers. All nine Swordfish attacked shortly after midnight, and one of them scored a hit on the most heavily-armoured, midships section of the *Bismarck*. They then managed to crown their exploit by returning unscathed to *Victorious* and landing safely – though two of the Fulmar fighters sent out with the Swordfish were forced to 'ditch' in the ocean and were lost. It was a superb effort, deserving a better success. *Bismarck* was undamaged; the morale of her crew, far from being dashed by this rapidly-mounted new attack, soared after beating off the aircraft – and the pursuit continued as before, *Bismarck* heading due south, still held by the British radar, *Suffolk* shadowing at extreme range while *Prince of Wales* and *Norfolk* brought up the rear.

Perhaps the tenacity with which the British had maintained contact for over twenty-four hours led to overconfidence; perhaps it was merely the sheer bad luck which had dogged them ever since the weather had closed in on the 22nd. At 0306 hours on the 25th, *Suffolk* obtained another fix on *Bismarck* and continued with her antisubmarine zig-zag course. Ten minutes later, completing the inner leg of the zig-zag, she confidently expected to find *Bismarck* reappearing on her radar screen – but the sea was empty. *Bismarck* had escaped – and this when Tovey's battle fleet was a mere 100 miles away.

The first reaction of the British was to look west to safeguard the Halifax convoy route. *Norfolk* and *Suffolk* were already searching on that quarter, and Tovey ordered *Victorious* to begin air searches there at dawn. He feared that *Bismarck* would rendezvous with a tanker somewhere south of Greenland and start commerce-raiding with her fuel tanks replete. Far to the east, *Rodney* was astride the track *Bismarck* would have to take to reach the Bay of Biscay. *Ramillies* was heading north, and was approaching *Bismarck* head-on, but was hundreds of miles to the south when contact was lost. And Force H, the 'long-stop' carrier squadron from Gibraltar, was heading northwest into the open Atlantic. Now that *Bismarck* had vanished again, it seemed only too likely that the meshes in this huge net, covering the entire North Atlantic, would be too wide to stop her from slipping through.

Ironically, Lütjens betrayed himself – and betrayed himself without doing himself any harm. Believing that *Bismarck* was still being tracked by the British radar, and that he had nothing to lose by breaking radio silence, he sent off a long report to Hitler describing the victory over *Hood* and *Prince of Wales* – a message which was easily picked up and tracked by the British. (They had plenty of time, as it took *Bismarck* some thirty minutes to transmit her victory message.) But to start with it was plotted with a disastrous inaccuracy which disrupted the entire British pursuit. The Admiralty assumed that Tovey's force included destroyers equipped with direction-finding apparatus, and so merely transmitted individual bearings received, not an actual position; and the plotters aboard *King George V* made the serious mistake of using a navigational chart – which distorts radio bearings – instead of the correct gnomonic chart.

The result was that *Bismarck*'s new 'position' was plotted some 200 miles north of where she actually was. This made it look as though she were heading back to the North Sea via the Iceland/Faeroes passage, and at 1047 hours the whole Home Fleet turned in its tracks to give chase, while – still undetected – *Bismarck* ploughed on along her south-easterly course, heading for France.

Bismarck had been given another reprieve. It did not last long – but by the time the error had been put right, and the Admiralty had signalled its new appreciation that *Bismarck* was in fact trying to get through to France, and Tovey had swung round to the south-east (at 1810 on the 25th) the Home Fleet was now 150 miles behind *Bismarck*'s estimated position. With fuel starting to run low, it seemed like an impossibly long chase. Meanwhile the weather continued vile – low cloud and high seas from the north-west – making conditions most difficult for the comprehensive air search being made by the long-range Catalina flying-boats of RAF Coastal Command. But at 1036 hours on the morning of 26th May one of these Catalinas sighted a lone warship through the murk, circled to investigate, and was rocked by furious anti-aircraft fire. *Bismarck* had been found.

She was now only 690 miles from Brest and could get there late on the 27th. Within twenty-four hours she would be under the air umbrella of the Luftwaffe. Tovey was 130 miles to the north, with his fuel situation now becoming critical. In fact *Prince of Wales* and *Repulse* were already out of the hunt, ordered to Iceland and Newfoundland to refuel, although *Rodney* was steering to join Tovey's force. Coming in from the west after leaving the convoy they had been escorting were the five destroyers of Captain Vian's 4th Flotilla. But there seemed to be little or no hope of the all-important battleships bringing *Bismarck* to action; they seemed in a hopeless position, 'a terribly long way off,' as Tovey later said, 'and again our only hope lay in the Fleet Air Arm.' Everything now depended on Force H – and the *Ark Royal*.

It was fitting that *Ark Royal* should have the chance of avenging *Hood*, for the two warships had sailed together for many months in Force H as 'chummy ships'. *Sheffield* was detached to locate the *Bismarck* at 1315 hours on the 26th while the first air strike was being prepared; and at 1450 hours fourteen torpedo-carrying Swordfish staggered one by one from *Ark Royal*'s storm-tossed flight-deck. They attacked an hour later – but with near-disastrous results, for *Sheffield* was by now deep within the target area and had been mistaken by the Swordfish for *Bismarck* in the atrocious conditions. Luckily, all the torpedoes either missed or blew up prematurely due to their over-sensitive magnetic pistols, and a tragedy was avoided. The Swordfish returned to *Ark Royal* – apologising to *Sheffield* for the 'kippers' before they left – and a second strike was prepared, this time with contact pistols fitted into the torpedoes.

The second strike, guided in this time by directions from *Sheffield*, made history. Fifteen Swordfish made successive attacks from 2047 hours, some of the aircraft receiving severe damage from *Bismarck*'s guns – still more than active, for all the weariness of their crews – and one torpedo exploded right aft as *Bismarck* was dodging to starboard, wrecking her steering-gear and jamming her rudder hard over. As the last Swordfish left the scene, *Bismarck* had made two tight circles and was staggering away to the north-west at a bare ten knots, turning her damaged stern away from pounding seas . . .

And now heading straight for the British Home Fleet. *Bismarck*'s engines were still intact, but she could not use full power until the rudder had been cleared. A diver was sent down to

89

The power of *Bismarck's* guns

investigate, but the task seemed impossible. The damage, Lütjens concluded after hearing the reports, was irreparable. But *Bismarck*'s guns were undamaged, and the crippled battleship would limp forward to meet her fate on the following day. A last exchange of heroics with Berlin produced a typical verbal rataplan from Hitler: 'To the crew of the battleship *Bismarck:* The whole of Germany is with you. What can still be done will be done. The performance of your duty will strengthen our people in the struggle for their existence.' Lütjens also radioed for a U-boat to take off *Bismarck*'s War Diary, but none arrived in time and she carried the War Diary to her end – a sad loss to future naval historians.

But was all this necessary? Gerhard Junack, engineer lieutenant-commander in the *Bismarck*, certainly thinks not. 'One cannot help wondering whether everything humanly possible was really done in order to try and save the *Bismarck* on this critical night. The ship had gone to sea well constructed and it is possible that the damaged rudder might have been blown out of the stern without damage to the propellors. But this risk was not attempted – nor was there any attempt to improvise a sea-anchor to stabilise the course. With three propellors capable of driving *Bismarck* at

28 knots, it is difficult to accept that there was no alternative but to head straight for the enemy at a slow speed.'

Had *Ark Royal*'s Swordfish failed in their second attack, Tovey would still have had a last chance to cripple *Bismarck* – Vian's 4th Flotilla, which now arrived upon the scene. All through the night until 0700 hours on the 27th, Vian's destroyers – *Cossack*, *Maori*, *Sikh*, *Zulu*, and the Polish *Piorun* – made attack after attack, keeping *Bismarck*'s exhausted crews closed up at their gun stations (and undoubtedly doing much to hasten the end the following morning by tiring them to the limits of endurance). Yet *Bismarck*'s gunnery remained voluminous and accurate, driving off the destroyers time and again. Vian himself later reported – in his typically imperturbable style: 'During these attacks, and throughout the night, the enemy obtained only splinter hits from near misses by her 15-inch guns, but she shot away *Cossack*'s wireless aerials, which was very inconvenient. A disconcerting aspect of being under the fire of such big guns, which we were experiencing for the first time, was that the shells could be seen on our radar screen as they raced towards us, thus inducing some unpleasant moments until the shells plunged into the sea, exploding with a violent concussion and throwing up huge pillars of water which seemed to tower above us.'

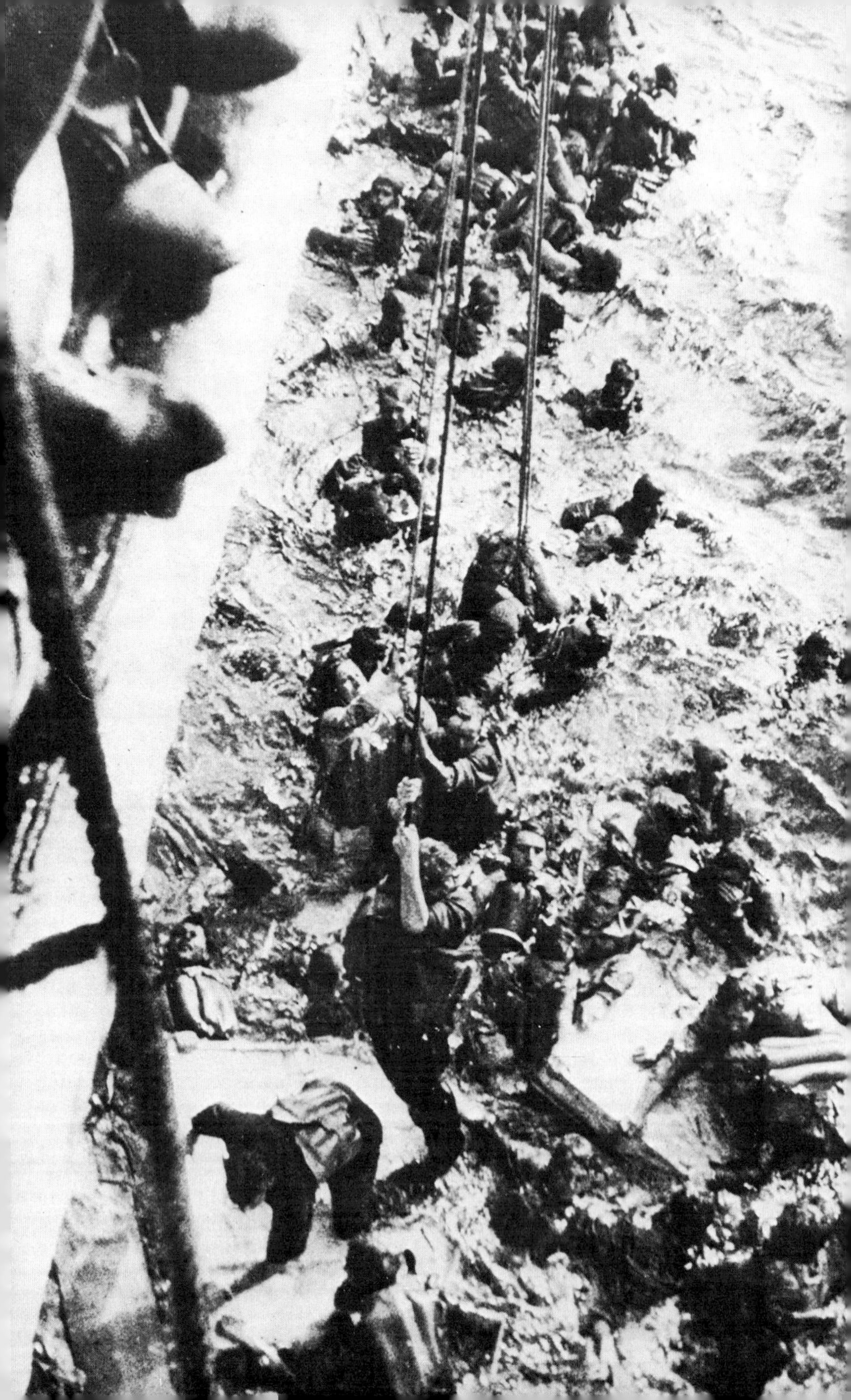

The end came with daylight on 27th May. Vian sighted *King George V* and *Rodney* soon after 0800, and homed them accurately onto the *Bismarck*. Unlike the unfortunate Admiral Holland with *Hood* and *Prince of Wales*, Tovey could afford to fight this battle as he chose. He waited until daylight. He gave *Rodney* full license to manoeuvre as her captain thought best, to give her gunnery full play. and the last fight of the *Bismarck* began when all three battleships opened fire between 0847 and 0849, with the range at about 16,000 yards.

True to her record, *Bismarck*'s first salvoes fell uncomfortably close to the *Rodney*, which had been selected for priority treatment as the strongest enemy (*Rodney* carried nine 16-inch guns). But the tired German gun crews could not maintain this accuracy – nor could the best gunnery in the world have availed against the torrent of 14-inch and 16-inch shells which started to pound the *Bismarck* shortly after 0900 hours. With an almost horrible simplicity, the British Official History states; 'Gradually the range was reduced to what can justly be described as point-blank target practice. By 10.15 the giant battleship had been reduced to a flaming shambles.'

So short of fuel oil were the British battleships after their long chase across the Atlantic that Tovey had to break off the action at 1023 and head for home, leaving the wallowing hulk of the *Bismarck* to be finished off with torpedoes from the cruisers and destroyers. Even so, she had to be helped on her way by the German engineers in her still-intact engine-rooms, who had ample time to prepare and explode demolition charges. *Bismarck* rolled over and sank at 1036 hours, her flag still flying; 110 survivors were picked up by the British and the German submarine U-74 saved another three, but over 2,200 of

The end. Exhausted *Bismarck* survivors are rescued after the final action

Fleet Commander Günther Lütjens

her crew died, including Admiral Lütjens. If ever a warship died a Wagnerian death it was *Bismarck*, scuttled by her own crew after her upper-works were ruined and her guns all knocked out, suffering certainly eight and possibly twelve torpedo-hits (out of a total launched at her, be it noted, of seventy-one). The British crews who fought the *Bismarck* marvelled at the fighting spirit of her crew against such terrifying odds, and at the fearful amount of punishment which their ship endured.

Prinz Eugen, meanwhile, having refuelled from the tanker *Spichern* far to the south of where she had parted from *Bismarck*, was in no commerce-raiding mood. Her Captain Brinckmann took her east to Brest as soon as he could, having accomplished nothing. Operation *Rheinübung* had reached its disastrous end. In two months the outlook for Hitler's High Seas Fleet had completely changed. The British strength at sea was unbroken, and many valuable lessons had been learned by the Royal Navy, which now turned with new vigour to the hunting down of the surface-raiders still at sea, and strengthened the blockade of the surviving warships of the German fleet.

Scharnhorst and Gneisenau

The loss of the *Bismarck* was a turning-point for Hitler's High Seas Fleet. Unlike his behaviour when he had heard of the loss of the *Graf Spee*, Hitler received the news quietly enough and went on to discuss other matters. But in fact the episode cancelled all the advantages and lost all the ground that Raeder had won by the fleet's successes to that date. Hitler had always been unhappy when the big ships were out; after the fate of the *Bismarck*, he would interfere increasingly in every movement of the fleet. Unknown to Raeder, the regular warships of the Reich navy had made their last war cruise against the Atlantic sealanes.

Bismarck was gone, and *Prinz Eugen*, after a cruise which can most kindly be described as abortive, had scuttled back to Brest as soon as possible, joining *Scharnhorst* and *Gneisenau* there. But the German disguised merchant raiders were still at sea, and were steadily increasing their score. Three more - *Michel*, *Stier*, and *Togo* - were being prepared for action, though none of them would go to sea during 1941. And it was the months after the sinking of the *Bismarck* which saw the end of the disguised raiders' 'happy time' (to borrow a phrase more commonly used of the heyday of the U-boat arm). One by one the raiders were forced to curtail their cruises and head for home. Some got there; some were hunted down and sunk, until by December 1941 no more disguised raiders were left on the high seas.

In fact, the process had begun even before *Bismarck* had put to sea in late May. On 23rd April, *Thor* arrived safely in the Bay of Biscay - after yet another battle with an armed merchant cruiser, the *Voltaire*, on 4th April, the *Voltaire* being sunk - and passed safely up-Channel to German waters, reaching Hamburg on the 30th. *Thor* had cruised for ten months, and had sunk eleven ships totalling 83,000 tons.

Within a week another raider, the

Pinguin, had also quitted the scene, but in a far more dramatic manner. On 8th May she was intercepted by the cruiser *Cornwall* in the Indian Ocean. Her failure to pass herself off as a Norwegian vessel (after much suspicious hesitation by the British captain) was followed by a vicious gunnery duel, and *Pinguin* blew up after eleven minutes with heavy loss of life, including Captain Felix Krüder. *Pinguin* was the first of the disguised raiders to be sunk by the British. She had cruised for ten months and had sunk twenty-eight ships totalling 136,551 tons; and her most impressive exploit had been the capture of an entire whaling fleet – two factory ships, a tanker, and eleven whale-catchers – in Antarctic waters on 14th and 15th January.

Orion was the next raider to return safely, arriving in Bordeaux on 23rd August. She had not been among the highest-scoring raiders of the 'first wave'; in company with *Komet*, she had accounted for seven victims totalling 43,744 tons, but her overall score (including the 'three-and-a-half' ships shared with *Komet*) was only 57,444 tons. An elderly vessel, *Orion* was never used again as a raider, but she had done an impressive job of keeping herself seaworthy for 510 days.

Komet, too, made a safe journey home. She quitted the Pacific on 18th October, rounding Cape Horn in company with her last prize, the Dutch *Kota Nopan*, which was carrying a valuable cargo of manganese and rubber. *Kota Nopan* safely arrived in Bordeaux on 17th November, while U-boats escorted *Komet* into Cherbourg on the 26th. She had been spotted in the Bay of Biscay, and had to run the gauntlet of several British air attacks as she made her final run up-Channel, but arrived undamaged in Hamburg on 30th November. *Komet*'s tally was 'six-and-a-half' ships of 42,959 tons, and she had cruised for fifteen-and-a-half months.

But *Kormoran*, cruising in the Indian Ocean, made the most spectacular exit of all. On 19th November she fell in with the Australian cruiser *Sydney* (namesake of the ship which had run the German surface raider *Emden* to earth in 1914) off the western coast of Australia. After the usual preliminary period of question-and-answer (Captain Theodor Detmers was trying to pass his ship off as a Dutchman) there was fought one of the most remarkable single-ship duels in naval history. By 1725 Detmers had decided that he would have to fight for it; the *Kormoran*'s gun-flaps were flung open, and *Sydney* (whose captain had most incautiously approached to within 2,000 yards) found herself being pounded by accurate, rapid-fire broadsides. Within minutes *Sydney*'s bridge was a wreck and she had also been hit by a torpedo from *Kormoran*, and soon her forward guns were silent. But her after turrets kept firing, and began to score damaging hits on *Kormoran*. Both ships began to burn fiercely, and at 1745 *Kormoran*'s engines broke down. The battle, however, did not end until about 1830, with both ships mortally damaged. *Sydney*, a blazing wreck, drifted helplessly away and vanished over the horizon. She was never seen again; there were no survivors. But *Kormoran*'s crew could not master the fire which was threatening her mine store, and Detmers ordered 'Abandon ship'; the crew took to the boats, and *Kormoran* blew up shortly after midnight. Some 315 survivors from her crew of 400 managed to reach Australia or were picked up. It was an extraordinary end to a cruise which had lasted eleven-and-a-half months and which had accounted for 68,274 tons of Allied shipping.

Of all the disguised surface raiders which had sailed since March 1940, only *Atlantis*, first of them all, was still at large – and she did not outlive the *Kormoran* by as much as three days.

Since the New Year of 1940–41, *Atlantis* had enhanced the impressive cruise-record of the surface raiders by virtually circumnavigating the world, like *Orion*. The summer months of 1941 had seen her cruise in the Indian Ocean and Australian waters for eighty days without finding a victim, and Captain Rogge decided to try the *Komet*'s hunting-ground in the Pacific. There, on 10th September, *Atlantis* took her last prize, the Norwegian *Silvaplana*, before replenishing from *Komet*'s supply-ship and heading for the Atlantic via Cape Horn, which she passed on 30th October.

Back in the Atlantic, *Atlantis* was ordered to take on the duties of a U-boat supply-ship before heading for home – and it was on 22nd November, when U-126 was in the act of refuelling from *Atlantis*, that the British cruiser *Devonshire* found the German raider. U-126 crash-dived, and the now-familiar game of bluff began – but this time the British captain was not to be hoodwinked. He kept well out of range. He radioed for confirmation that the ship *Atlantis* was claiming to be could not possibly be there – and when he got it he immediately opened up with his 8-inch guns, with *Atlantis* out-ranged, unable to reply, and her crew forced to take to the boats while their ship blew up and sank. Unlike *Pinguin* and *Kormoran*, *Atlantis* in her last fight was unable to prevent the British achieving anything less than a one-sided, bloodless success. But she had set up a record for surface raiding and long-range cruising which remained unbeaten for the rest of the war: over twenty months at sea, and twenty-two ships totalling 145,697 tons sunk or captured.

Thus by November 1941 the British had succeeded in clearing the high seas of German surface raiders. It had taken them far longer than in the First World War, and the problem could only be considered solved for the present. Far more vital during this round-up of the merchant raiders was the menace in home waters: *Scharnhorst*, *Gneisenau*, and *Prinz Eugen* in Brest harbour, a potent battle-squadron in themselves, not to mention the possibility of *Bismarck*'s sister-ship *Tirpitz* breaking out to join them. There still seemed every chance of Raeder's original *Rheinübung* plan becoming a reality. And on 22nd June the invasion of Russia had begun. Within weeks the catastrophic losses of war *materiel* set Stalin demanding supply-convoys to Russia, adding a third geographical dimension, the Arctic, to the Royal Navy's commitments in the Atlantic and the Mediterranean. The German warships in Brest, therefore, were justly regarded as a most dangerous 'fleet in being'. The difficulties of destroying them were already well known; every effort was therefore made to immobilise them and make it impossible for them to sally out and fall upon the Atlantic convoys.

The bombers tried. Churchill had proclaimed the Brest squadron a number-one target, and a number-one target it remained for the rest of the year. Three-quarters of the total tonnage of bombs dropped by Bomber Command during 1941 were aimed at Brest, bombs which otherwise would have been aimed at targets in the Reich. Perhaps never has a remotely-based 'fleet in being' diverted so much enemy effort from its homeland.

The Germans' luck soon ran out. On 24th July five bombs struck home on *Scharnhorst*, which had made a brief cruise from Brest to La Pallice, and she struggled back to Brest with an impromptu cargo of 3,000 tons of flood water. Earlier in the month, *Prinz Eugen*, too, had been immobilised by a bomb hit at Brest. By the end of July 1941, therefore, *Scharnhorst*, *Gneisenau*, and *Prinz Eugen* were all undergoing dockyard surgery after the attentions of the RAF. There was no chance for another sortie from Brest during the summer of 1941; and the German Naval High Command, on the insistence of Hitler, was forced to reconsider the value of heavy units of the fleet based on the Biscay ports.

Above: Shrouded with camouflage netting, *Prinz Eugen* lurks in Brest after her escape from the *Rheinübung* fiasco. *Below:* Conference aboard *Scharnhorst*

The damage suffered by the ships in Brest reinforced Hitler's 'intuition' that Norway was the crucial zone in the West, and that it was futile to keep vital units of the fleet away from it. Had the British been able to read the Führer's mind, they could hardly have done more to encourage this view, for in 1941 they started to launch their first big Commando raids – against targets in Norway. On 4th March they attacked fish-oil factories and shipping in the Lofoten Islands. Between 25th August and 3rd September they evacuated the Norwegian and Russian population of Spitzbergen and wrecked the coal mines there. And right at the close of the year, on 27th December, they raided the coastal trade focus of Vaagsö Island, knocking out coastal batteries, destroying 16,000 tons of shipping, and taking ninety-eight prisoners. Within forty-eight hours a full report was on Hitler's desk. The Führer deliberated; his 'intuition' produced a solution; he pronounced:

'If the British go about things properly they will attack northern Norway at several points. By means of an all-out attack by their fleet and ground troops they will try to displace us there, take Narvik if possible, and thus exert pressure on Sweden and Finland. This might be of decisive importance for the outcome of the war.

'The German fleet must therefore use all its forces for the defence of Norway. It will be expedient to transfer all battleships and pocket-battleships there for this purpose.'

Raeder fully agreed that *Tirpitz* should go to Trondheim as soon as possible to act as a one-vessel naval deterrent in Norwegian waters. But – unlike Hitler – he refused to believe that the Brest squadron could be returned to Germany up-Channel, under the noses of the British. True, the fuel oil situation was not good, and the ships in Brest would not be able to make a prolonged cruise in the Atlantic (planned by Raeder for March-April 1942). It might, in the long run, be best to bring them back to Germany around the north of Iceland. But there was no shortage of diesel fuel, and Raeder wanted *Admiral Scheer* to make another long-range cruise. The situation in the Far East had been transformed by Japan's entry into the war on 8th December, and now every port in the Japanese Empire could be used as a refuge by German raiders. But Hitler's obsession with Norway steam-rollered Raeder into submission. The Grand Admiral's hopes were wrecked and his objections overruled. And it was on this note that the preparations for the famous gamble known as the 'Channel Dash' were begun.

It was very much Hitler's plan. It appealed to him: an opportunity to flex his 'intuition' by overcoming the objections of his military experts to a daring venture carried out under the nose of the enemy. For once, however, it was a plan that had a lot to it. There could be no denying that the Channel was by far the quickest route back to German waters. More important, the string of German fighter bases along the Channel coast would be able to lay on virtually continuous air cover. To protests that the German ships would be equally exposed to heavy British air attacks (not quite true, especially with regard to the home stretch along the Dutch coast, for the RAF bases would be further away), Hitler replied with appeals for boldness, with references to the supreme advantage of surprise – and with the straight ultimatum that the ships must either attempt the Channel route or be decommissioned, broken up where they were, and have their crews, guns, and armour sent north to build heavy coastal defence batteries in Norway.

Air power was the key. On 1st January, 1942, Major-General Hans Jeschonnek, Chief of the Luftwaffe General Staff, gave an advance briefing to the fighter ace Adolf Galland, newly promoted to be C-in-C of the German fighter arm. He warned

Galland what was brewing in the Führer's mind, and that only the strongest possible fighter protection would make the Naval High Command consider the Channel venture. On 12th January there was a decisive conference at Hitler's HQ in East Prussia, *Wolfsschanze*, the 'Wolf's Lair'. Raeder was there; so were Jeschonnek and Galland, together with Vice-Admiral Otto Ciliax, the new commander of the fleet in Brest. After many arguments between Raeder and Jeschonnek, the following decisions were made: minimum movements of the ships before the breakout; departure by night, so as to run the Dover Narrows in daylight; and an all-out effort by Galland's fighter strength along the Channel coast. In his summing-up, Hitler forecast that the British would not react fast enough to stop the ships – and repeated his ominous diagnosis that the ships in Brest were like 'a patient with cancer who cannot be saved unless he submits to an operation'. His 'surgeons', who immediately began work on detailed plans, were to be Ciliax and Galland.

'Thunderbolt-Cerberus', as the Germans code-named the Channel Dash ('Thunderbolt' for the Luftwaffe and 'Cerberus' for the navy), was one of the extremely rare successes in co-operation between the services which the German High Command achieved in the Second World War. Galland, who master-minded the air umbrella over the ships, later wrote: 'The technical co-ordination of this typical combined operation was planned in such a way that the Luftwaffe was not placed under the navy, but had to rely on teamwork. I must say here in advance that this co-ordination worked without friction . . .

'Between the different naval command centres and the air force, liaison officers were exchanged during the preparations in order to give the best chance of teamwork. My most important liaison with the naval C-in-C was established by Colonel Ibel

Otto Ciliax, C-in-C Brest squadron

as 'Fighter Command Afloat'. With him was an officer in charge of operations and interception, two further interception-officers, as well as Colonel Elle in charge of the necessary wireless personnel. This staff was to be on board the flagship during the operation. In the *Gneisenau* and *Prinz Eugen* there were a pilot officer and a wireless operator.' Meanwhile, on shore, Galland amassed about 250 day fighters (Me-109s and FW-190s), with 30 Me-110 night fighters to cover the dawn and evening periods.

The weather was vital. Bad conditions were essential, to blind the British as long as possible without grounding the German fighters. At the same time, a day had to be picked with a strong tide to speed the ships up-Channel. The tide problem narrowed down the choice for a suitable date to between 7th and 15th February and an ideal weather forecast for the ships (if less favourable for the fighters) was obtained for 12th February. As darkness fell on 11th February, the final preparations were made. Seven destroyers – the 'safety belt for the capital ships', as Galland puts it – headed for the exit of Brest harbour, while *Scharnhorst*, *Gneisenau*, and *Prinz Eugen* prepared to follow.

99

Then, at the very worst moment for the German vessels, the sirens sounded. A British air raid was coming in, and the ships were rushed back to their berths. As had happened so often in the past eleven months, Brest harbour was rocked by bombs but the ships escaped unscathed. The last bombers droned away – and within minutes the ships were renewing their preparations for sea. Shortly after 2300 hours – two hours behind schedule – the flotilla was on its way, unharmed and undetected.

The British had always thought it likely that the Germans might try to run the ships through the Channel, and had laid their plans accordingly. Coastal Command patrols had watched the concentration of destroyers in Brest, not to mention the stepping-up of German minesweeping operations in the Channel. The British, too, had tidal charts and were watching the weather reports. And on 2nd February the Admiralty had issued a prophetic 'appreciation': 'At first sight this passage up the Channel appears hazardous for the Germans. It is probable, however, that, as their heavy ships are not fully efficient, they would prefer such passage, relying for security on their destroyers and aircraft, which are efficient, and knowing full well that we have no heavy ships with which to oppose them in the Channel. We might well, therefore, find the two battle-cruisers and the 8-inch cruiser with five large and five small destroyers, also, say, 20 fighters constantly overhead (with reinforcements within call), proceeding up the Channel...'

Next day the order went out for Operation 'Fuller': the bringing to readiness of all available trained air and naval strike forces. These were scattered up and down the country, from Cornwall to Scotland – 42 Squadron, for example, had been moved to Leuchars in Scotland when *Tirpitz* was transferred from Kiel to Trondheim on 22nd January. No 42 had thirteen Beaufort torpedo-bombers.

At Thorney Island, near Portsmouth, was 217 Squadron with seven Beauforts. At St Eval in Cornwall was 86 Squadron, new and inexperienced, with thirteen Beauforts. At Manston on the tip of Kent, in the very throat of the Channel, were six Fleet Air Arm Swordfish under the command of Commander Eugene Esmonde, the man who had led the first air strike against the *Bismarck*.

As for the Royal Navy, its strength in the Narrow Seas was at a low ebb. The Home Fleet was hundreds of miles to the north in Scapa Flow, and it had to stay there as long as the *Tirpitz* was in Trondheim. Six elderly destroyers based on Harwich, and a handful of torpedo-boats; some thirty torpedo-bombers, dispersed across Britain about as widely as they could be; and half a dozen Swordfish – such was the force that could be sent against the German flotilla and its dominant air umbrella – *if* the Germans were spotted in time, *if* they fulfilled the expectations of the British by coming through at night, and *if*, by some miracle, the supporting British fighters and the strike crews could create, on the spot, a system of co-operation which only months of intense training could have given...

Things went wrong for the British right from the start. To begin with, the bombers which had raided Brest on the evening of the 11th reported – naturally enough – that all was normal at Brest and the ships were still there. This need not have mattered unduly, since Coastal Command was flying three patrols (Lockheed Hudsons, fitted with radar), off Brest itself, along the north coast of Brittany, and between Le Havre and Boulogne. But neither of the first two picked up the German squadron, and the third was still too far to the east to have been able to do so. The ships had rounded Ushant shortly after midnight. At 0114 on the 12th they were swinging east into the Channel, steaming at twenty-seven

100

Above: Scharnhorst takes the lead as 'Thunderbolt-Cerberus', the Channel Dash, begins. *Below:* Vividly-camouflaged torpedo-boats of the close escort

Below: Me-110s of the low-level air umbrella mustered by Adolf Galland

knots. They passed Alderney at 0530; the first torpedo-boats joined the destroyers' to form the outer escort off Cherbourg; and the first Me-110 night fighters were over the squadron by 0850, shortly before dawn, flying low over the water on the port quarter – from which the British attacks would come.

Soon afterwards the Germans began heavy jamming of British radio frequencies, but as they had been doing this at intervals for weeks it evoked no undue suspicion until it became continuous at about 1020. Soon the British radar began to register large concentrations of aircraft over the French coast, and patrolling Spitfires began to report considerable activity by torpedo-boats further up the Channel. But not until 1042 did two Spitfires, in hot pursuit of a couple of Me-109s, fly right over the German ships. They broke off at once and headed for base, landing at 1109 with the electrifying news: the Brest squadron was not only out, but steaming at close to thirty knots into the Straits of Dover.

Air Vice-Marshal Joubert, head of RAF Coastal Command, had about six hours of daylight left to get his strike forces into action, knowing that the Germans had won a 300-mile lead over his existing plans. There could be no question of a united attack. The St Eval Beauforts had been left far to the west, and it would take hours to move them eastwards to a base within range; the Thorney Island Beauforts were all within range but unprepared for an immediate attack (three of the seven aircraft there were armed with bombs, not torpedoes); while the Beauforts at Leuchars, which Joubert had ordered south on the 10th, had been diverted to Coltishall in Norfolk and were just about to land there when the German ships were sighted in mid-Channel. The best chance for an immediate strike lay with Esmonde's Swordfish at Manston – and it would have to be an immediate one, for with the German squadron making thirty knots up-Channel those single-engined, lumbering biplanes would soon be hopelessly out-ranged by the speeding warships. Esmonde, then, would lead the first strike. He did not hesitate.

It was one of the saddest yet most heroic missions of the war. Everything went wrong. Only one of the five squadrons of Spitfires which had been promised for Esmonde turned up at the rendezvous on time, and Esmonde had to make the agonising decision to go in without adequate fighter cover. None of the six Swordfish returned: all were hacked down by the swarming German fighters and the heavy flak from the ships. Esmonde was last seen pressing through a hail of flak bursts, in flames. Only five men survived out of eighteen; one of them vividly remembered the astonishing sight of FW-190 fighters flying with wheels and flaps down in an attempt to get their speed down to that of the plodding 'Stringbags'. Esmonde was awarded a posthumous VC, but none of his gallant force had scored a hit; and by early afternoon the German ships were heading out into the North Sea, still undamaged.

Joubert now planned a strike by the Thorney Island Beauforts, hoping to score one or more hits which might slow down the squadron until the combined strength of the St Eval and Coltishall Beauforts could be mustered. There were repeated breakdowns in communication between the British fighters and strike planes. On the German side, Galland meanwhile had given the order to break radio silence, and he had stepped up his fighter cover from sea-level to higher altitude to fend off the medium-bombing attacks which were launched in sporadic fashion during the afternoon. But when the first of the pursuing Beauforts caught up with the German ships, they noticed an exciting difference in their formation: one of the battle-cruisers seemed to have dropped out. After all the previous disappointments for the British, had the Germans' luck finally run out? This was so – but it was not due to the British air strikes. At about 1430 hours – roughly two and a half hours after passing the Dover Narrows – *Scharnhorst* shook to a violent explosion and came to a dead stop while the rest of the flotilla thundered past her. She had hit a mine, and for a while it seemed she would be lucky to reach a Belgian or Dutch port. Admiral Ciliax and his Luftwaffe liaison officer transferred to the destroyer Z-29, and he set off in pursuit of his command. By 1505 hours, however, *Scharnhorst* was under way again, and brilliant emergency repairs enabled her to work up to much of her original speed. Meanwhile, the Harwich destroyers had made torpedo attacks on the German ships, only to be beaten off with severe damage to the destroyer *Worcester*.

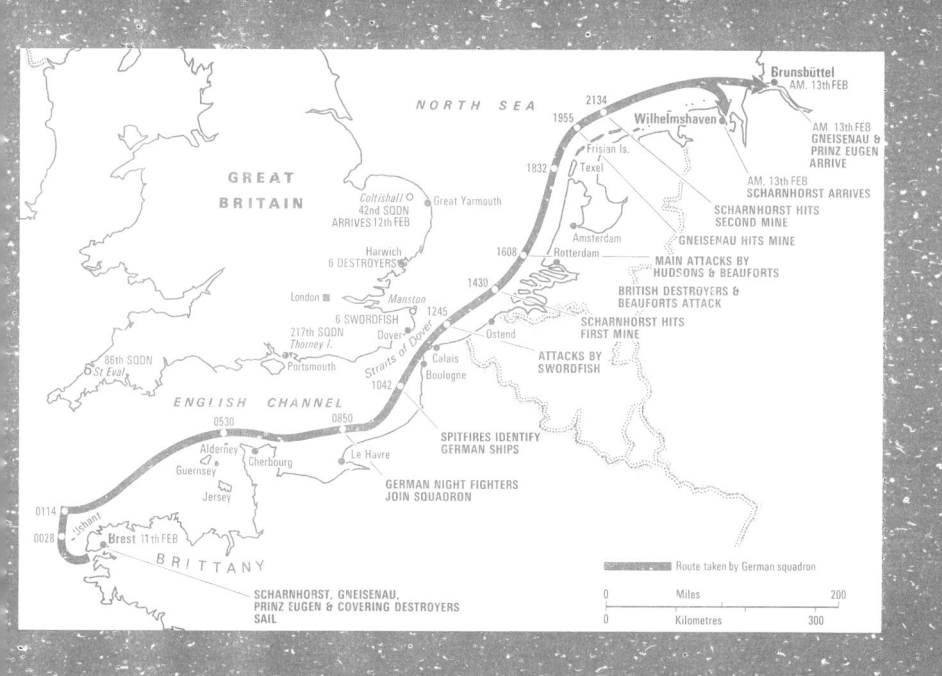

Damage to Z-29, however, soon forced Ciliax to shift his flag again – and while he was still in the cutter taking him across to the destroyer *Hermann Schömann*, with another whirling air battle in full swing overhead, he had the mingled mortification and satisfaction of seeing *Scharnhorst* race past at twenty-five knots. As dusk drew in, the weather conditions worsened as if to help the German warships home. The last of the Coastal Command Beauforts – those rushed east from St Eval – never made contact, let alone attack. The ships were passing the Frisian Islands when, at 1955, *Gneisenau* hit a mine. Like *Scharnhorst*, however, she was able to carry on after emergency repairs, and reached Brunsbüttel safely with *Prinz Eugen* – the only one of the trio to come through the ordeal unscathed – at 0700 on the 13th. *Scharnhorst*'s trials, however, were not yet over. At 2134 she hit another mine in approximately the same waters as had *Gneisenau*, and this time was badly damaged. *Scharnhorst*'s engines were both silenced and she took on 1,000 tons of water. It took her almost another hour to get under way again, and she limped into Wilhelmshaven

103

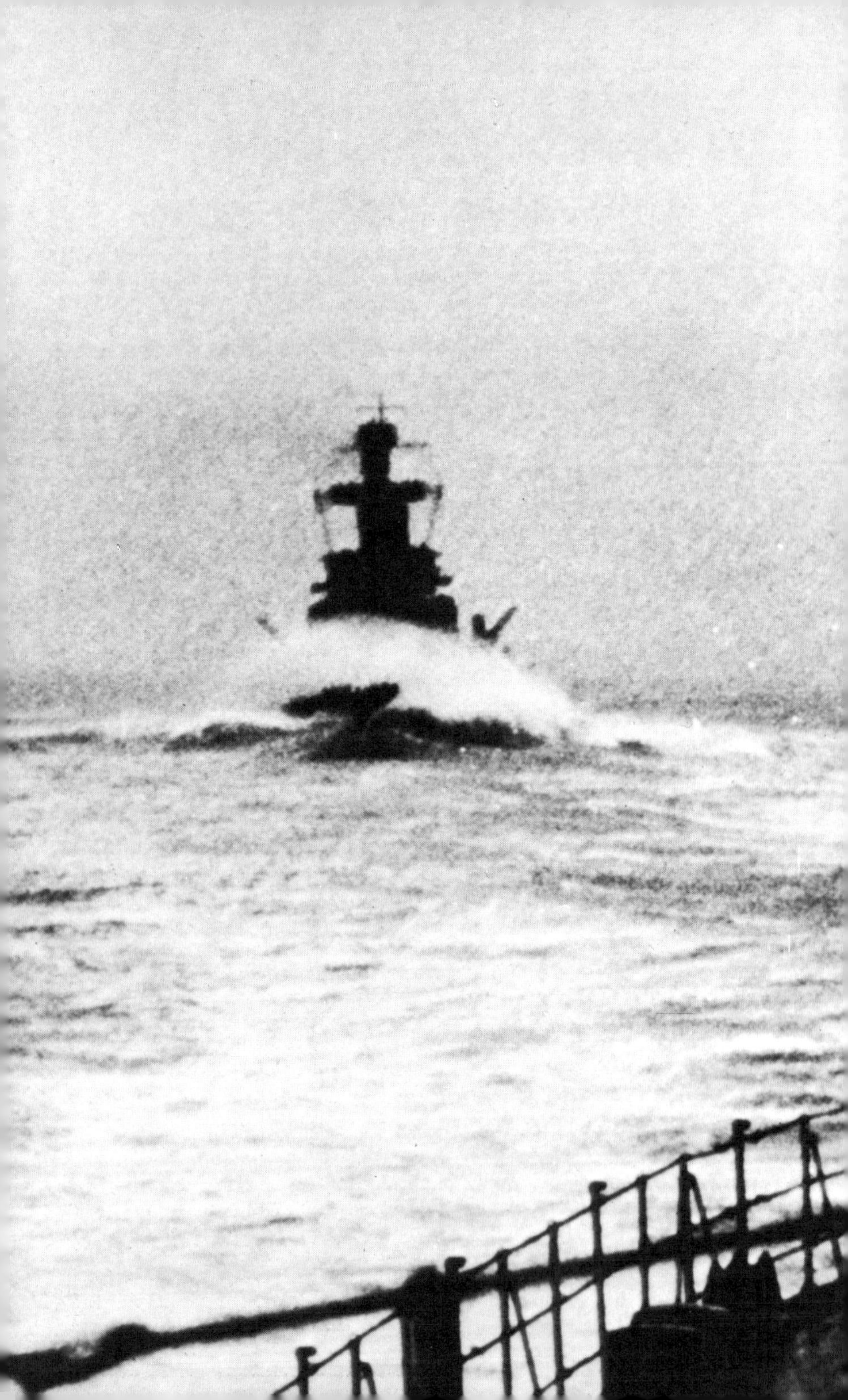

in the early hours of the 13th.

There was fury in Britain – and a full Board of Enquiry – after the failure to stop the Channel Dash. Whatever the strategic advantages may have been in the German withdrawal of their battle fleet from Brest – whatever relief the Allies would now find in the Battle of the Atlantic – there was no doubt that the British had suffered a humiliating defeat. A full-blown German fleet had deliberately courted every form of attack the British could throw at it – in their own home waters, what was more – and had survived the lot. For almost twelve hours, moreover, German warships had cruised the English Channel without even being spotted. Even the stoic *Times* lost its self-control far enough to thunder 'Vice-Admiral Ciliax has succeeded where the Duke of Medina Sidonia [commander of the Spanish Armada] failed' – a somewhat fatuous comparison when one considers that Ciliax was trying to sprint through the Channel without looking for trouble, which was the complete opposite of what the Armada was trying to do.

Although 'Thunderbolt-Cerberus' was undoubtedly one of the most spectacular performances by Hitler's High Seas Fleet, it marked the end of the line for the *Scharnhorst-Gneisenau* partnership. Once again, as back in Brest, both battle-cruisers were back in dock for repairs – but this time the luck of the *Gneisenau* had run out. On the night of 26th February she received two grievous hits from heavy bombs as she lay in dry dock in Kiel, undergoing her mine-damage repairs. A full year's repair programme was necessitated, which soon suffered the stop-go treatment which had kept the aircraft-carrier *Graf Zeppelin* in a state of uncompleted limbo since 1940. *Gneisenau* was de-

Left: **Centre ship in the squadron, *Gneisenau* ships water over her bows.**
Right: Scharnhorst and *Gneisenau* lead *Prinz Eugen* home to Germany

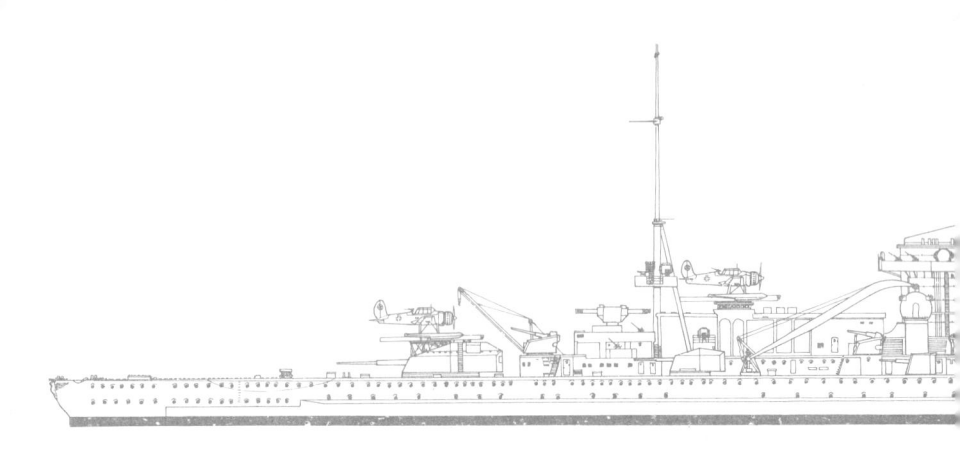

Scharnhorst after her conversion, with clipper bow. The most obvious feature which distinguished her from *Gneisenau* was her mast, a tripod structure stepped further aft. In both these ships, the 11-inch gun was adopted as the main armament rather than a heavier calibre, to allow for greater weight of protection. *Displacement:* 32,000 tons. *Length overall:* 741½ feet. *Beam:* 98½ feet. *Draught:* 24¼ feet. *Max speed:*

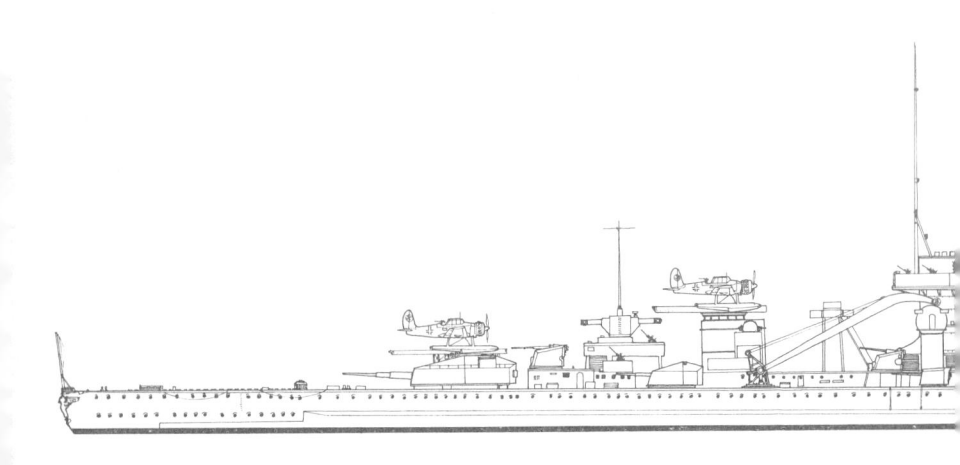

commissioned in July 1942. Her repairs were finally abandoned in January 1943. Her guns were taken out of her for coastal defence. In March 1945, what had once been one of the finest capital ships ever built suffered a final ignominy: *Gneisenau*'s rusting, disarmed hulk was sunk at Gdynia as a blockship against the Russians.

But with the success of the Channel Dash in mid-February 1942, Hitler had got his way. The German surface fleet could now be concentrated in what he still believed to be the 'zone of destiny' – Norway and its fjords. And as the summer of 1942 drew on, the fear of the German fleet would heap peril on peril for the men of the Allied merchantmen heading 'north-about' for the ports of Murmansk and Archangel. The ordeal of the Russian convoys was about to begin.

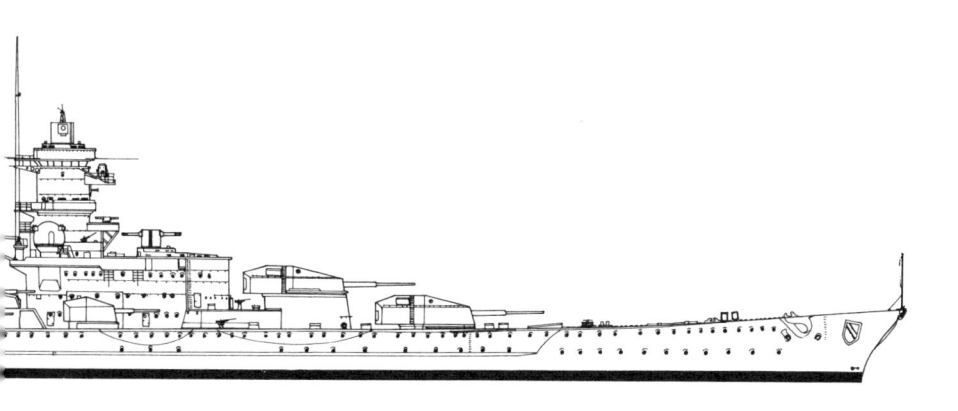

31½ knots. *Radius:* 10,000 miles at 19 knots. *Armour:* Main belt 12-13 inch, turrets 12 inch, deck 6 inch. *Armament:* Nine 11-inch, twelve 5.9-inch, fourteen 4.1-inch AA, sixteen 37-mm AA, ten (later 28) 20-mm AA; six 21-inch torpedo-tubes; four aircraft *Complement:* 1,800

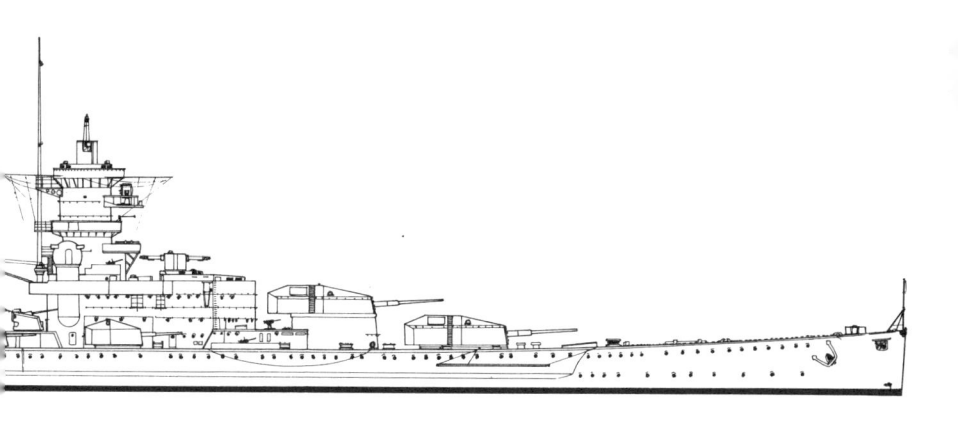

Gneisenau as originally built, with straight bow. Later (as with *Scharnhorst*) she was given a clipper bow and a funnel screen. The 'enlarged *Deutschland*' format is obvious. Among the toughest battle-cruisers ever built by any nation, *Scharnhorst* and *Gneisenau* were also referred to as 'small battleships'; and when the Second World War broke out they formed the only modern battle squadron in the German navy. *Displacement:* 32,000 tons. *Length overall:* 741½ feet. *Beam:* 98¼ feet. *Draught:* 24½ feet. *Max speed:* 31½ knots. *Radius:* 10,000 miles at 19 knots. *Armour:* Main belt 12-13 inch, turrets 12 inch, deck 6 inch. *Armament:* Nine 11-inch, twelve 5.9-inch, fourteen 4.1-inch AA, sixteen 37-mm AA, ten (later 38) 20-mm AA; six 21-inch torpedo-tubes; four aircraft. *Complement:* 1,800

Arctic menace

Within weeks of the launching of 'Barbarossa' on 22nd June 1941, most of European Russia had been overrun, two-thirds of the Red Army's prewar strength had been annihilated, German spearheads were driving towards Leningrad, Moscow, and Rostov, and the bulk of Russia's industrial centres west of the River Don had been either captured or destroyed. By herculean efforts many vital industries had been evacuated lock, stock, and barrel to sites in the Urals, but their production could not be resumed before the winter. Long before that, with first Leningrad and then Moscow under siege, it seemed that Hitler's boast, 'We only to kick in the front door and the whole rotten structure will come tumbling down', would prove only too true of the Soviet Union.

In his broadcast on the first day of the German invasion of Russia, Churchill had stated: 'We shall give whatever help we can to Russia and the Russian people.' One 4th September, M Maisky, Soviet Ambassador in London, relayed Stalin's request for 'a second front somewhere in the Balkans or France, capable of drawing away from the Eastern Front 30 to 40 divisions, and at the same time . . . ensuring to the Soviet Union 30,000 tons of aluminium by the beginning of October next and a *monthly* minimum of aid amounting to 400 aircraft and 500 tanks (of small or medium size) . . .' A week later, Stalin told Churchill: 'It seems to me that Great Britain could without risk landing in Archangel twenty-five to thirty divisions, or transport them across Iran to the southern regions of the USSR . . .'

On this note the planning of British (and, after Pearl Harbor on 7th December, of American) aid to Russia began.

But Britain had precious little to give. Anything she sent to Russia in 1941 would be a drop in the ocean of the vast demands of the Red Army on the Eastern Front. A Second Front was out of the question until the Mediterranean had been made an Allied lake. Yet Churchill insisted that despite the additional strain thrown on the responsibilities of the Home Fleet, a regular system of convoys to Russia's northern ports should start to run as soon as humanly possible, sending whatever arms and supplies could be spared.

The Russian convoys were to traverse one of the most hideous stretches of water in the world: the Barents Sea. Lashed by sub-zero winds off the polar icecap which sometimes reach hurricane strength, the sea can become tortured into nightmare waves seventy feet high. Spray freezes immediately, forming a top-heavy shroud on decks, guns, and stanchions which must be chipped away to prevent 'tender' ships with high centres of gravity from rolling over from excess weight. The icy sea is a killer, biting off the human circulation within minutes. There is fog, caused by the warm Gulf Stream blending with the Arctic Ocean. There is snow. And in summer, in those far northern seas, there is the Midnight Sun – a nightmare in war to ships and men trying to remain concealed from a vigilant enemy.

There is also the ice edge, fluctuating widely with the seasons. It was the ice that laid down the two main tracks of the Russian convoys. In winter, convoys could only use Mur-

Hitler's dream fulfilled: *Scharnhorst* **reaches the seas of the Far North**

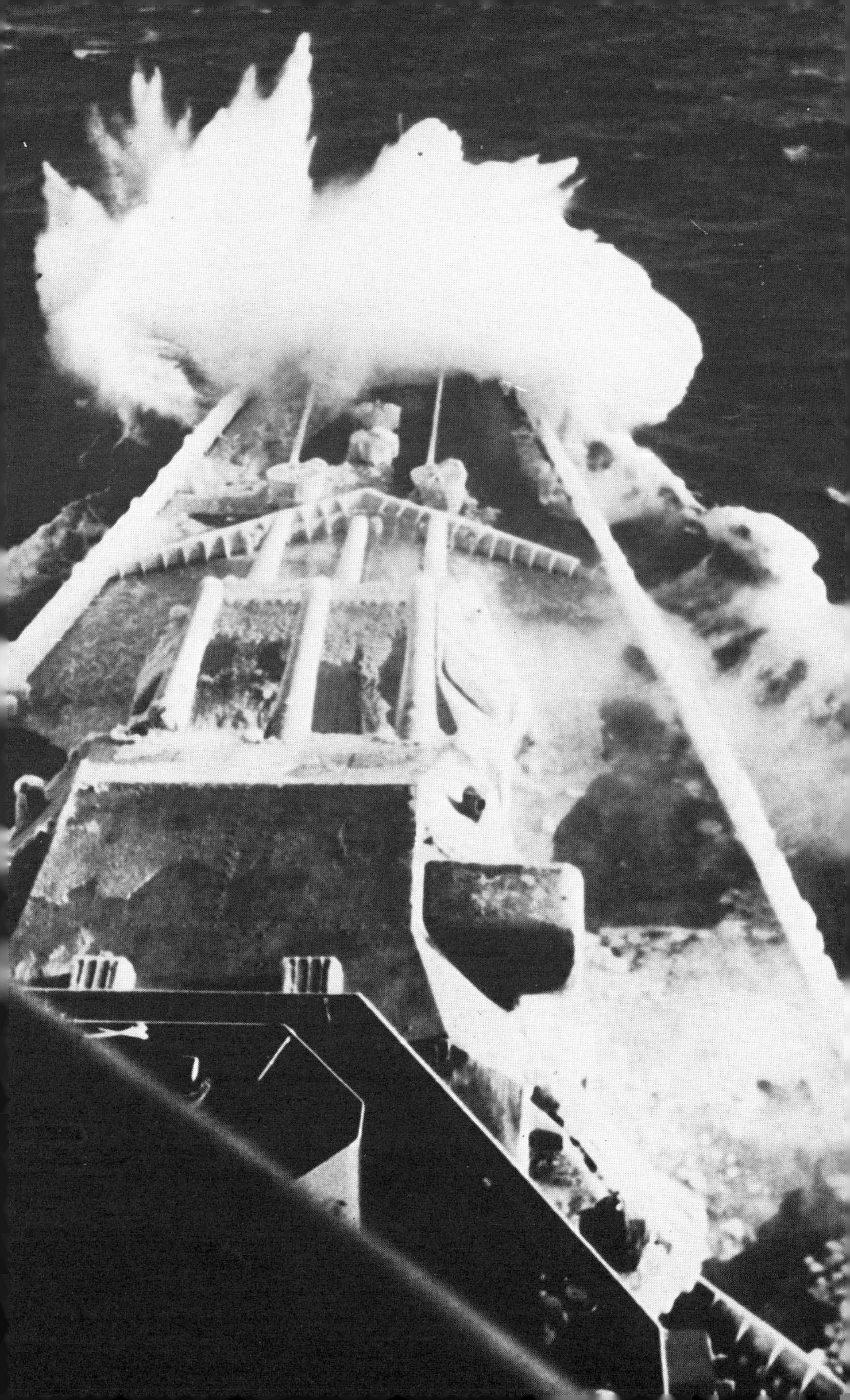

mansk, for the White Sea and Archangel are sealed off by ice. In summer the ice retreats northwards, opening the White Sea. And when the Russian campaign began, Murmansk rapidly became the most important of these two ports.

It became, in fact, virtually a front-line base. Murmansk was a target that Raeder needed to clinch his control of the coastal traffic in the far north. The German troops in northern Norway, with their Finnish allies, made repeated attempts to capture Murmansk. They never got it, but the port remained open to heavy bombing raids by aircraft based on the nearby German airfields at Kirkenes and Petsamo; and one of the most welcome early items of Allied aid was the RAF's 151 Fighter Wing (Hurricanes), despatched from Iceland on 21st August. The aircraft-carrier *Argus* flew off twenty-four Hurricanes which landed at Vaenga airfield, near Murmansk, while fifteen more crated Hurricanes were delivered at Archangel with six merchantmen. On 28th September the first homeward-bound convoy – QP-1 – left Archangel and the first outward-bound convoy – PQ-1 – sailed from Iceland, arriving safely in Archangel on 11th October. The Russian convoys were off to an uneventful start.

It took the German Naval High Command several months to realise the opportunities offered by the Russian convoys. Ironically, on 17th September Raeder had attempted to counter Hitler's insistence on sending the fleet to Norway by claiming that the big ships would be unable to attack Allied commerce there. A lot of this inertia was due to the extremely threadbare state of German air reconnaissance. Luftflotte V, the air fleet responsible for Norway, had had its strength depleted by the needs of 'Barbarossa', but that was not the whole story. As previously mentioned, there was never a unified German High Command staff working to co-ordinate the mutual needs of the navy and of the Luftwaffe. Raeder spent most of his time at loggerheads with Göring – on subjects, for instance, like aircraft and crews for the aircraft-carrier *Graf Zeppelin* – and he was constantly complaining to Hitler over the defects in air reconnaissance, which was cramping the style of the U-boats as well as of the surface fleet.

Nor was the German fleet in any condition to make an immediate challenge to the Russian convoys. In the autumn of 1941 it was pretty fairly dispersed. *Scharnhorst, Gneisenau,* and *Prinz Eugen* were all still in Brest. *Lützow,* finally repaired after the Norwegian campaign, had been making her way up the Norwegian coast, heading for Trondheim, when a lone Beaufort from a RAF air strike crippled her with a torpedo on 13th June, and she had to go back to Germany for repairs. *Admiral Scheer* was operational, but Hitler would not authorise her move north, let alone sanction another high seas cruise as Raeder wanted. She set the British Home Fleet on tenterhooks in mid-September when she was spotted in Oslo Fjord, but by the end of the month she was back in the Baltic. *Hipper* was operational, but was still in the Baltic – and so was the most important unit of the Fleet, *Bismarck*'s sister-ship, *Tirpitz.*

Simultaneously, however, the strength of Admiral Tovey's Home Fleet was dramatically cut by the decision in October to send the battleship *Prince of Wales* and the battlecruiser *Repulse* out to Singapore to form the nucleus of a British Pacific Fleet (to be sunk with alacrity by Japanese bombers eight days after getting there). This left Tovey to face the threat of a sortie by *Tirpitz* with one battleship (*King George V*), one aircraft-carrier (*Victorious*), three 8-inch gun cruisers, and three 6-inch gun cruisers. He needed carrier support to watch the *Tirpitz*; if the Germans chose to strengthen their defences in the Far North and begin heavy attacks on the Russian convoys, he would need at least one more carrier to give the merchantmen air cover: and there were none to spare, what with the heavy demands of the Mediterranean theatre. The latter were increased on 14th November when *Ark Royal*, the carrier which had crippled the *Bismarck* in May, was torpedoed and sunk twenty-five miles off Gibraltar. Yet already the Royal Navy was at work in the far north. The submarines *Tigris* and *Trident* had been sent to operate off Murmansk in August, and by the end of September British and Russian submarine activity had completely disrupted German traffic along the Murmansk coast, forcing the Germans to send supplies for their troops in the north overland through Finland. Energetic German countermoves could clearly be expected in the near future: the painless passage of the early Russian convoys must be considered too good to last.

The German build-up started, sluggishly enough, in mid-November, when Raeder moved five of the new destroyers – 'Narviks', tough ships, armed with 5.9-inch guns – to northern waters. He also ordered Dönitz to set up a patrol-line of three U-boats to cover the approaches to the Barents Sea and Murmansk. But the real catalyst came with the resounding success of the British Commando raid on Vaagsö on 27th December followed within forty-eight hours by a tense Führer Conference. The shipping losses and damage done at Vaagsö were blamed by the navy on insufficient Luftwaffe defence, which was duly ordered to be strengthened. And this was the conference which saw *Tirpitz* definitely earmarked for Arctic waters, together with all other heavy surface units of the fleet. Even so, the Germans had to concede defeat in the first round of the battle for the Russian convoy route: by the end of 1941 seven convoys had sailed through unscathed, delivering some 750 tanks, 800 fighter aircraft, 1,400 vehicles, and over 100,000 tons of stores. The Royal Navy had originally wanted a period of forty days between sailings; Churchill, to placate Stalin, had cut this down to ten days, and the actual period had worked out at about fifteen days.

12th January 1942, saw the conference which agreed on the transfer of the *Tirpitz* and the gamble of the Channel Dash. British reconnaissance located *Tirpitz* in Aas Fjord, fifteen miles from Trondheim, on 23rd January. For the German navy, as shown in the previous chapter, the next fortnight was taken up with the final preparations for the Channel Dash, which reached its triumphant conclusion with the arrival in German waters of *Scharnhorst, Gneisenau,* and *Prinz Eugen* in the early hours of 13th February. It was decided to waste no time in moving the undamaged *Prinz Eugen*, together with the pocket-battleship *Admiral Scheer*, into the comparative safety of Norwegian waters, where the myriad fjords would offer them a much safer hiding-place while the battle-cruisers were being repaired.

On 20th February the British Admiralty warned the Home Fleet and the RAF strike wings that a German naval sortie seemed imminent; the Beauforts combed the North Sea and the Skagerrak, but had no luck. By 1500 hours on 22nd February, both ships had been located in Grimstad Fjord, near Bergen – the second time round for *Prinz Eugen*, which had last been there nine months before with *Bismarck* on the eve of the ill-fated *Rheinübung* venture. The next day, on the last leg of her journey to join *Tirpitz* in Aas Fjord, *Prinz Eugen*'s luck ran out when she was torpedoed by the submarine *Trident*. She had about twenty feet of her stern blown off, but was able to join *Tirpitz* and *Scheer* in Aas Fjord towards the end of the day. Apart from this mishap, the German build-up was going according to plan. Hitler's High Seas Fleet had concentrated a powerful battle squadron in Norwegian waters.

111

threatening a chess-game 'fork' dilemma for the British Home Fleet. Admiral Tovey was under no illusions about the seriousness of the position and he stated the problem bleakly. 'No disposition of the British Home Fleet', he pointed out, 'could adequately protect both the Russian convoys and the northern passages [into the Atlantic] from this threat.'

Meanwhile, convoy after convoy had been fighting its way through the unbelievable conditions of winter in the Far North. For the loss of one merchantman sunk and another damaged but towed into Murmansk's Kola Inlet, Convoys PQ-7, PQ-8, PQ-9, PQ-10, and PQ-11 had delivered the cargoes of fifty-six merchantmen to Murmansk by the last week of February. A grim episode had occurred on 17th January, when the escort destroyer *Matabele* was torpedoed and sunk. A rescue-ship was on the spot in minutes – but picked up only two survivors. The rest of her complement of 200 who had taken to the water had all frozen to death.

Tovey was sure that the German concentration in Aas Fjord presaged a sortie by the German surface fleet in the near future, and asked that the next two convoys to sail – PQ-12 and the return convoy QP-8 – should be co-ordinated so that the Home Fleet could offer maximum cover to both. The convoys sailed on 1st March, the first to have the chance of such protection – and it was just as well. On the evening of 8th March, the British submarine *Seawolf*, patrolling off Trondheim, raised the alarm that a 'battleship or heavy cruiser' was at sea. *Tirpitz* was out with three destroyers, heading north under the command of Admiral Ciliax to intercept the outward-bound convoy which a long-range Focke-Wulf Kondor had reported at noon on the 5th.

Apart from *King George V* and *Victorious*, Tovey had with him the newly-joined battleship *Duke of York* (another 'KGV'), the battle-cruiser *Renown*, the cruiser *Berwick*, and twelve destroyers. He headed east on the morning of the 7th to intercept the enemy raider. The weather was vile, preventing aircraft from being flown off either from *Victorious* or from *Tirpitz*, which had its own spotter plane. The British Official History aptly describes the manoeuvres of 7th March as a 'game of blind man's buff'. By noon, *Tirpitz* was within miles of the two passing convoys, and under ninety miles from the Home Fleet, which Ciliax had no idea was so close. For the British, this was the most dangerous moment of the sortie: as the gap between the two convoys widened, the chance of a decisive blow against them lessened. Ciliax detached his destroyers to sweep to the north – one of them sank a Russian merchantman from QP-8 at 1830 – and later sent them back to Norway to refuel, continuing the search alone.

This groping game continued until 2000 hours on 8th March, when Ciliax gave up and headed for shelter in Narvik's Vest Fjord, south of the Lofoten Islands. As usual, the British Admiralty was monitoring the German wavelengths, and warned Tovey that the German warship seemed to be heading south, and he changed course to intercept. At this moment he was about 200 miles west of the *Tirpitz*, and was pinning his hopes on an air strike from *Victorious* the following morning. At 0800 on the 9th, *Tirpitz* was spotted and twelve Albacore torpedo-bombers headed in for the attack. Dramatic photographs taken aboard the *Tirpitz* record how narrowly the speeding battleship, zig-zagging violently, evaded torpedo after torpedo. No hits were scored and two Albacores were lost. Tovey had missed his chance to engage *Tirpitz* before she reached the shelter of the Vest Fjord, and he returned to Scapa Flow. Anchoring off Narvik on the evening of the 9th, *Tirpitz* made the home run down the Norwegian coast between 1100 hours on the 12th and 2100 on the 13th, when she arrived back in her former berth. None of the des-

Above: A dockyard case – *Prinz Eugen* after having her stern blown off by the British submarine *Trident*. *Below:* Torpedoes from British Albacores lance through the wake of the violently zig-zagging battleship *Tirpitz*

Admiral Hipper at anchor in a Norwegian fjord

troyers and submarines deployed to intercept even sighted her. The first sortie of the *Tirpitz* was over.

It was a bitter disappointment for the British, a disappointment as great as Scheer's escape with the High Seas Fleet after Jutland in 1916. On 25th January, Churchill had sent another of his 'directive' minutes to the Chiefs-of-Staff Committee. 'The destruction or even the crippling of this ship is the greatest event at sea at the present time. No other target is comparable to it...' Now the Royal Navy had been given its chance to trap the *Tirpitz* at sea. It was never to get another.

Raeder was only too well aware of how narrow *Tirpitz*'s escape had been, and that she owed 90% of her luck to the weather. He was appalled how close *Tirpitz* had come to following *Bismarck*'s fate on her very first war cruise. The lesson was clear: far more support from the Luftwaffe was essential, both in reconnaissance and attack. It soon came. Luftflotte V began to receive heavy reinforcements in bomber units. Not only did Raeder demand that the British aircraft-carriers be made the primary targets for the bombers: he declared that the German carrier *Graf Zeppelin* must be completed and sent to join the fleet as soon as possible. (Raeder even got Hitler to agree to converting the liners *Gneisenau*, *Europa*, and *Potsdam*, as well as the uncompleted heavy cruiser *Seydlitz*, into auxiliary carriers but although work did begin on the *Seydlitz* nothing came of the scheme, which never came anywhere near completion.) With the build-up of German air power in the far north however, the first crisis of the Russian convoys was at hand. PQ-12, which *Tirpitz* had missed so narrowly, was in fact the last of the early convoys to run the gauntlet to Russia unscathed.

To compensate for the immobilisation of *Prinz Eugen*, *Hipper* was sent north to join the fleet in the maze of fjords around Trondheim, where she anchored on 21st March. This move coincided with the sailing of the next two convoys, PQ-13 and QP-9. The homeward-bound convoy had an uneventful run, and one of its escorting minesweepers, *Sharpshooter*, managed to ram and sink U-655. But PQ-13 soon ran into bad trouble. To start with, it was scattered and separated from its escorts by a storm on the 24th, and within forty-eight hours its troubles began in earnest. Luftwaffe reconnaissance picked up the scattered merchantmen and air attacks began on the 28th, sinking two stragglers. In addition, three destroyers of the 'Narvik' class – Z-25, Z-26, and Z-27 – alerted by the Luftwaffe, sortied from Kirkenes and sank a straggler from PQ-13 in the early hours of 29th March.

At 0900 the same morning, they ran into the cruiser *Trinidad* and the destroyers *Fury* and *Eclipse*, and battle was joined. Z-26 was sunk, but

Eclipse was badly damaged, while *Trinidad* achieved the extraordinary feat of torpedoing herself. She fired a torpedo which ran wide of the mark, and whose steering-mechanism went beserk in the intense cold. In course of her manoeuvres against the German destroyers, *Trinidad* steered across the erratic track of this torpedo and was badly hit in her boiler-rooms. By 30th March–1st April the survivors of PQ-13 had won through to Murmansk. For the first time, a Russian convoy had been severely mauled. A quarter of its merchantmen had gone down: two ships had been sunk by the Luftwaffe, two by U-boats, and one by the destroyers. It was a grim story, with a promise of worse to come.

The British naval leaders knew what was going to happen. As summer drew on, the improving conditions in the far north would make it far easier for the Luftwaffe to locate large convoys. Ideally the convoys should be suspended for the summer months – the period of perpetual daylight. Failing that, they should be spaced out nearer to the forty-day period originally recommended, to enable larger escorts to be sent with each convoy. Certainly the number of merchantmen per convoy should be kept down. But the demands of the Grand Alliance overrode naval commonsense. Whatever arrived in Murmansk, the Russian response was the same: there was never enough of it. And Roosevelt was pressurising Churchill to feed more American merchantmen into the Russian convoys, and not to keep so many loaded ships awaiting passage to Russia.

PQ-14 was therefore larger still: twenty-four merchantmen, sailing on 8th April. (The flagship of the escort, the cruiser *Edinburgh*, was carrying steel plating to repair *Trinidad* in Murmansk, for Russian facilities there were so bad that not enough material could be provided for the job.) Ice was the first enemy faced by PQ-14: it had drifted further south than usual, and sixteen ships turned back to Iceland. Seven of the remaining eight ships won through to Murmansk, while one was sunk by a U-boat. As for the return convoy of sixteen ships – QP-10 – U-boats and the Luftwaffe accounted for four merchantmen.

While these convoys were still at sea, Hitler was at last beginning to take notice of the increasing numbers of Allied ships carrying supplies to Russia. He ordered Raeder to make further such convoys the navy's primary objective, and intervened in yet another Raeder-Göring wrangle with the order that torpedoes were to be made available to the Luftwaffe. (Here Göring, for once, had a good point. His own bone-headed insistence that the navy should not have the wherewithal for an independent air arm was nothing, in comparison to the navy's obstinacy in declaring the torpedo to be an exclusively naval weapon.) Thus a new danger – torpedo-bombers – had been added to the existing threats from dive-bombers, U-boats, and surface attack by the time PQ-15 and QP-11 sailed, on 26th and 28th April respectively.

This time the Germans attacked with everything they had tried to date, but their score of merchantmen was low. Torpedo-bombers sank three out of PQ-15's twenty-five ships; QP-11 was attacked by three destroyers: the *Hermann Schömann*, veteran of the Channel Dash, and Z-24 and Z-25, 'Narviks'. A torpedo from one of the destroyers sank a Russian straggler from QP-11, but the three ships retreated before the defiant manoeuvres of the heavily out-gunned British destroyer escort, whose bluff, to their relief, succeeded. (*'I would hate to play poker with you'*) signalled one of the British ships to the leader of the destroyers, Commander Richmond of the *Bulldog*.) But QP-11 was deprived of the protection of *Edinburgh*, which was torpedoed by a U-boat and turned back for Murmansk; and the German destroyers followed to finish her off. They managed to inflict mortal

115

damage on *Edinburgh*, but this time they were out-fought as well as out-bluffed by the weaker British escort. *Hermann Schömann* was lost, and the two 'Narviks' retreated. It was the British escorts, not the merchantmen, which took the lion's share of the punishment during the sailing of PQ-15 and QP-11, but they had proved that the caution which paralysed the capital ships of the German fleet also applied to its destroyer arm.

Once again the British naval pundits gave their verdict on the convoys. 'If they must be continued for political reasons,' declared Tovey, 'very serious and heavy losses must be expected.' The convoys continued.

PQ-16, of thirty-five ships, sailed on 21st May the largest convoy yet. As before, a return convoy – QP-12, of fifteen ships – coincided with the outward-bound convoy. Once again, the battle fleet shadowed the convoy, out of the Luftwaffe range, to counter the German fleet if it came out. This time, destroyers were not the only threat: *Admiral Scheer* and *Lützow* had both been located in Narvik by 26th May, and *Scheer* had already shown what pocket-battleships could do to convoys when given the chance. But PQ-16 was the Luftwaffe's target. Never before had a Russian convoy encountered air attacks of such volume or intensity. On 27th May, attacks by 108 German aircraft – torpedo-carriers and dive-bombers – were counted by the harrassed convoy. For five days and nights the air attacks continued; thanks to the gallantry of the escorts, losses were kept down to six, but it was a fearful experience.

These losses were considered acceptable – but what made the difference was the hitting-power of the Luftwaffe in the far north, now at its peak. Massed on the airfields around the North Cape – Banak, Bardufoss, Tromsö, and Kirkenes – were some forty-two He-111 torpedo-bombers, 102 Ju-88 level- and dive-bombers, and thirty Ju-87 'Stuka' dive-bombers, not to mention fifteen He-115 torpedo floatplanes and a reconnaissance force of seventy-four machines: Focke-Wulf Kondors, Ju-88s, and Blohm-und-Voss 138s. The previous convoys were used to the distant drone of the long-range Luftwaffe reconnaissance planes, circling the Allied ships well out of gun range, and sending back accurate fixes for the bombers, U-boats, and surface forces. In addition, Admiral Dönitz was ordered – much against his will – to switch more U-boats from the Atlantic convoy routes to the far north. Ten would be available for shadowing and attacking the next convoy.

Such was the terrifying threat facing the Allied naval planners as they prepared for the next convoy, which would prove the most notorious of the war: PQ-17. Nothing could be done in June, for the Mediterranean campaign was reaching its greatest crisis. Rommel was driving east again. Malta, its garrison reaching the limits of endurance, seemed likely to fall, and a relief venture – Operation 'Harpoon' – was essential. So was the transfer of warships from the Home Fleet to cover the Malta convoy. But on 28th June the German army launched its summer offensive to reach the Caucasus and the Volga. It was the summer of Stalingrad, and the urgency of sending supplies to Russia was greater than ever. As soon as the Mediterranean situation had been shored up, PQ-17 must sail as soon as possible and face the consequences.

Raeder was determined that the fleet should justify its existence by attacking the next Russian convoy to sail. He prepared an ambitious plan: *Rösselsprung*, 'Knight's Move', a co-ordinated strike by the available warships of the surface fleet, which were divided into two groups: 'Trondheim' and 'Narvik'.

Trondheim Group consisted of *Tirpitz*, flying the flag of Vice-Admiral Otto Schniewind (who had replaced Ciliax as Fleet Commander), *Hipper*,

Fleet Commander Otto Schniewind

and six destroyers. Narvik Group included the pocket-battleships, *Lützow* and *Admiral Scheer*, also with six destroyers. It would be the most powerful German fleet sent to sea since the outbreak of war, and the plan was carefully worked out. The luckless convoy, to start with, would be steaming through waters dominated by the Luftwaffe, which would be under orders to attack only merchantmen or aircraft-carriers. Any escort forces which were found with the convoy would be dealt with by *Tirpitz* and *Hipper*, while the pocket-battleship squadron liquidated the merchantmen.

Hitler rejected Raeder's plan as it stood. The British Home Fleet carrier force, he insisted, must be neutralised by the Luftwaffe before any attack by the fleet could be considered. This, obviously, Raeder could not hope to guarantee. But instead of getting himself bogged down in a lecture on the basic realities of modern war at sea, he promptly suggested a revised, two-stage operation which would keep the warships in safety for as long as possible. When the Luftwaffe had located the convoy, Narvik Group would move at once to Alten Fjord, near the North Cape, while Trondheim Group would move up to Narvik. When the Führer was satisfied that the Home Fleet could not hope to intervene – and only then – he himself would give the order which would send both groups to rendezvous 100 miles north of the North Cape before falling on the convoy well to the east of Bear Island.

Raeder's suggestion was a typical product of Nazi court politics, but it worked. Hitler agreed: Raeder's fleet would still be given its chance to annihilate PQ-17.

Such was the formidable opposition waiting for PQ-17 when the convoy sailed on 27th June. As Admiral Tovey put it, quite simply: 'The strategic situation was wholly favourable to the enemy.' The Barents Sea was dominated by U-boats and the Luftwaffe and there was nothing the Home Fleet could do about it. The German fleet, with *Tirpitz* at its core, was poised to strike, and Tovey's battle fleet, though eager to bring its German opposite number to action, dare not keep close enough to the convoy to offer any effective support because of the Luftwaffe's command of the air, which could not be challenged with merely the planes of *Victorious*'s air group.

Thirty-three merchantmen made up PQ-17 (of the original thirty-five one grounded on leaving Iceland and another turned back because of ice damage). Russian port facilities at Murmansk had recently been wrecked by Luftwaffe raids, and so the convoy was routed to Archangel. An Anglo-American cruiser force of four warships, under the command of Rear-Admiral Sir Louis Hamilton, together with three destroyers, formed the close escort which would accompany PQ-17 at least as far east as Bear Island.

The long-range escort joined the convoy on 30th June: six destroyers, four corvettes, two submarines, and the anti-aircraft ships *Palomares* and *Pozarica*. The following day PQ-17 was located by the Luftwaffe and by U-boats, and shadowing began. PQ-17 and the homeward-bound convoy, QP-13, crossed on the afternoon of the 2nd, and the same evening PQ-17 beat off its first Luftwaffe torpedo attack without loss. By the evening of the 3rd, PQ-17 was thirty miles to the north of Bear Island. The next day every American merchantman in the convoy hauled down the Stars and Stripes and saluted the 'Fourth of July' by running up gleaming new ensigns. Heavy Luftwaffe attacks on the 4th sank three ships, but as evening approached the convoy was still ploughing eastwards towards Archangel and things looked hopeful. Morale was high, and the discipline of the convoy had been excellent from the start.

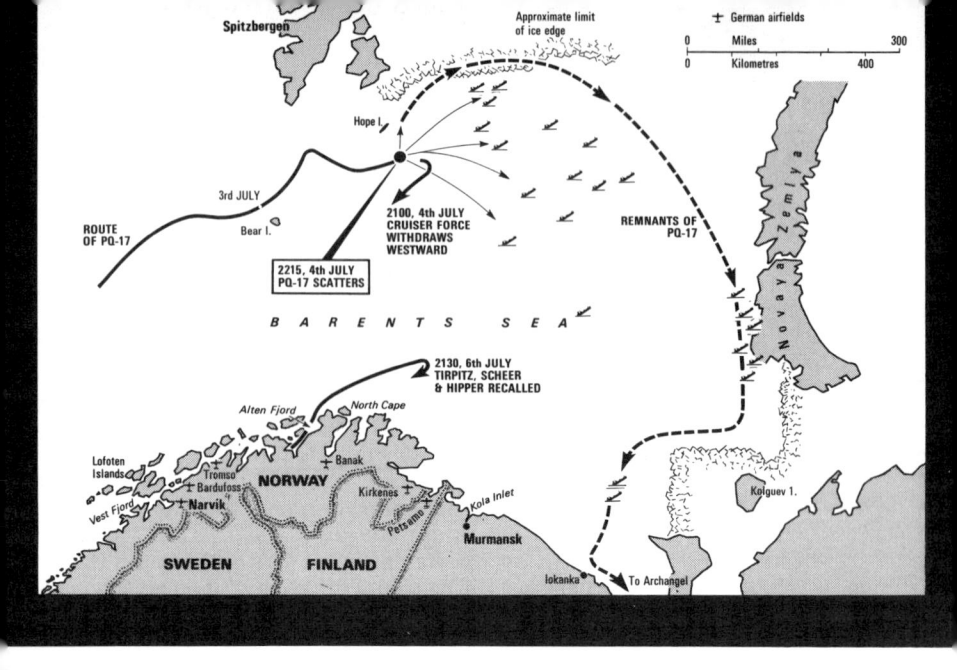

Then, shortly after 2100 hours, three dramatic Admiralty signals sounded the death-knell of PQ-17, coming out of the blue, astounding the men of both convoy and escort.

c. 2100 hours: 'Most immediate. Cruiser force withdraw to the westward at high speed.'

2123 hours: 'Immediate. Owing to threat from surface ships the convoy is to disperse and proceed to Russian ports.'

2136 hours: 'Most immediate. Convoy is to scatter.'

To the British Admiralty, it seemed that the worst fears of the last few weeks were about to be realised. On 2nd July, after PQ-17 had been located coming up from the west, Raeder had set *Rösselsprung* in motion – but the operation got off to a shaky start. Three of Trondheim Group's four destroyers ran aground, so that *Hipper* and *Tirpitz* arrived at Narvik with only one; and *Lützow* also went aground. All other ships in the operation, however, reached their destinations safely – and by afternoon of 3rd July the British knew that both *Tirpitz* and *Hipper* had quitted Trondheim. Unhappily, they were unable to make a detailed reconnaissance of Narvik, and could not rule out the probability that both German warships were heading north to attack PQ-17.

As Raeder had foreseen, he was unable to undertake the disabling of

Above: The doomed convoy PQ-17 as spotted by the pitiless eye of German air reconnaissance. *Below:* PQ-17 merchantman – a U-boat's easy victim

Below: Survivors from the *Carlton*, an American member of PQ-17

The threat that never was – the abortive sortie by *Tirpitz*, *Hipper*, and *Scheer* never came near PQ-17

the British carrier *Victorious*, as Hitler had demanded. But he did get permission to go ahead and move *Hipper* and *Tirpitz* up to Alten Fjord, which was done on the night of 3rd July. On the morning of the 5th, when the withdrawal of the British escorts had been reported, Hitler agreed to the fleet making a limited strike against PQ-17; *Hipper*, *Scheer*, *Tirpitz*, and seven destroyers sallied out of Alten Fjord in the afternoon and headed east to cut the track PQ-17 was most likely to take on its route to Archangel. But even as the fleet put to sea, the stunning news of PQ-17's scattering and almost immediate decimation by Luftwaffe bombers and U-boats was beginning to come in, and at 2130 – some twenty-four hours after the fatal order for the convoy to scatter had gone out from Whitehall – Schniewind's fleet was recalled to Alten Fjord. It was by now quite obvious that the U-boats and bombers could finish the job of annihilating the scattered convoy without the need for any help from the surface ships.

The doomed convoy had carried out its last order with impeccable discipline. As the last warships of the escort were vanishing over the western horizon, the merchantmen were breaking up their well-drilled lines and 'starring' – some heading north towards the edge of the ice barrier, some east towards Novaya Zemlya, some south-east, direct for Archangel. Their ordeal began almost immediately, and it is better briefly told. Out of the thirty-three ships of PQ-17, twenty-three were sunk, ten of them by U-boats. The Luftwaffe threw 202 aircraft against the scattered convoy. All in all, Soviet Russia was deprived of 430 tanks, 210 aircraft, and 3,350 vehicles – 'sufficient', as Admiral Schofield points out in *The Russian Convoys*, 'to have equipped an army.' It was not only one of the greatest tragedies of the entire naval war: it was a crushing military defeat.

The pros and cons of the British Admiralty's decision to scatter PQ-17 form a complex and delicate controversy in themselves. Two inescapable facts are relevant here: the decision was made because British air reconnaissance could not pinpoint where the German warships were at the vital moment. And the Admiralty, assuming that they were most probably heading out to attack the convoy, sent out a series of peremptory and clear-cut signals which indicated the likelihood of imminent attack, and which certainly made the danger appear greater than it actually was.

Although the bombers and the U-boats were the direct instruments of PQ-17's destruction, the surface ships of the German navy were the prime movers. Once again, the strategic power of a 'fleet in being' had proved itself. The fear of Hitler's High Seas Fleet had inflicted a major naval disaster on the Allies without the German warships having to fire a shot.

After the PQ-17 disaster the decision was made: the Russian convoys would be suspended for the rest of the summer. Even without such a tragedy occurring on the Russian run, the convoys would have had to have been suspended for the Mediterranean theatre now dominated the scene. On 4th July, the day PQ-17 scattered, Auchinleck had managed to fight Rommel's *Panzerarmee* to a halt at El Alamein, but Egypt was still in grave danger. Help was on its way – on 21st June, after Tobruk had fallen to Rommel, President Roosevelt had promised 300 Sherman tanks for the down-at-heel armoured divisions of Eighth Army, but they would take months to arrive and be worked up into battle-worthy units. In the meantime it was still possible for the Axis to win control of the Mediterranean and send Rommel enough supplies to break through at Alamein and sweep the British out of Egypt. Here Malta was the key, and Malta's fate hung in the balance. A massive relief operation was again essential, and it was launched in August. Operation 'Pedestal' it was called – and it was the PQ-17 of the Malta convoys. Five out of 'Pedestal's' fourteen merchantmen, burned, battered, and sinking, had struggled through to Malta by 15th August, but their precious cargoes were enough. Malta could now hold out until December, and with the centre of gravity of the Mediterranean war switching from the blitz on Malta to the crisis on the Alamein line, the Allied lifeline through the Mediterranean was given the respite it so badly needed.

This halting of the Axis run of success in the Mediterranean, and the suspension of the Russian convoys, is a convenient point to tell of the 'second wave' of German disguised merchant raiders, now making its bid to equal the successes of the 'first wave' in 1940-41. There were three vital differences: the raiders no longer dared to try the Denmark Strait entrance to the Atlantic: the British and Americans had more warships with which to hunt the raiders; and with Japan in the war, the ports of the Japanese Empire could now be freely used. All three raiders of the 'second wave' – *Thor*, *Stier*, and *Michel* – were passed down-Channel to the Biscay ports before beginning their high seas cruises.

Thor sailed from Bordeaux on 14th January, and made straight for the Antarctic, the idea being to repeat *Pinguin*'s savaging of Allied whaling fleets. After a month's fruitless search, she returned north to rendezvous with her supply-ship *Regensburg* in the South Atlantic, sinking a Greek merchantman on 23rd March – her first victim in the six weeks of her cruise. After sinking five ships totalling 23,626 tons, *Thor* headed into the Indian Ocean where she cruised during the summer months of 1942 before heading into friendly Japanese waters. On 30th November, *Thor* was lying alongside the German tanker *Uckermark*

121

(none other than *Graf Spee*'s old running-mate *Altmark*, which had been renamed) in Yokohama, when *Uckermark* blew up, an explosion which completely burned out *Thor*, ending the raider's career. On her second cruise, she had scored ten ships of 56,037 tons.

Michel, under the command of the notorious Captain Helmuth von Rückteschell, sailed from Kiel on 9th March, reached La Pallice on the 17th, and headed out into the Atlantic two days later. *Michel* was carrying a formidable torpedo-boat, which had two 14-inch torpedo tubes and a speed of thirty-seven knots, and which Rückteschell was soon to put to effective use. Within four months, *Michel* had sunk eight ships totalling 56,731 tons in the South Atlantic. By the end of October she had moved into the Indian Ocean, and, using her torpedo-boat, sank two more merchantmen there. By the New Year, *Michel* was back in the South Atlantic – but British air power had so greatly extended in the past months that Berlin told Rückteschell not to attempt to return to home waters but to make for Japan. By this time – January 1943 – *Michel* had sunk fourteen merchantmen totalling 87,332 tons, and was to continue her career in the Pacific in 1943.

Stier had had to fight for it during her run down-Channel from Rotterdam, which she had left on 12th May. She was undamaged, though two of her escorts were sunk, and she sailed from the Gironde on 20th May. Her cruise, which included a mid-ocean rendezvous with *Michel* between 28th July and 1st August, was limited to the Atlantic, and netted only four ships totalling 29,406 tons. The fourth victim, the American Liberty ship *Stephen Hopkins*, encountered on 27th September, ended *Stier*'s cruise by hitting back valiantly with her single 4-inch gun and starting a fatal fire aboard the German raider before being sunk. *Stier*'s crew were picked up after abandoning ship by the blockade-runner *Tannenfels*, operating in the area as a supply-ship; but only fifteen of *Stephen Hopkins*'s gallant crew survived.

Last of the disguised surface raiders which tried for a high seas cruise in 1942 was the *Komet*. She left Flushing on the night of 7th October, and her cruise – which, like that of *Thor*, would have been her second – was short and sharp. *Komet* was hunted down by British destroyers and motor torpedo-boats and sunk off Cherbourg in the early hours of 14th October.

By mid-October, therefore, the 'second wave' of disguised merchant raiders had met with far more abrupt treatment than the 'first wave' – a clear indication that times had changed since the intoxicating months of 1940–41. After these cruises, the German Admiralty virtually pinned its entire hopes for future commerce-raiding on the U-boat arm. But by this time there were far more urgent matters afoot in northern waters. The Russian convoys had started again, with the Germans hoping to repeat their success against PQ-17, and the British experimenting with new and significant defensive tactics.

What the British did not know was that the German High Command had not grasped the real reason for PQ-17's martyrdom: the offensive potential of the German surface fleet. There was a feeling of confidence that the fleet was not necessary for the annihilation of outward-bound Russian convoys, which could, it was felt, be left to the U-boats and the Luftwaffe. The fleet should content itself with limited strikes against homeward-bound convoys in the Barents Sea.

For their next convoy, the British applied every lesson learned so painfully from PQ-17's ordeal. First came air reconnaissance. A mixed air group was sent to Russia to operate from airfields near Murmansk: long-range Catalina scouts, Hampden torpedo bombers, and Spitfire fighters. Next came protection for the convoy, which was to be fought through, this

Convoy PQ-18 under German air attack

time, without breaking up: a 'fighting destroyer escort' of sixteen ships, which would corset the entire convoy, covered by the air support of the escort-carrier *Avenger* – Sea Hurricane fighters to tackle the Luftwaffe bombers and Avenger anti-submarine aircraft for the U-boats. Finally, there would be no 100% divorce between the Admiralty and the C-in-C Home Fleet at sea. Tovey planned to stay in Scapa Flow, in telephone contact with the Admiralty, delegating the long-range shadowing by the battle fleet to his second-in-command, Admiral Sir Bruce Fraser.

The result was that the German fleet in Alten Fjord – *Admiral Scheer*, *Hipper*, and the light cruiser *Köln*, which moved up from Narvik – remained under careful scrutiny by the Russian-based Catalinas when PQ-18 sailed, forty strong, on 2nd September. German air reconnaissance first picked up the convoy on the 8th, and the first ships were torpedoed on the 13th. There followed over five days of the fiercest fighting, which saw the heaviest Luftwaffe and U-boat attacks ever thrown against a Russian convoy.

The vital difference was that this was the most heavily-defended Russian convoy yet to sail. The Germans managed to sink thirteen out of PQ-18's forty ships – but they lost forty-one aircraft and four U-boats in doing it, and there was much gloom in the German High Command. The only alarm for the British caused by the German fleet was when *Tirpitz* suddenly vanished from Trondheim for four days 14th–18th September. But all she had done was to cruise up to Narvik's Vest Fjord for seagoing exercises before heading back to her base at Trondheim.

Meanwhile, Rear-Admiral Burnett's 'fighting escort', with the all-important carrier, stepped across to the return convoy QP-14 (mostly remnants of PQ-17), with the result that only two of the homeward-bound convoy's fifteen ships were lost. The German fleet did not come out. To have a British battle fleet at sea was nothing new, but with PQ-18 proving so decisively that the Luftwaffe's control of the Barents Sea was in dispute Raeder's veto on the fleet's proposed strike was not surprising.

The tide had turned for the Russian convoys, but this was not merely due to the exertions of PQ-18 and its hard-fighting escort. Grand Strategy was now making itself felt again. The demands of the Mediterranean theatre meant that the Luftwaffe's formidable strike force must be moved south from its bases in Norway. Again unknown to the British, the immense air attacks which had savaged PQ-16, PQ-17, and PQ-18 would never be repeated, while the Luftwaffe's domination of the northern seas would never be restored. The convoys would continue, using improved tactics for their defence; but after PQ-18 the German fleet could no longer score remote-control victories by sitting in port and looking menacing. Sooner or later, it must come out and fight.

123

The last battles

After PQ-18's battle-scarred survivors arrived at Archangel on 20th September 1942, the Allies again suspended the sailing of outward-bound convoys to Russia. They had to. It was not a question of 'supply and demand': some forty merchantmen were awaiting passage to Russia by the end of September 1942, while the Stalingrad-Caucasus campaign was becoming more and more critical for the Russians with every week. But to force through another Russian convoy with a full fighting escort at this stage would only have meant the postponement of the first major Anglo-American stroke in the European theatre: Operation 'Torch', the invasion and retention of Algeria and Tunisia, intended to trap Rommel's Italo-German *Panzerarmee* from the west while the Eighth Army launched its offensive at Alamein from the east. Once Rommel had been driven from North Africa, the Mediterranean crisis would be over for ever, and the Allies could then pick their targets for the 'second front' so long demanded by Stalin: Sicily and Italy, southern France, or the Balkans.

Until 'Torch' had been well and truly lit in north-west Africa, there would simply not be enough warships available to escort set-piece convoys to Russia, and so such convoys were postponed until December 1942. Yet there were still isolated sailings – between October and December 1942, thirteen merchantmen sailed for Russia, of which three turned back, four were sunk, one was wrecked, and five got through. And the last of the 'PQ' series of convoys – QP-15 – cleared a residue of twenty-eight merchantmen out of Archangel before the annual freezing of the White Sea. It sailed on 17th November, and was soon scattered by appalling weather which worked against the Germans: only two of QP-15's ships fell victim, and they were sunk by U-boats.

Even if the demands of other fronts had not bled off the Luftwaffe's summer concentration of strike aircraft from the Far North, the aircraft would have had to pass the onus of anti-convoy operations to the U-boats for the winter. Weather conditions in the winter months made accurate air surveillance, let alone air strikes, virtually impossible. Thus the heavy ships of the fleet now reassumed the important rôle which should have been theirs from the start.

The German surface fleet's inaction was due to other forces at work besides the restrictive caution transmitted from Hitler via the Naval High Command to the captains of the ships. By late 1942 the shortage of fuel oil was getting serious. This fuel shortage lay behind the decision not to transfer *Prinz Eugen* (now operational again) to northern waters. As before, however, diesel fuel was plentiful, and so *Lützow* came north to replace *Admiral Scheer*, due for refit. The light cruiser *Nürnberg* also moved north, to Narvik, and on 18th December *Lützow* joined *Hipper* and *Köln* in Alten Fjord. *Tirpitz*, meanwhile, had

The camouflaged *Lützow* in a Norwegian fjord, behind her anti-torpedo nets

been sent down to Trondheim for an extensive dockyard refit. For all this, Raeder was still obsessed with the notion that his fleet must prove itself at the expense of the Allied convoys; but this obsession had virtually robbed him of all strategic purpose. He wanted to concentrate on homeward-bound convoys, which he considered would provide easier targets for the surface ships – while in fact the only valid target for the fleet in the Far North should have been the interdiction of outward-bound supply convoys to Russia!

However, the Allied suspension of the convoys forced Raeder to think again. Disguised merchant raiders of the 'second wave' were still at sea, and Raeder still hankered after a high seas cruise for the *Lützow*. But Hitler refused even to consider this without a prior success being scored in Arctic waters when the convoys

Lützow under way. She formed one of the converging pincers in Kummetz' attack during the Barents Sea battle

should be resumed. The result was the evolution of Operation *Regenbogen* ('Rainbow'): a strike against an unspecified convoy, using *Hipper* and a destroyer squadron to engage the convoy's escort (with the vital condition that such an escort must be found weak enough), while *Lützow* savaged the convoy itself.

Once again, there was nothing wrong with the plan itself. But also once again, it was doomed from the start because the seagoing commanders were given absolutely no licence to fight a flexible battle on their own initiative.

On the Allied 'side of the hill', plans for resuming the Russian convoys were proceeding apace by the end of November. These new convoys would not repeat the costly tactics of the 'PQ' series. As a starter, their very code-name was changed from 'PQ' to 'JW', and they would start at number 51, for security reasons. Admiral Tovey's new prescription was to sail each convoy in two successive instalments, 'A' and 'B', thus forming smaller convoys which could be more easily handled as well as more easily defended.

The new convoys got off to a flying start. JW-51A – fifteen merchantmen with seven destroyers and five smaller escort vessels – went right through to Murmansk without a hitch, sailing on 15th December and arriving in the Kola Inlet on Christmas Day without losing a ship. Rear-Admiral Burnett's cruiser escort – *Sheffield* and *Jamaica*, with two destroyers – then turned back to bring through JW-51B, which had sailed a week later and which was now coming up from the west, escorted by six destroyers and five smaller escorts under the command of Captain R Sherbrooke in the destroyer *Onslow*. A battle fleet was bringing up the rear: Vice-Admiral Sir Bruce Fraser in the new 'KGV' battleship *Anson*, with the cruiser *Cumberland* and three destroyers.

But JW-51B had less luck than its predecessor. Five days out, its port wing column was separated by a tremendous gale before Burnett's cruisers could join up. And on 30th December U-354 sighted the main force in bad visibility and radioed back the description of six to ten ships with a weak escort. To Raeder, it seemed that the ideal chance had come for the fleet to win an easy success, and he immediately ordered *Regenbogen* into operation. With luck, *Hipper*, *Lützow*, and their destroyers would present the Third Reich with a resounding victory at sea as a New Year's gift.

Regenbogen was planned as a cruiser operation, and so it was entrusted not to Ciliax or Schniewind but to Vice-Admiral Oscar Kummetz, Flag Officer, Cruisers, flying his flag in the *Hipper*. Here it is necessary to examine the long chain of inhibiting command which connected Kummetz on his bridge with the Armed Forces High Command. Above Kummetz was Admiral Otto Klüber at Narvik, the Flag Officer, Northern Waters. Above him, in Kiel, was Admiral Rolf Carls, C-in-C Naval Group North. Above him was Raeder at the Admiralty in Berlin, which kept in direct touch with Hitler via Admiral Theodor Krancke, once captain of the *Scheer* during her triumphant war cruise, now naval representative at Hitler's HQ at *Wolfsschanze* in East Prussia. As soon as JW-51B was reported, Carls duly signalled Klüber to alert Kummetz, whose preliminary orders included the caution 'Avoid a superior force, otherwise destroy according to tactical situation.' On this note Kummetz put to sea, leaving Alten Fjord at 1800 hours on 30th September, with *Hipper*, *Lützow*, and six destroyers.

Kummetz had worked out a sound enough tactical plan. *Hipper* and *Lützow* would separate and approach the convoy from astern. The big ships would attack from two directions,

Oscar Kummetz, Flag Officer, Cruisers

which should enable at least one of them to make contact with the escort before the other, enabling one of them to get through to the merchantmen unmolested. He kept all six destroyers with *Hipper* to start with, intending to allot three of them to *Lützow* as the operation developed. But at the last minute Raeder issued a reminder of the Führer's obsession with the need for caution – which resulted in Carls signalling Klüber, who in turn signalled Kummetz within an hour of his putting to sea, 'Contrary to the operational order regarding contact against the enemy, use caution even against enemy of equal strength, because it is undesirable for the cruisers to take any great risks.' It was a message which could hardly have been expected to inspire the 'Nelson touch' in the most enterprising of admirals. But it was typical of the spirit in which the commanders of Hitler's High Seas Fleet went into battle.

What made matters still more unfortunate for the Germans was the fact that to start with Kummetz found himself, without knowing it, presented with one of the most vital ingredients of victory: luck. *Hipper* and *Lützow*, steaming to the north-

127

east, separated at 0240 hours on 31st December. At 0715, *Hipper* passed across the wake of the convoy, twenty miles behind, and within minutes unidentified ships were sighted from *Hipper*. Kummetz ordered the destroyer *Friedrich Eckholdt* to investigate, swinging *Hipper* to offer a bows-on silhouette to the mystery ships. *Friedrich Eckholdt*, however, soon lost touch with the flagship, and was followed by the other destroyers: *Richard Beitzen* and Z-29 of *Hipper*'s group, and *Theodor Riedel*, Z-30, and Z-31 of *Lützow*'s group. By 0800 the latter three were edging eastwards in *Lützow*'s direction, while *Friedrich Eckholdt* and her consorts continued to shadow the convoy.

By 0830 the situation was looking good for Kummetz's squadron – on paper. He was on the convoy's port quarter; *Lützow* was approaching from the starboard. JW-51B itself was 220 miles north-west of Murmansk, heading east with Sherbrooke's destroyer escort in attendance. Thirty miles to the north were Rear-Admiral Burnett's cruisers, *Sheffield* and *Jamaica*, sweeping to the north-east in search of the convoy. The problem was that none of these groups knew of the others' position: visibility was very poor, while Burnett's cruisers were out of radar range. It was the destroyers who first made contact. *Obdurate*, one of Sherbrooke's escort, sighted three destroyers, was ordered to investigate, and promptly came under fire at a range of four miles. Sherbrooke in *Onslow*, sighting the gun flashes, immediately ordered *Orwell*, *Obedient*, and *Obdurate* to join him, and headed into the fray. It was 0915 hours. The Battle of the Barents Sea had begun.

When the shooting started, Kummetz in *Hipper* had very little idea of what he was up against. He certainly had no idea of the superb positioning of his force. 'Visibility very poor', he noted at 0915. 'Everything seems hazy. Cannot make out whether I am dealing with friend or foe. A total of ten ships now in sight, some of which look like destroyers. It cannot be said for certain whether our shadowing destroyers are not among them.' What was certain was that one of those destroyers was streaking along between *Hipper* and the convoy, laying a dense smokescreen (*Achates*, the only destroyer left by Sherbrooke to stiffen the lighter warships of the convoy's escort) and *Hipper* swung round and loosed off several inaccurate broadsides. Simultaneously, however, Sherbrooke in *Onslow* sighted *Hipper*, broadside-on as she was to the British destroyers, and ordered a mock attack, racing in and then wheeling as if to launch torpedoes.

Here was precisely the threat Kummetz had always dreaded: a 'serious risk' from an enemy of less than 'equal strength'. He broke off and ran for it, steaming away from the convoy, at the same time opening fire on the *Onslow*.

At 0957 Kummetz decided to try another attack, hoping to smash these defiant British destroyers or at least manoeuvre them away from their blocking position between *Hipper* and the convoy. The German cruiser made several lunges against *Onslow* and *Orwell* (Sherbrooke had sent *Obdurate* and *Obedient* back towards the convoy to check the German destroyers). And soon after 1000 *Onslow* picked up a signal from *Sheffield*, telling Sherbrooke that Burnett's two cruisers were on their way south to help.

The two British destroyers desperately needed help. Aboard *Onslow*, two of her four 4.7-inch guns were frozen up, which meant that between them *Orwell* and *Onslow* could only fire 'broadsides' of 220lbs, while *Hipper* was firing eight 8-inch and six 4.1-inch guns – a formidable broadside totalling 2,200lbs. So far the destroyers had led a charmed life, but this tenfold disparity in hitting-power was too much. About 1020 *Hipper*'s gun crews at last found *Onslow*'s range and landed two devastating salvoes in succession, crippling *Onslow*, knocking out her guns, and inflicting injuries on Captain Sherbrooke which forced him to hand over command to Lieutenant-Commander Kinloch in *Obedient*.

And then – exactly like Langsdorff of the *Graf Spee*, after knocking out the *Exeter* in the Battle of the River Plate – Kummetz managed to snatch defeat out of the jaws of victory. His hitting-power was vastly superior and his ship was undamaged. He had just crippled one of the destroyers which were keeping him away from the convoy, and his gunners had the range to shift target and eliminate the other. Instead, Kummetz now took *Hipper* out of action again, retreating to the north-east at 31 knots, disappearing into a snow squall at about 1035.

While *Onslow* fought her fires and fell back to take position ahead of the convoy in order to 'home' Burnett's cruisers to the scene of action, Kinloch in *Obedient*, with *Orwell* and *Obdurate*, headed south to overtake the convoy, which was now heading south-east. Within minutes, however, a new crisis materialised for the British: the escort corvette *Rhododendron* reported unidentified ships to the south at 1045 hours. *Lützow*, with her three destroyers, had closed to within two miles of the convoy before being sighted. Unlike Kummetz in the *Hipper*, Captain Stänge in *Lützow* had no British destroyers to challenge him. The convoy was all his – but *Lützow*, too, turned away in a snow squall, her log recording, at 1050, 'Impossible to ascertain whether dealing with friend or foe because of the poor light...' *Regenbogen* had reached the threshold of success, but Stänge's caution was fatal. When he appeared, at 1100, he found Kinloch's destroyers between *Lützow* and the convoy.

Burnett's cruisers, meanwhile, had been repeatedly diverted from their approach from the north. The first distraction had come at 0900, when radar contacts located ships to the north. This was the trawler *Vizalma*, escorting a straggler from JW-51B; and Burnett sighted them shortly afterwards before heading south. The vivid gun flashes from Sherbrooke's action with *Hipper* were sighted next and at 0955 Burnett steered towards them – only to be distracted again by the need to investigate two long-range mystery radar contacts to the east. Before this problem could be solved, however, another burst of gunfire flared up to the south of Burnett's flagship, *Sheffield*. It was in fact coming from the *Hipper*, which had run across the minesweeper *Bramble*, detached to search for stragglers from the convoy. *Hipper* made short work of the diminutive *Bramble*, but her triumph was short-lived. *Sheffield* sighted *Hipper* at 1045, minutes before Kummetz turned south to make another attempt to close with the convoy and its escorts. *Hipper*'s descent from the north coincided with the second sighting of the *Lützow* detachment. As the British destroyers made smoke to shield the convoy from *Lützow*, *Hipper* sighted the *Achates* and smashed her into a sinking wreck. Kummetz then turned his fire to the *Obedient*, knocking out her radio before flinching away, once again, from the threat of a torpedo attack.

At this point the tables were turned with a vengeance when *Hipper* suddenly came under fire from the north. *Sheffield* and *Jamaica* had arrived at last, and now Kummetz found himself threatened by cruisers to the north while his erstwhile victims – the British destroyers – separated him from *Lützow* to the south. *Sheffield* and *Jamaica* opened up at a range of seven miles and scored three rapid hits, flooding a boiler-room and dropping *Hipper*'s speed to twenty-eight knots. Five minutes later, the German destroyers *Friedrich Eckholdt* and *Richard Beitzen* blundered across the paths of *Sheffield* and *Jamaica*, which

129

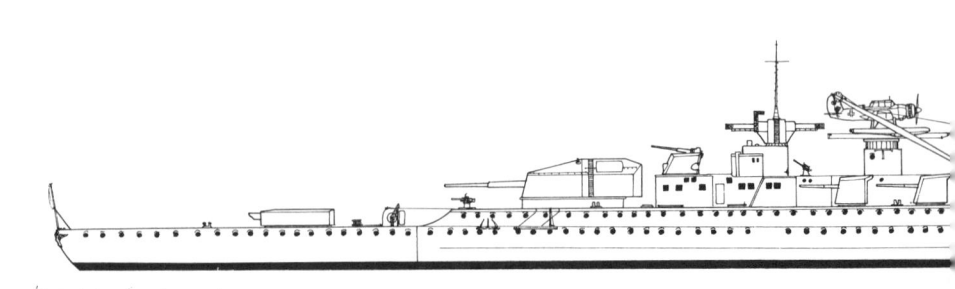

Admiral Scheer, second of the pocket-battleships. Like *Graf Spee*, she was originally built with a heavily-armoured fighting mast, but this was soon removed in an extensive refit and replaced with the slimmer mast as carried by *Deutschland*. *Scheer*'s triumphant high seas cruise (October 1940-March 1941), in which she sank 17 ships totalling 113,223 tons, proved what excellent raiders the pocket-battleships were – if given the chance. *Displacement:* 12,100 tons. *Length overall:* 609 feet. *Beam:* 70 feet. *Draught:* 21½ feet. *Max speed:* 26 knots. *Radius:* 19,000 miles at 19 knots. *Armour:* Side 4 inch, turrets 2-5½ inch, deck 1½-3 inch. *Armament:* Six 11-inch, eight 5.9-inch, six 4.1-inch AA, eight 37-mm AA, ten (later 28) 20-mm AA; eight 21-inch torpedo-tubes; two aircraft. *Complement:* 1,150

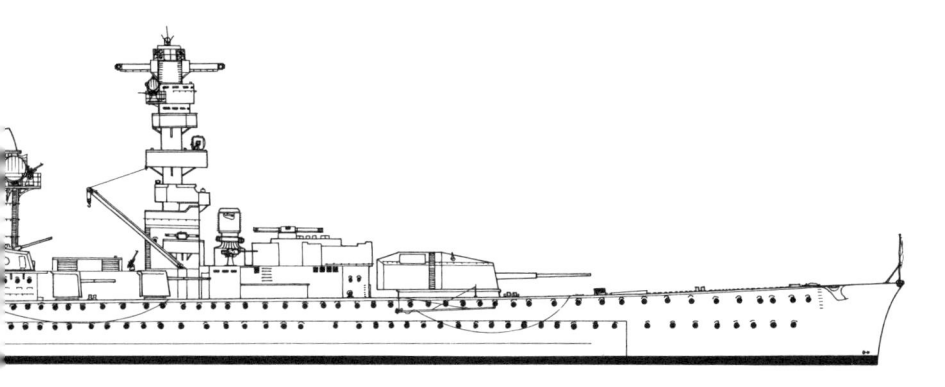

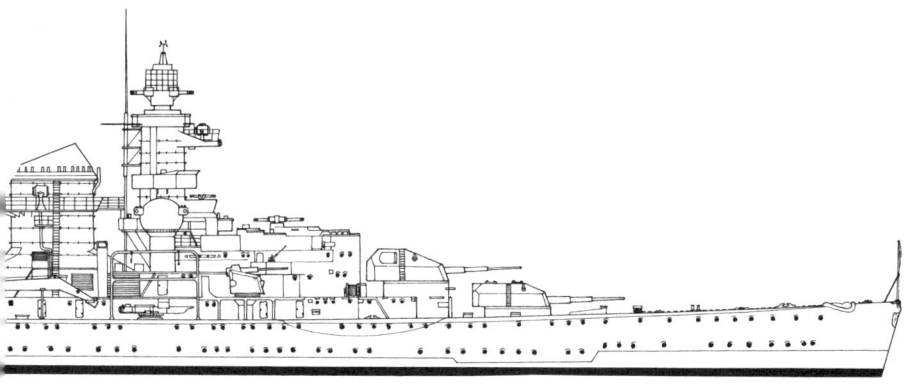

Admiral Hipper, first of the heavy cruisers ordered for the German navy in the 1930s. Of the five *Hipper*-class cruisers, only *Hipper*, *Blücher*, and *Prinz Eugen* entered service. *Lützow* was sold to the USSR in 1940; *Seydlitz* was to have been converted to an aircraft-carrier, but this was never completed. *Hipper* had an eventful career, but chronic engine trouble prevented her from being a success as a long-range high seas raider. *Displacement:* 13,900 tons. *Length overall:* 640 feet. *Beam:* 70 feet. *Draught:* 15 feet. *Max speed:* 32 knots. *Radius:* 6,800 miles at 18 knots. *Armour:* Side 5 inch, deck 4 inch, turrets 5 inch. *Armament:* Eight 8-inch, twelve 4.1-inch AA, twelve 37-mm AA, eight (later 28) 20-mm AA; twelve 21-inch torpedo-tubes; three aircraft. *Complement:* 1,600

Hipper, Kummetz' flagship during the abortive attack in the Barents Sea

immediately attacked. *Friedrich Eckholdt* was sunk and *Richard Beitzen* driven off. Meanwhile, at about 1140, Stänge in *Lützow* had actually opened fire on the convoy, slightly damaging a merchantman before the destroyers laid a fresh smokescreen and the pocket-battleship ceased fire. And at 1149 Kummetz signalled the order for all German vessels to withdraw.

A wild, confused affair it had been, lasting nearly four hours, but the Battle of the Barents Sea was over. Kummetz headed back to Alten Fjord with Burnett on his heels. The British Admiral called off the chase at 1400; darkness had fallen, and it was desirable to rejoin the convoy, which sailed on unscathed and reached Murmansk on 3rd January.

For Kummetz to put the blame for the *Regenbogen* fiasco – as he subsequently did – on the very poor weather conditions was just not good enough. The British, after all, had had to cope with the same weather. And there were so many other things that should not have gone wrong on the German side. From start to finish, the performance of the German destroyers, when compared to the gallantry, dash, and initiative of their British opponents, had been lamentable. Stänge's inactivity in the *Lützow* at the crucial moment had ruined the whole plan. Even Kummetz – who had played his part well, drawing the British destroyers by his repeated lunges at the convoy's left flank – had made the human but basic mistake of not knowing when he had won his battle. The result had been a well-earned victory for the British, with Sherbrooke of the *Onslow* receiving the VC. As Admiral Tovey commented, 'that an enemy force of at least one pocket-battleship, one heavy cruiser and six destroyers, with all the advantages of surprise and concentration, should be held off for four hours by five destroyers, and driven from the area by two 6-inch cruisers is most creditable and satisfactory.'

But if justice is to be done to Kummetz, one has to remember the underlying thread of restrictive caution which had characterised the planning of the whole operation. To be really fair, one has to admit that such caution was not peculiar to the German navy in the Second World War, either. The movements of Jellicoe's Dreadnought battle fleet in the First World War had been cramped in much the same way by the eternal dread of losing the whole fleet to German torpedo-boat attacks. On 31st December 1942, Kummetz was forced to find out, the hard way, that the execution of the most perfectly-planned operation cannot be divorced from some element of risk. The German Naval High Command realised this well enough, but always preferred to echo the caution radiated by Hitler whenever a move by the fleet was being contemplated. Perhaps if the one man in a position to remonstrate with Hitler over naval strategy – Grand Admiral Raeder – had had more seagoing experience himself in his earlier career, his arguments would have carried more weight and the fleet's whole story would have been very different.

As it was, the repercussions of the Barents Sea battle were disastrous both for Raeder and for his fleet. This latest failure could hardly have come at a worse moment. Menaced from east and west, Rommel was falling back along the North African coastline, retreating towards the Mareth Line on the frontier of Tunisia. The Allies had only been prevented by the narrowest of margins from taking Bizerta and Tunis. Paulus and his Sixth Army were cut off in Stalingrad, hundreds of kilometres behind the advancing Russian lines. And now the surface fleet, so far from even interrupting the Allied convoys to Russia, had sunk a minesweeper and a des-

Raeder with Hitler at Armed Forces High Command. Hitler had never really understood Raeder's strategy – and the Barents Sea fiasco proved fatal

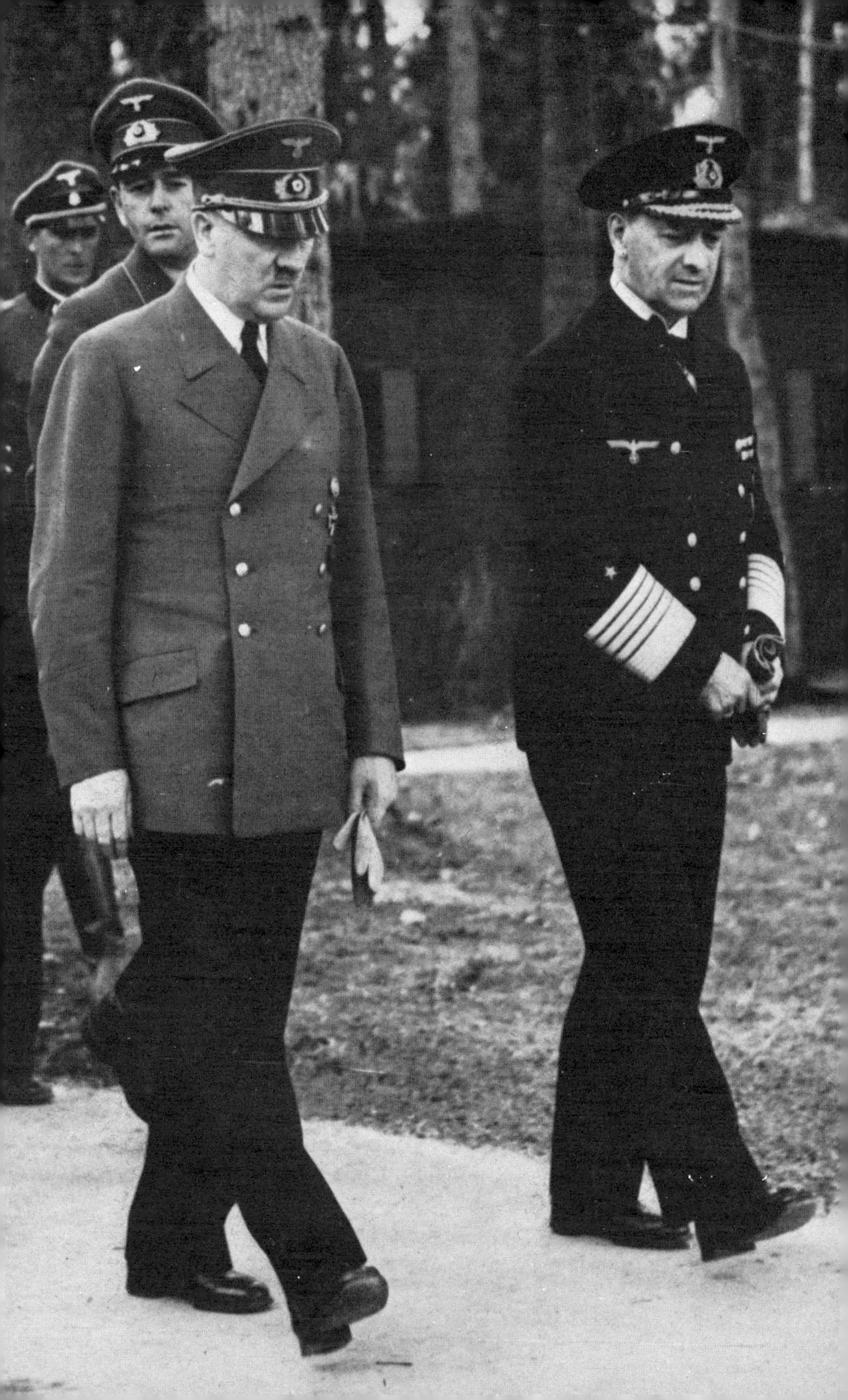

troyer, lost one of its own destroyers, and had scurried ignominiously back to port with nothing more to show for its efforts but shell damage. Incensed beyond all reason, Hitler exploded with one of his most startling edicts of the entire war. The fleet had never earned its keep; it had been given a last chance, and had achieved nothing but another humiliating failure; the entire surface fleet was therefore to be scrapped – right down to destroyer level – and its guns, crews, and armour at last put to profitable use as part of the defences of the Reich's 'Western Wall'.

Erich Raeder now fought his last battle as Commander-in-Chief of the German navy: to save the fleet which he had brought into being, which he had seen plunged into a premature war, and which he had never been allowed to use according to its full potential. He prepared an exhaustive memorandum, pointing out the fleet's rôle as a deterrent. He argued that the scrapping of the fleet would present the Allies with a strategic victory, freeing powerful squadrons of Allied warships for far more dangerous service elsewhere. Banking on Hitler's fascination with military hardware and statistical hard facts, Raeder even produced the figures for exactly what could be gained by the irrevocable act of cannibalising the fleet: the services of 8,800 officers and men (14% of the navy's total personnel), and 125,800 tons of high-grade steel (about one-twentieth of the Third Reich's total requirements *per month*). Some fifteen coastal batteries could be armed with the fleet's guns – but the first of these batteries could not possibly be completed within a year. And he repeated: 'The paying-off of the large surface vessels will be a victory gained by our enemies without any effort on their part.'

Hitler's reply only heaped insult on injury. The fleet, he retorted, never even considered battle without counting the odds to the point of timidity. 'The army', he positively sneered,

Rolf Carls, Raeder's nominee

'does not follow this principle. As a soldier, the Führer demands that, once forces have been committed to action, the battle be fought to a decision.' Against such a futile argument it was useless for Raeder to point out that the fleet's so-called timidity was merely a faithful carbon-copy of the Führer's own apprehension whenever the big ships were out. He therefore played his last card: resignation. Hitler was shaken, but refused to go back on his decision; and on 30th January 1943, Grand Admiral Erich Raeder ceased to be commander of the German navy. As his successor, Hitler selected Karl Dönitz, the only Admiral he knew to have made a significant contribution to the war at sea by his work as head of the U-boat arm.

Perhaps Raeder's main defect had been his main virtue: his inability to secure the Führer's confidence, standing aloof as he did from the squalid in-fighting of Nazi court politics. It was a mistake which the new Grand Admiral, Dönitz, never made. Having won Hitler's confidence by the achievements of his U-boats, Dönitz was determined to keep that confidence by his personal influence, maintained by regular meetings and discussions with the Führer. He was to succeed so well that he would become one of the most trusted members of the 'inner circle' of the Third Reich's leaders, and would in time be nominated as Hitler's successor.

Yet for all his mastery of the realities of Nazi politics, Dönitz remained a hundred per cent professional when it came to running the German navy. And one of the first things he realised on taking up the supreme command was that the surface fleet must not be sacrificed as Hitler wanted. By all means, he argued, it could be cut down, but it must not be liquidated. Within three weeks of becoming C-in-C, Dönitz had succeeded where Raeder had failed. The fleet got its reprieve. The old pre-Dreadnought battleships, *Schlesien* and *Schleswig-Holstein*, were to be decommissioned. The same went for the damaged *Hipper*, which would not be repaired after the Barents Sea battle, and for some of the light cruisers. The aircraft-carrier scheme was to be abandoned and all work halted on *Graf Zeppelin* and *Seydlitz*. *Lützow*, *Scheer*, and *Prinz Eugen* would be used mainly for training in the Baltic. But *Scharnhorst*, operational again after the repairing of the damage suffered during the Channel Dash, and now the second most powerful warship in the fleet, would go north to join *Tirpitz* as a deterrent threat to the Russian convoys.

If Hitler had had his way, the Allies would have been given an unbeatable lead in the war at sea. They would have been able to throw the full strength of the Home Fleet into the fight against the U-boats in the Atlantic, while continuing to sail convoys to Russia virtually without fear of molestation. Because of the work of Dönitz, none of this was possible. By late March, 1943, British air reconnaissance had located the strongest German battle squadron yet assembled in northern waters: *Tirpitz*, *Lützow*, and *Scharnhorst* – battleship,

Karl Dönitz, Raeder's successor

pocket-battleship, and battle-cruiser, packing a collective big-gun broadside of eight 15-inch and fifteen 11-inch guns – all of which had been moved up to Alten Fjord. And it was the news of this formidable concentration which persuaded the British Admiralty to insist on the suspension of the Russian convoys for the summer months of 1943.

This was not because of recent losses due to enemy action; on the contrary, the Russian convoys of the winter of 1942–43 had an excellent record to show. Convoys JW-52, RA-52, JW-53, and RA-53 delivered thirty-five ships to Russia and brought thirty-six home, while four Russian vessels made successful independent runs. The Luftwaffe and the U-boats only managed to pick off four ships, while another was sunk by foul weather. In addition, two independently-routed ships were sunk. But the case for halting the Russian convoys was unanswerable. The Battle of the Atlantic was reaching its greatest crisis, and the Atlantic convoys were crying out for escorts which could only be provided at the expense of the Russian route. Churchill informed Roosevelt: 'The sinkings in the North Atlantic of seventeen ships in two days [17th–19th March] in

135

convoys HX-229 and SC-122 are a final proof that our escorts are everywhere too thin. The strain upon the British Navy is becoming intolerable.'

More escorts could only be provided by switching forces from the Home Fleet; and if Russian convoys sailed without proper escorts during the summer – silhouetted against the pack-ice by the eerie pallor of the midnight sun – the result might well be more PQ-17s. And now the Germans had concentrated a battle squadron which would need all the vigilance of the Home Fleet if it were to be prevented from escaping into the Atlantic, let alone from attacking convoys to Russia.

Churchill therefore made his decision. He broke the news of the need for suspending the convoys to Stalin by telegram on 30th March, resigning himself to the torrent of not-so-diplomatic reproach and sarcasm which streamed from Moscow during the next five months. So it was that the huge Eastern Front battles of summer 1943 were fought without Russia receiving any fresh weapons or supplies via the Arctic convoy route, while the German battle squadron swung idly round its anchors in Alten Fjord with no convoys to attack.

At this point, two important changes were made in the high commands of the British and German navies. Dönitz streamlined the cumbersome chain of command which linked the German Admiralty with its Fleet Commander, amalgamating the post of Flag Officer, Northern Waters, with that of the C-in-C, Group North. From now on, the competent Admiral Schniewind, Commander-in-Chief, Northern Group, would relay movement orders from his post at Kiel to Admiral Kummetz at Alten Fjord. And on the British side, the Home Fleet got a new C-in-C when Admiral Tovey hauled down his flag on 8th May 1943, and handed over to his second-in-command, Admiral Sir Bruce Fraser. Tovey had had to do a thankless job with forces which were nearly always insufficient. For two and a half years he had covered the northern approaches to the Atlantic as well as the Russian convoys, managing to make bricks without straw even when the politicians gave him impossible tasks to achieve and deadlines to meet. His greatest achievement, for which he will always be remembered, was leading the hunt for the *Bismarck* in May 1941. But no less important was the fact that when his spell of command ended, he was able to hand over a fleet which was superbly trained and in magnificent fighting order. Fraser, Tovey's successor, was a worthy heir. He was fully experienced in overcoming the practical difficulties of the job, and was to make admirable use of the weapon which Tovey passed to him.

The year 1943 also saw the end of the German commerce war by surface raiders on the high seas. On 10th February the British spotted the disguised raider *Togo* coming down-Channel under a heavy escort. The Dover batteries opened up without scoring any hits, but Whirlwind bombers landed a bomb on *Togo* forcing her to put into Boulogne. She headed back towards Germany, reaching Dunkirk, where she was hit by another bomb, and struggled back to Kiel on 2nd March. *Togo* never tried to run the gauntlet of the Channel defences again, and this left only one raider at sea: *Michel*, out in the Pacific. The day *Togo* returned to Kiel, 2nd March, *Michel* anchored at Kobe, Japan, after stopping off at Batavia and Singapore. She set off on a new cruise in May heading south to Indonesian waters and sinking two merchantmen before turning east into the open Pacific. On 11th September she sank her last victim, the Norwegian tanker *India* near Easter Island. And on 18th October, when three days out of Yokohama, she was sent to the bottom by the US submarine *Tarpon*.

Michel's fate is a reminder of the

efficiency of America's submarine arm, which virtually annihilated Japan's mercantile fleet in the Pacific in return for minimal losses to their own submarines – a startling contrast to the German U-boat wolf-packs in the Atlantic. The German raider had been at sea since March 1942, and had sunk seventeen ships totalling 121,994 tons, most of them in the South Atlantic. The last of the German high seas commerce raiders had gone, and now the only sea in which Hitler's High Seas Fleet could make its presence felt was the Arctic.

By autumn 1943, *Scharnhorst* was tying with the heavy cruiser *Prinz Eugen* as one of the luckiest of the German Navy's heavy warships. She had escaped from the Norwegian campaign of 1940, two Atlantic cruises, a year of bombing attacks by the RAF while in Brest, the Channel Dash, and the breaker's yard; and in late September 1943 her luck saved her again.

On 8th September there occurred the last sortie made by a German battle squadron in the Second World War. *Tirpitz, Scharnhorst,* and ten destroyers sailed out of Alten Fjord to destroy shore installations on Spitzbergen. This was in fact the only time when *Tirpitz* could be said to have fired her 15-inch main armament 'in anger', and both ships returned to Alten Fjord with their escorts after this dubious feat of arms. But *Scharnhorst*'s target-practice against the immobile defences on Spitzbergen had been so atrocious that her captain had insisted on putting to sea for further exercises despite the chronic shortage of fuel oil; and while the battle-cruiser was out of her berth on this gunnery shoot, British X-craft midget submarines got into Alten Fjord on the night of 22nd September, determined to sink the German squadron.

The X-craft had mixed successes and heavy losses. *Lützow* had moved her berth since the last reconnaissance and could not be found; *Scharnhorst* was out on exercises – but *Tirpitz* was thoroughly crippled by four explosive charges, and completely immobilised. None of the three X-craft which struggled through the net defences to attack the *Tirpitz* got back to Britain, but their mission had been accomplished. *Tirpitz* could not possibly be repaired before April 1944 at the very earliest. And on the 23rd *Lützow* left Alten Fjord to refit in the Baltic. Here was a dramatic change in the far north's naval balance – and it opened the next chapter in the story of the Arctic convoys.

It so happened that Moscow had opened another barrage of demands for more supply convoys only twenty-four attacks before the X-craft attack on Alten Fjord, which meant that now – for once – the requirements of British diplomacy and naval strategy were compatible. But it took a month of knuckle-duster diplomacy before Churchill could make Stalin understand that Britain could not bind herself to a set timetable of convoy sailings, or to a set volume of deliveries. It was not until 15th November that the first of the new set of outward-bound convoys – JW-54A – set out for Russia, followed a week later by JW-54B, both of which arrived untouched.

Admiral Fraser was eager for any challenge the *Scharnhorst* might care to make, and made the decision to accompany the next convoy, JW-55A, right the way through to Murmansk with his battle squadron – a decision unprecedented in the entire history of the Russian convoys. No challenge came from Alten Fjord, and JW-55A reached Russia safely. Fraser left the Kola Inlet on 18th December, after a two-day stay in Russian waters, and the return voyage, too, had no trouble.

But now that the Russian convoys had started again, Dönitz was determined to send the *Scharnhorst* against them, and in this he was backed by both Schniewind and Kummetz. Schniewind, in fact, had gone on record back on 16th April as stating: 'All commanding officers of the

Salvo from *Tirpitz*. Her only offensive operation of the war was in the target-practice at Spitzbergen

Northern Task Force are in no doubt that the main purpose of their ships is to fight.' Yet this fighting spirit could not eliminate the difficulties of which Dönitz and his fellow admirals were only too well aware from painful experience: foul weather conditions, superior British radar, the danger of destroyer attacks from the close escort, and threadbare support from the Luftwaffe. There was undoubtedly a marked degree of uncertainty whether the first foray would be by destroyers alone, or whether *Scharnhorst* would in fact be sent out as well.

The man with the best first-hand experience of these problems was Admiral Kummetz, but early in November he was sent on 'prolonged leave'; and he was replaced as C-in-C Battle Group by the erstwhile Flag Officer, Destroyers, Rear-Admiral Erich Bey. All Bey's main wartime experience had been with the destroyer arm, and he thought of attacking the Russian convoys mainly in terms of destroyer strikes. He also professed a strong belief in luck, in striking when the iron was hot (which had done him little good during the Second Battle of Narvik, when his destroyer force had been wiped out). He had come to his present post after the *Scharnhorst*'s Spitzbergen venture, and he had not organised her working-up and the gunnery drill. Yet it was Bey who would lead the Battle Group out of Alten Fjord when the next Allied convoy came within its reach.

On 19th December, Dönitz informed Hitler that the *Scharnhorst* would attack the next Allied convoy to Russia, and on the following day his prospective victim set out: Convoy JW-55B, nineteen merchantmen with an escort of ten destroyers. It was the mixture as before: Fraser was shadowing the outward-bound convoy with his battle fleet while Burnett's cruisers *Sheffield*, *Belfast*, and *Norfolk* escorted the return convoy, RA-55A, which sailed from Murmansk on the 23rd. Fraser 'felt very strongly that the *Scharnhorst* would come out and endeavour to attack' this time, and he was keeping as close as he could to the convoy without betraying his presence. The German Naval High Command, on the other hand, which ordered the Battle Group to readiness when JW-55B was sighted on 22nd December, seems to have anticipated a comparatively easy attack on the convoy. It was soon to be undeceived.

By Christmas morning, the Luftwaffe's constant shadowing of JW-55B, compared with the undetected progress of RA-55A, made it fairly obvious which of the two was being selected for treatment. Fraser switched four destroyers from RA-55A, thus increasing JW-55B's escort to fourteen destroyers, and at the same time ordered JW-55B to head further to the north. And at 1400 on the 25th, Dönitz ordered the sortie to proceed. Operation *Ostfront* ('Eastern Front'), he called it – the clearest proof that, as he later claimed, this sortie by *Scharnhorst* represented a vital part of German Grand Strategy and was aimed at taking pressure off the German armies in Russia (an optimistic programme if ever there was one).

Dönitz later claimed that he ordered Bey to go out because the convoy 'could not hope to escape'. The method of attack was also left to Bey. It seemed that for the first time a full degree of initiative would be permitted for this sortie – but within hours of putting to sea Bey, exactly like Kummetz twelve months before him, received a qualifying signal from the Naval High Command. He was to 'exploit the tactical situation boldly' but to 'disengage if heavy forces are encountered', and he was to conduct the operation according to 'accurate information about the enemy' – a facility which was to be singularly lacking on the German side in the following twenty-four hours.

Unlike Kummetz, Bey had not had

Erich Bey: lost with the *Scharnhorst*

the experience of co-ordinating the movements of capital ships and destroyer squadrons in the difficult conditions of an Arctic winter. It is most uncertain whether or not, like Kummetz, he had in mind a plan for distracting the escort vessels with one part of his force while attacking the merchantmen with another. It is interesting to note that the time of sailing had to be postponed in order to allow Bey to shift his flag to the *Scharnhorst*, which would indicate that he had not expected the battlecruiser to be included in the operation. But by 1900 hours on 25th December, *Scharnhorst* was heading out into the Barents Sea with a force of five destroyers.

Bey headed north at twenty-five knots. The weather was vile – it had been deteriorating since the morning of the 25th – but with the sea astern his ships were able to make good speed to the north. And at midnight Bey made the first in a series of fatal miscalculations: he broke radio silence to swap messages with Naval Group North about weather conditions and future movements, which were promptly picked up by the British.

At 0339 hours on the 26th, Fraser received the news that the *Scharnhorst* was out. At that point in time, Bey was about 100 miles from the convoy,

139

heading north, Fraser was 200 miles away, heading east, while Burnett's cruisers were 150 miles away, heading west. Thus JW-55B's situation was a critical one, with Bey's squadron heading for it on a converging course. At 0628, Fraser signalled the convoy to head north-east, which would add to *Scharnhorst*'s difficulties in finding it. But Bey was having quite enough troubles as it was. German radio Intelligence had picked up none of Fraser's signals asking Burnett and the convoy to report their positions, and he was operating on reports which were both out-dated and misleading. In a report timed at 1510 hours the previous day, he had been told that no enemy ships had been located within fifty miles of the convoy. Bey must have realised that such delayed reports, in the prevailing weather conditions, were of little value; but he had nothing else on which to plan his tactics.

He made his second fatal mistake at 0700 when he turned to the southwest and ordered his destroyers to fan out ahead and scout for the convoy. Here was a compound error. The destroyers, led by Captain Johannesen in Z-29, now had to struggle into a head sea and had to cut down their speed to ten knots; and Bey was also deliberately diffusing his force in extremely uncertain conditions. Even so, he was still in a good position for continuing the search, between Burnett's cruisers and the convoy – until, at 0820 hours, he swung round to the north again, without informing his destroyers, He was now on a converging course with Burnett, and the range fell rapidly. At 0840 hours the inevitable happened: *Scharnhorst* was picked up by *Belfast*'s radar at a range of seventeen and a half miles, and Burnett's force continued to close. At 0921 hours, when *Sheffield* suddenly sighted the *Scharnhorst*, the range was down to six and a half miles.

What is now known as the Battle of the North Cape began at 0929 when Burnett's cruisers opened fire on the German battle-cruiser; but only the *Norfolk* managed to land a couple of 8-inch salvoes before Bey swung *Scharnhorst* away to the south-east, and then round to the north in an attempt to side-step the British force. Burnett meanwhile, knowing that four destroyers were on their way to join him from the convoy's escort, steered to put his cruisers between the *Scharnhorst* and the convoy. Bey had been taken completely by surprise, and certainly overestimated the British strength. Gun for gun, he could have played havoc with any of Burnett's lightly-armoured cruisers while courting little danger – though it is possible that the records of the bad gunnery during the Spitzbergen affair may have made him shy of a set-piece gunnery duel. And he did not have the added fire-power of his five destroyers – all of them armed with 5.9-inch guns – which would have favoured him even more in a gun action. This he attempted to put right by ordering the destroyer group to head north-east towards *Scharnhorst* as she continued to search for the convoy.

In an impressive feat of co-ordination and seamanship, Burnett's force sprinted in the direction of the convoy and formed a defensive screen ten miles ahead of it. This move transformed the scene for the British. Burnett's force was now the powerful spring of a trap – with the convoy as bait – into which *Scharnhorst* was heading. Fraser had known all along that he was unlikely to get a chance of intercepting *Scharnhorst* unless she were engaged by Burnett's force; and now, if Bey persisted in his attempts to get at the convoy, he would have his hands full indeed. Meanwhile, however, he had made his fourth mistake. At 1158 he threw away his chance of concentrating his force by ordering the German destroyers to re-commence their search for the convoy. Once again, Johannesen's destroyers had to turn back into sea and slog back to the west.

140

Then, at 1205, Belfast's radar picked up *Scharnhorst* again. This time the positions were reversed, with Burnett's ships to the west of Bey, and the British cruisers opened fire at 1221 hours. *Scharnhorst* shied away again, which prevented the British destroyers from making torpedo attacks; but there was an interchange of fire lasting twenty minutes, during which *Norfolk* definitely came off worst. She was hit twice by 11-inch shells, one turret was wrecked, and only one of her radar sets was left in action. Burnett called off his ships at 1241 hours and they settled down to the chase. In his second cruiser action, Bey had once again suffered from the absence of his destroyers, and the course he now took could hardly have been better calculated to give Fraser the chance he needed to intercept: south-south-east at twenty-eight knots. Bey could have coped with the threat of Burnett's force in one of two ways: he could have continued the gunnery duel, which would have obliged the British cruisers to withdraw out of range of *Scharnhorst*'s formidable broadside; or he could have steamed flat-out into the pounding seas at a higher speed than the lighter British ships could have endured. He did neither.

Then came the episode which made it inevitable that Fraser would have a good chance of intercepting *Scharnhorst*. Bey was relayed a message from Luftwaffe Group Lofoten which repeated a reconnaissance report of three hours before, to the effect that several small ships and *one heavy ship* had been located to the west. The repeat, however, omitted any reference to the heavy ship. If at this point Bey had been warned that there was a battleship coming up from the west, he could have acted accordingly; but as it was, he stood confidently on to the south-east. His destroyers were still doggedly heading west, and had in fact passed within about ten miles of the convoy around 1300 hours. They continued their search until, at 1418 hours, Bey ordered them to leave off and return to Alten Fjord. He had called off the sweep against JW-55B; once again, the surface threat to the Russian convoys from Hitler's High Seas Fleet had fizzled out – and *Scharnhorst* was on her own.

At 1617 hours, *Duke of York*, twenty-two miles to the south-west, picked up the *Scharnhorst* on her radar for the first time, and now her position was being plotted by two sets of radar. *Duke of York*'s gunnery radar started tracking at 1632 hours at a range of fourteen miles; at 1650 *Belfast* lobbed over a salvo of starshell, illuminating *Scharnhorst*, which immediately came under fire from *Duke of York* and *Jamaica*. The Battle of the North Cape was entering its last phase, with Bey surprised for the third time – this time by an enemy battle group. This time, however, he had Burnett's cruiser-destroyer force on his left flank, preventing him from swinging away. And so, still heading for the Norwegian coast, *Scharnhorst* began to engage *Duke of York* with ripple salvoes, which soon became uncomfortably accurate, from her 11-inch guns.

It was now a running fight, and there was still a faint chance that *Scharnhorst*'s superior speed might shake off Burnett and cheat Fraser. Already Burnett's destroyers were falling behind, and soon *Jamaica* ceased fire, last of the cruisers still in range. But as *Scharnhorst* gradually crept away, the trajectory of *Duke of York*'s 14-inch shells became steeper and steeper – and therefore more lethal. Two 11-inch and one 5.9-inch turret were knocked out – and then, at 1820, a 14-inch shell smashed through into her No 1 Boiler Room, severed a steam pipe, and cut off power from her turbines. Her speed fell off, and the destroyers began to close in again. *Scharnhorst*'s fire-power, like that of *Bismarck* during her last fight, was still formidable. She managed to put two 11-inch shells through *Duke of York*'s masts, and the British battleship ceased fire at 1824 – the same moment

141

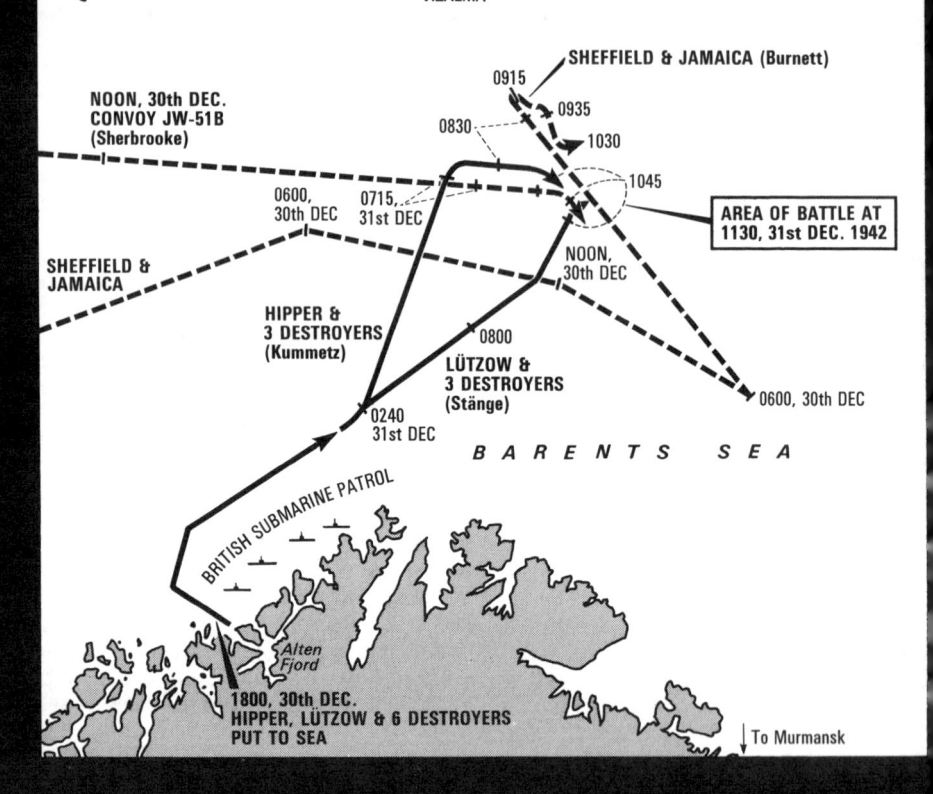

Battle of the Barents Sea: *Hipper* and *Lützow* snatch defeat from the jaws of victory

that Bey sent off a signal assuring his Führer 'We shall fight to the last shell.'

Now it was the turn of the destroyers – the British *Savage*, *Saumarez* and *Scorpion*, with the Norwegian *Stord*. In they came, braving the powerful 5.9-inch secondary armament of *Scharnhorst*, with the battle-cruiser looming bigger and bigger until one startled seaman aboard *Scorpion* exclaimed, 'Get out wires and fenders – we're going alongside the bastard!' Twisting and turning, *Scharnhorst* could not escape this attack, and took four torpedo-hits which reduced her speed again. What the Swordfish of *Ark Royal* had done to *Bismarck* back in 1941, the destroyers had done to *Scharnhorst*: crippling her and allowing the battleships to close in for the kill.

At 1901 hours, *Duke of York*, seconded again by *Jamaica*, reopened fire at the range of five miles. *Scharnhorst*'s last fight began with the battle-cruiser completely ringed in by cruisers and destroyers, and mercilessly pounded by 14-inch shells. The British crews sighted repeated hits, fires, and explosions through the pall of smoke which spread over the dying warship. By 1930 her engines were still turning over, giving her a speed of five knots; but she was listing so heavily that none of her guns could bear on her tormentors, and she sank after a tremendous explosion at about 1945 hours. During her last fight, she was

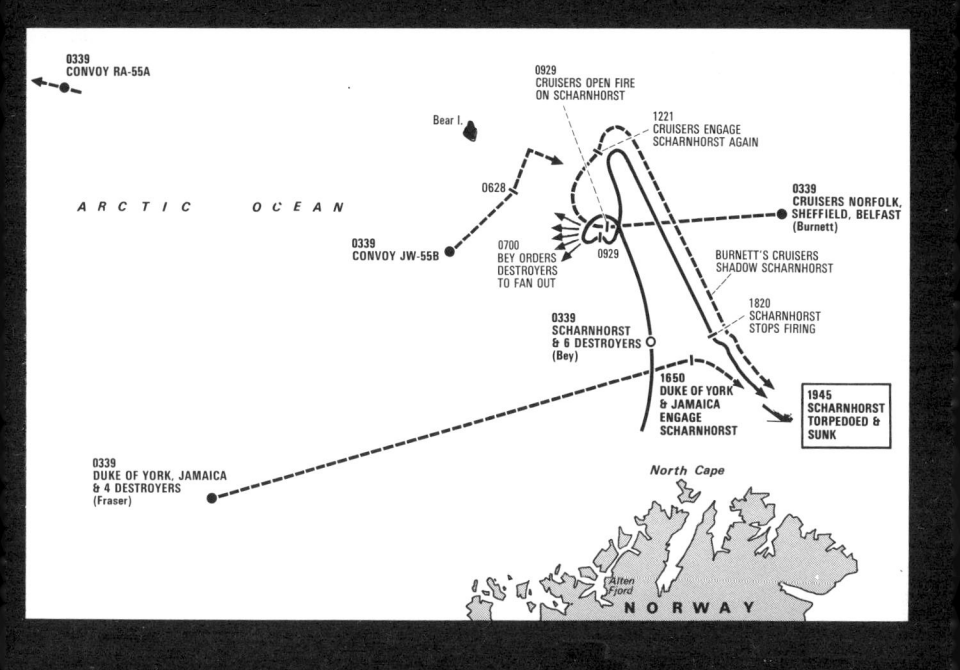

Battle of the North Cape: the last fight of the *Scharnhorst*, 26th December 1943

the target of some fifty-five torpedoes, of which eleven had hit. Only thirty-six out of her complement of 1,839 officers and seamen – which had included forty cadets having their first training cruise of the war – were picked up by the British.

The mistakes which led to the loss of the *Scharnhorst* in the Battle of the North Cape can partly be explained by Admiral Bey's continual lack of accurate information – but he knew the limitations under which he sailed, and it must be concluded that he took his ship into conditions which gave her no chance. For their part, the British admirals had fought a difficult battle with flexible tactics, and had earned a just reward. Their victorious ships sailed on with the undamaged convoy, JW-55B, to reach Murmansk on 27th December.

The last fight of the *Scharnhorst* was not only the last time that Hitler's High Seas Fleet challenged the Royal Navy. It was the last time that battleships engaged in a running fight in the style of Jutland, with aircraft taking no part in the battle apart from preliminary scouting. After *Scharnhorst* had gone, all attention now turned to the last battleship left in the German Fleet, immobile, camouflaged, but still the only warship capable of pinning down a British fleet by the very fact of her existence: *Tirpitz*, the 'Lone Queen of the North'.

143

Lone queen of the north

'A ship's best characteristic', Grand Admiral Alfred von Tirpitz had pronounced, 'is that provided it can stay afloat and horizontal it is a gun platform.' The founder of Germany's first High Seas Fleet may have hoped that one day the German navy might name a warship after him; but never could he have imagined that his 'gun platform' thesis could one day be taken as the epitome of the career of the battleship *Tirpitz* in a manner unique in history.

From January 1942, when she moved from Germany to Trondheim, until November 1944, *Tirpitz* was the one ship the Royal Navy could not ignore. She was its most dangerous potential opponent in the western hemisphere. Her existence triggered off a series of episodes in the war at sea which no other single ship in history has equalled. They are worth remembering, for they occurred in a period which was bidding fair to demonstrate the complete obsolescence of the battleship as an effective naval weapon – and no battleship has ever had a history like that of the *Tirpitz*.

The aura of fear and respect which *Tirpitz* generated was largely inherited from her sister-ship *Bismarck*. Never in the war did the Royal Navy have to conjure up such spontaneous improvisation as it did when hunting down the *Bismarck*. And when *Tirpitz* entered commission and moved to Norwegian waters, poised, as it seemed, to emulate *Bismarck*'s exploit, the British spared no effort to keep her pinned down.

First came the drama of the St Nazaire raid. Only in St Nazaire was there a dry dock big enough to hold a warship of *Tirpitz*'s bulk, and possibly refit her if she broke out into the Atlantic and made for France as *Bismarck* had tried to do. The raid which countered this threat was built round the plan of ramming an ancient destroyer, packed with high explosive, into the lock gate, and wrecking it by detonating the charge with a time-fuse after scuttling the destroyer

Tirpitz at sea on a gunnery shoot

in position. The raid, carried out with great gallantry on 28th March 1942, succeeded with frightful losses to the Commandos, soldiers, and sailors involved; but it eliminated the possibility of the Germans keeping *Tirpitz* operational in a Biscay port.

A fascinating question poses itself with regard to the St Nazaire raid. Admiral Darlan, the often-reviled Vichy leader, was never more vociferous in conference with German naval strategists than when he repeatedly asserted that, while it might be possible to get *Tirpitz* into the huge dock at St Nazaire, it would be virtually impossible to get her out. He repeated this time and again in the months before the raid put an end to the debate. Whether or not he was giving the Germans sound professional advice as a collaborator, or whether he was trying to argue them out of making a second Wilhelmshaven out of a French port, will probably never be known. But such was his argument, and it has to remain as yet another facet of the *Tirpitz* story.

Tirpitz was bombed repeatedly when she lay in Trondheim, but she was still undamaged when she scored her greatest victory: on 4th-5th July 1942, when the fear that she was at large caused the British Admiralty to scatter Convoy PQ-17 and send twenty-three merchantmen to their destruction by U-boats and bombers. She was one of the most potent reasons for the suspension of the Russian convoys during the crucial summer of 1942, and the desirability of her destruction was greater than ever.

In the First World War, Winston Churchill, as First Lord of the Admiralty, had come in for much displeasure by his boast that if the High Seas Fleet did not come out and fight, it would be 'dug like rats' from its ports. The officers of Jellicoe's Grand Fleet regarded this as mere bombast, but in the Second World War

145

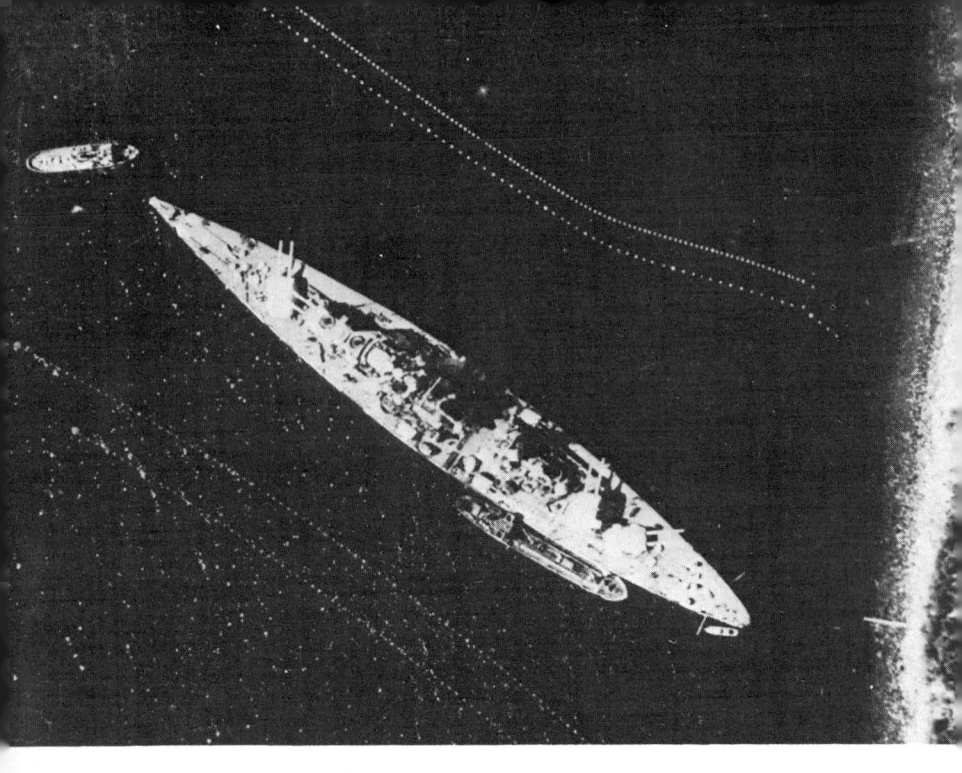

Above: **The Lone Queen in one of her many heavily-defended Arctic hideaways**
Below: **British X-craft penetrated the defences and crippled** *Tirpitz*

there were weapons for making this possible. The next line of attack tried by the British used one of them: human torpedoes. On 26th October 1942, Norwegian Resistance leader Lief Larsen headed for Trondheim in the fishing boat *Arthur*, towing two of these unwieldy weapons. Once the harbour had been entered, the idea was to ride the torpedoes underwater to where *Tirpitz* lay and leave their explosive warheads, with their fuses activated, beneath the battleship's hull. The operation ended in fiasco: five miles out from Trondheim, after being cleared by a German coastal patrol, the crew of the *Arthur* found that the torpedoes – 'Chariots', as they were known – had broken adrift from their towlines and were lost. *Tirpitz* had escaped again.

The next threat to the giant battleship's existence came from Adolf Hitler, when he sentenced every capital ship in the German Fleet to death by scrapping after the failure of Operation *Regenbogen* in the Battle of the Barents Sea on 31st December, 1942. But, as seen in the previous chapter, this peril was overcome by the arguments of Grand Admiral Dönitz, and *Tirpitz* was sent north to Alten Fjord to continue her deterrent rôle. From Alten Fjord she sailed in early September 1943 on the only mission when she used her 15-inch guns: the shelling of Spitzbergen on 8th September. And it was in Alten Fjord that the British X-craft midget submarines found her when they attacked on 22nd September.

It was with the X-craft attack that the shadows began to close in on the story of the *Tirpitz*. Captain Hans Meyer, having captured four crewmen from one of the disabled X-craft, had shifted his ship as far as possible from where it was guessed the explosive charges had been placed, but it was not enough. Any submarine explosion has a devastating effect, because the shock waves are concentrated by the water – and the X-craft had laid eight tons of amatol explosive beneath *Tirpitz*, all of which went up together.

When it came, the blast lifted the great ship bodily, it was calculated, by as much as six feet. It wrecked her lighting system, immobilised two turrets, twisted a rudder, and badly damaged all her main engines. Later, the German engineers found that many of the frames of her hull had been distorted, which meant that she would never be able to reach her designed full speed again. But she could be repaired; her guns could still fire; and as long as that was the case the British dare not leave her alone.

By the spring of 1944 it was calculated that her repairs were nearing completion, and the British prepared for yet another attack: this time a massed air strike from aircraft-carriers, since Alten Fjord was out of range of the RAF's land-based bombers. In a low-level attack on 3rd April, 1944, forty-two Barracuda dive-bombers gained complete surprise over the German defences in Alten Fjord and showered the *Tirpitz* with bombs, scoring fourteen hits and causing several fires. Some 122 of the battleship's crew were killed and 316 wounded. But the 1,600-lb bombs used in the raid had been dropped from too low an altitude to drill through her armour, and most of the damage was comparatively superficial. The vital point for the British, which made the attack worthwhile, was that it took another three months to repair it.

The success of the Fleet Air Arm's initial raid was never repeated, although attempt after attempt was made throughout the summer of 1944. These failed respectively because of adverse weather, because of the smokescreen with which *Tirpitz* was shrouded when attacked, and because of faulty bombs which failed to explode. Yet here was this fleet of aircraft-carriers, which could have been put to far more effective use in other seas, concentrating month after month on one solitary ship: the *Tirpitz*. The 'Lone Queen of the North',

147

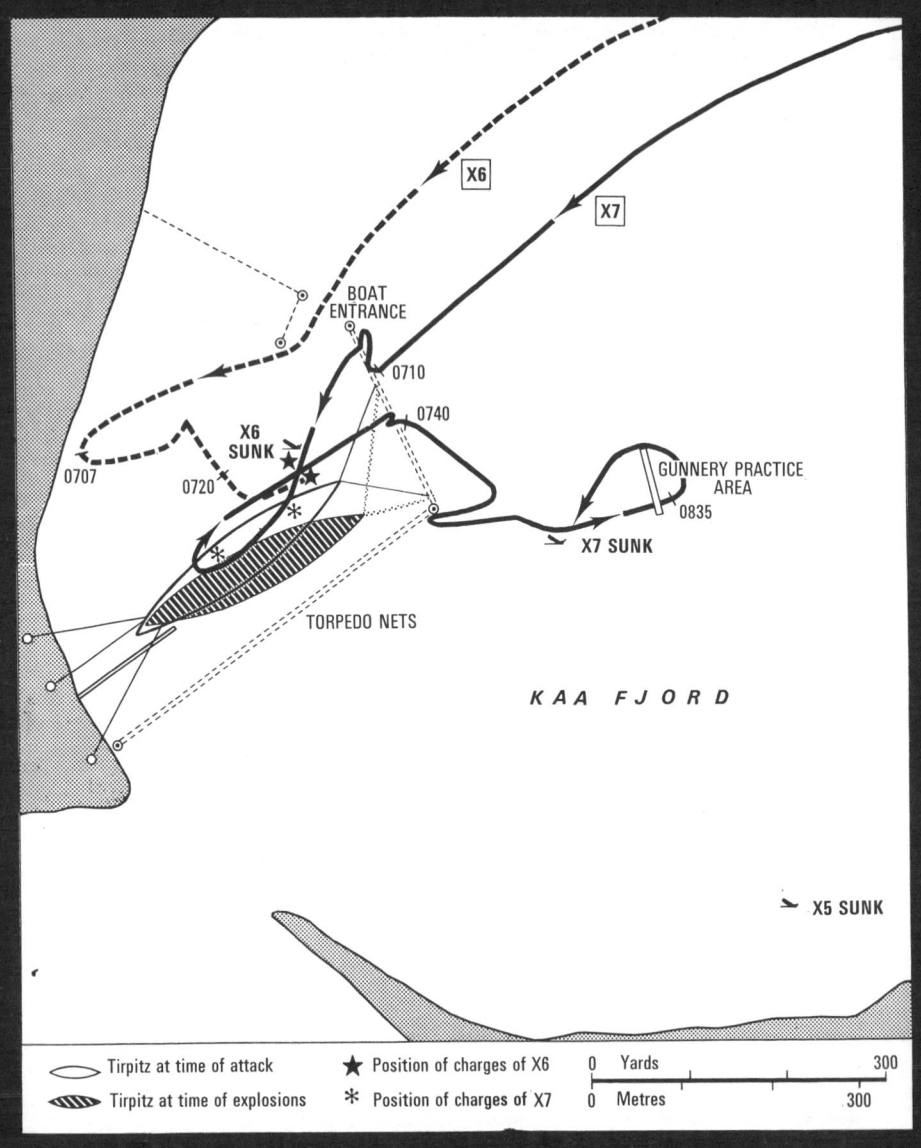

The monster and the midgets: how the British X-craft got through *Tirpitz*'s defences

Above: Fleet Air Arm Barracudas on their way to bomb *Tirpitz* in Alten Fjord
Below: The German smoke-screen drifts across to shroud *Tirpitz*

Below: Direct hit on *Tirpitz*. The Barracudas mauled her badly, but not fatally

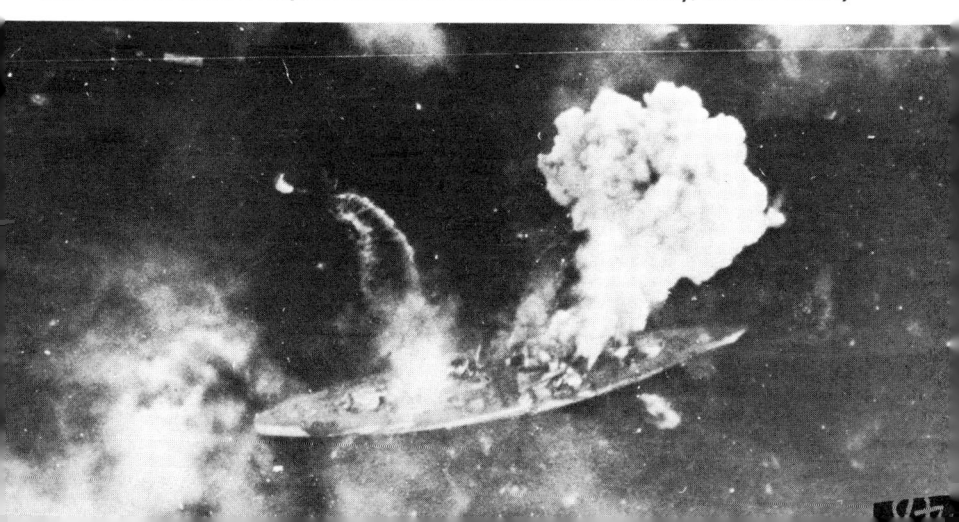

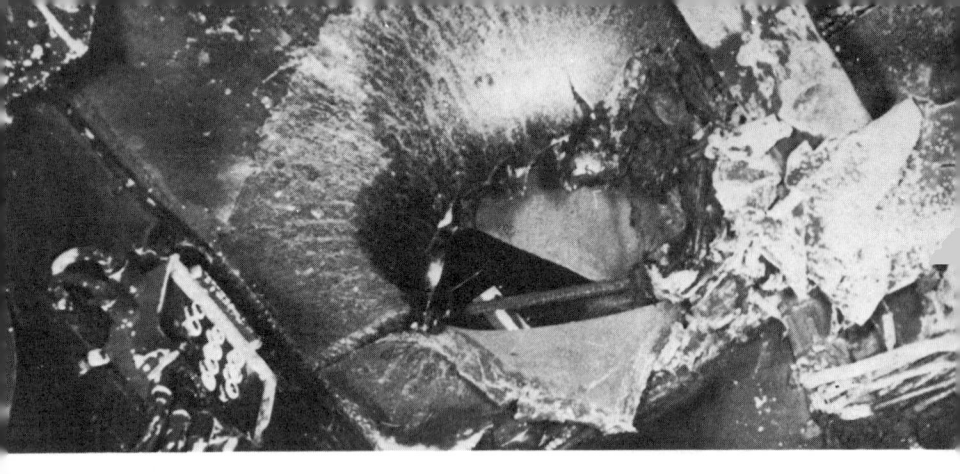

In the wake of the Barracudas. *Above:* Bomb hole in the upper deck. *Below:* The wrecked searchlight platform on the aircraft deck

Below: The wrecked seaplane hangar with its burned-out spotter plane

as the Norwegian Resistance dubbed her, was playing a vital part in the war at sea without stirring an inch from her berth.

The British now planned to use the giant 'earthquake bombs' devised by Barnes Wallis, who had produced the weapons which had smashed the Ruhr dams the year before. As an out-and-return trip could not be managed by Lancaster bombers, a strike force was sent to operate from Yagodnik airfield in north Russia, including No 617 Squadron, 'The Dambusters', Bomber Command's specialist bomber squadron. On 15th September, twenty-eight Lancasters took off from Yagodnik and attacked Alten Fjord overland from the east. As they made their runs, the anticipated smokescreen flooded over the target area – but one of the 12,000-lb 'Tallboy' bombs smashed through *Tirpitz*'s forecastle and burst deep in her hull. The bombers flew back to Yagodnik, their crews lamenting how close they had come to achieving success – and unaware that they had done just that.

For the damage suffered in the raid of 15th September meant that *Tirpitz* could never be made seaworthy again. At best she would be able to crawl along in coastal waters at a pitiful eight knots. And yet she could still fulfil Admiral von Tirpitz's ideal of being a 'gun platform', and that was what Dönitz now ordered for her. She would become a coastal defence battery for the Norwegian garrison; and the site chosen for her was off Haakoy Island, three miles down Tromsö Fjord. For the last time, *Tirpitz* quitted Alten Fjord, where she spent so many months, and was towed ignominiously south to Tromsö. There the Germans began to build a sandbank for her, for she was anchored, not beached; and it would be necessary to take precautions against further attacks from the air, because at Tromsö she could be reached by Lancasters based in Britain.

The Lancasters soon came – minus all dispensable armour-plate and their mid-upper turrets; crammed with extra fuel tanks, and powered by the latest Merlin 24 engines in order to get them to the target. The first attempt to bomb *Tirpitz* at Tromsö, on 29th October, failed because of bad visibility, and the Germans reacted by basing a fighter wing on nearby Bardufoss airfield. The Lancasters needed clear weather to drop their 'Tallboys' accurately; their defensive armament had been weakened to get them to the target area. Such a combination looked good from the point of view of the German defences – and yet, on Sunday, 12th November 1944, everything went wrong for the *Tirpitz*.

Twenty-nine Lancasters took off from Lossiemouth in Scotland, led by Wing Commander J B Tait of 617 Squadron (who had also led the raid on the *Tirpitz* flown from Yagodnik). They made a wide detour, approached from inland – and caught the *Tirpitz* unawares, while the German fighters based on Bardufoss were preparing to fend off what looked like being a raid on their own airfield. What should have been a fairly encouraging situation for the *Tirpitz* – clear weather, weakened bomber defences, and plenty of fighters on call – was fatally transformed within minutes: no smokescreen, no fighter defence, and no chance.

The smokescreen (whose apparatus had not yet been fully installed since the move from Alten Fjord) started to drift across the anchorage – far too late – as the Lancasters roared in. Two 'Tallboys' exploded on *Tirpitz*'s deck. Others gouged away the uncompleted sandbank around her by near-misses which carved great cavities in the bed of the fjord. *Tirpitz* began to list to port, and counter-flooding to bring her level again had hardly been started when her after magazines went up with a tremendous explosion. It was the end. *Tirpitz* rolled bottom-up, her superstructure coming to rest on the bottom, partly concealed from the observers overhead in the Lancasters by her own

The end: bottom-up in Tromsö Fjord, with over 1,000 members of her crew entombed in her massive hull

belated smokescreen.
 Even in the inglorious demise of the *Tirpitz*, there was a link with the legacy of the first High Seas Fleet: a desperate heroism, which stands beside that shown during the last fights of the *Bismarck* and the *Scharnhorst*. Over 1,000 crewmen were trapped below decks when *Tirpitz* turned turtle; some eighty of them managed to crawl upwards through the dead battleship and hammer on the bottom plating, to be released via a hole cut in the hull. Others were not so lucky –

but as the rescue parties strove to reach them, they heard, coming from deep within the hull, strains of *Deutschland über Alles* before the rising water silenced them. In exactly the same spirit, Admiral Graf von Spee's sailors had cheered and sung as their shattered cruisers sank beneath them in the Battle of the Falklands. The passive career of the 'Lone Queen of the North' had ended violently and ingloriously, but she was honoured by her crewmen, who might well have been expected to have had all the spirit rotted out of them by over two and a half years of defensive inactivity.

Eclipse

With the sinking of the *Tirpitz* in November 1944, Hitler's High Seas Fleet lost the last and most influential unit of its battle fleet. It marked the end of Germany's naval war in northern waters; but, in reality, the decline of the fleet's fighting value had begun with the Battle of the Barents Sea in December 1942.

Until the *Tirpitz* quitted the scene, the fleet's strategic influence extended north to the Arctic. After she was sunk it was limited to the Baltic: to the subsidiary, defensive rôle, in fact, from which Alfred von Tirpitz had devoted his career to raising it. Nothing could have reflected this more clearly than the Allied invasion of Normandy in June 1944. The armada of shipping which landed and supplied the spearhead of Operation 'Overlord' went about its business without any challenge from the surviving cruisers and destroyers of the surface fleet. These units – apart from *Tirpitz*, as long as she lasted up at Tromsö – were nearly all serving in the unit known as the Baltic Fleet Training Squadron. By autumn 1944 the eternal shortages of fuel was regulating and curtailing every voyage they made; and the fleet's situation was not improved when, on 15th October, *Prinz Eugen* collided with the light cruiser *Leipzig*, ramming her broadside-on between funnel and bridge. *Prinz Eugen*'s clipper bow gouged deeply into the flimsy cruiser, slicing her right down to her keelplate. It was the end of the *Leipzig*'s active career; she was towed back to port for makeshift repairs, but she finished the war as a floating battery.

With the New Year of 1945 the fleet entered its last five months of existence in the limited rôle of army support. The lightning Russian Vistula-Oder offensive, which carved through eastern Germany, reached the Baltic, and cut off East Prussia, began on 12th January. One of the most symbolic missions carried out by the fleet during this disastrous campaign, which ended with the Russians on the Oder, fifty miles from Berlin, was when the light cruiser *Emden* evacuated the coffin of Field-Marshal von Hindenburg from Königsberg, after it had been removed from the Tannenberg Memorial to prevent desecration by the advancing Russians.

On that note the last months began; months of evacuating troops and refugees from the eastern regions of the Reich; months which saw the Allied bombing offensive reach a crescendo, singling out the heaviest ships for destruction; months which saw the gigantic vice of the Allied land offensive from east and west relentlessly crush Germany in two. As the pressure increased, communications in the dwindling area of German-held territory became ever more chaotic, virtually ending all movement of remaining fuel stocks. Yet the fleet's greatest success in this period was an impressive and often-forgotten achievement. As early as the Führer's conference of 28th January, Dönitz reported the successful evacuation of some 62,000 refugees

Another fiasco: *Prinz Eugen* **rams the light cruiser** *Leipzig,* **writing her off as a seagoing fighting ship**

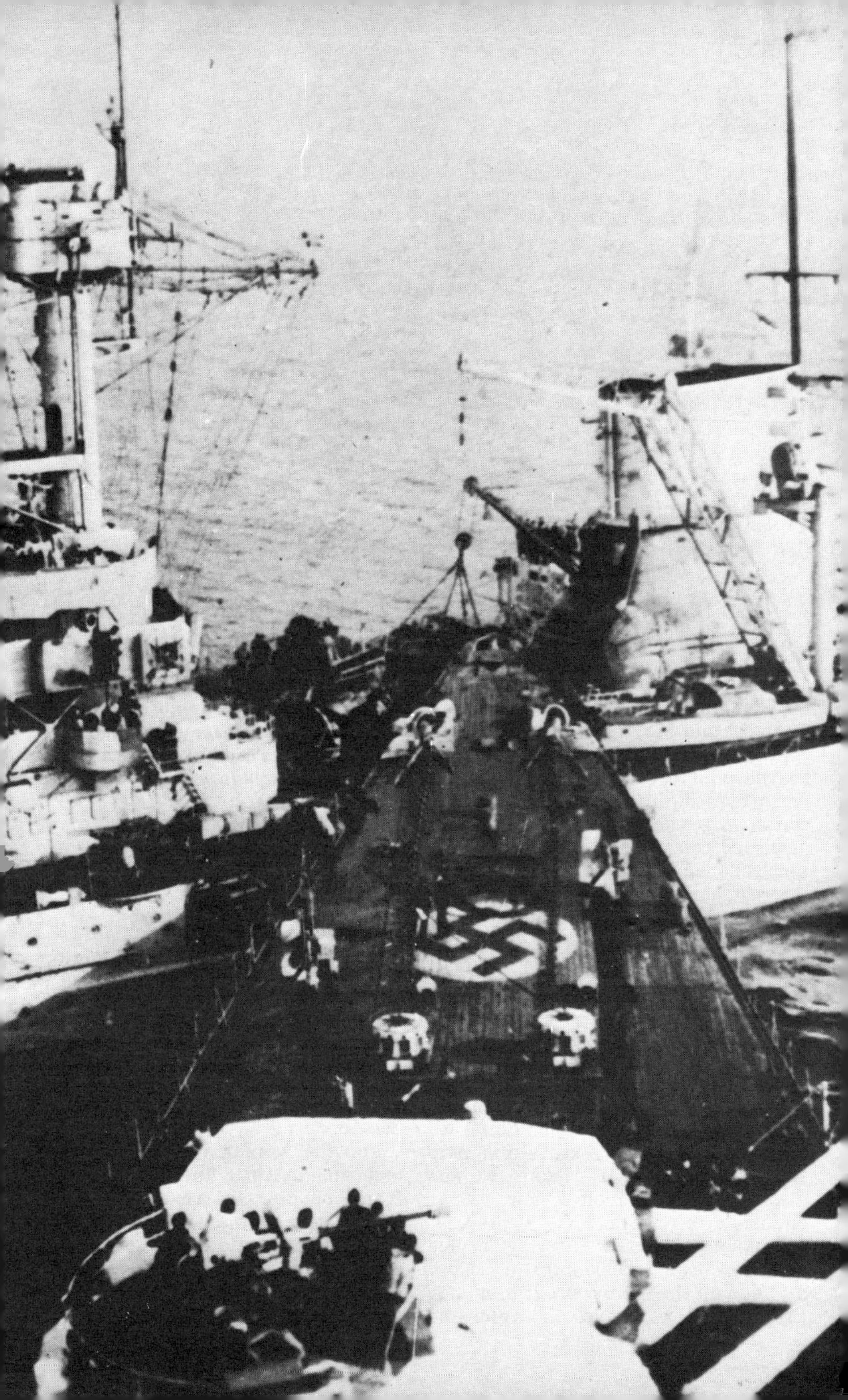

from the east by the navy. Between January and May 1945, the number of evacuees rose to 2,000,000, largely due to the efforts of the fleet. It was a performance which, all in all, certainly ranks with the 'miracle of Dunkirk' as a successful use of sea power in the teeth of enemy opposition.

Wrestling with the increasing chaos in northern Germany was Grand Admiral Dönitz, the last high-ranking commander to whom Hitler was still prepared to leave anything like a free hand. He held supreme responsibility for directing the evacuations. He had to take over the job of distributing the Reich's coal reserves. He had to provide ever-increasing detachments of naval personnel to fight alongside army units and help shore up the crumbling fronts. He was also trying to launch a new U-boat offensive, for the superb 'Type XXI' submarines were now entering service and were being rushed into action. To keep up the sailing programme for this U-boat offensive, in which he

Above: Dönitz with his staff. *Right:* The last great achievement of the fleet was Germany's Dunkirk – the evacuation of some two million refugees from the eastern Baltic

was pinning so much faith, Dönitz was forced to immobilise the diesel-powered *Admiral Scheer* and *Lützow*. In short, the Grand Admiral was tackling a task which was as impossible as it was gigantic. But – unlike all the generals and field-marshals who were facing problems of similar magnitude with land campaigns – Dönitz retained the full confidence of Hitler as the Reich's position grew more and more desperate.

For the warships of the fleet, the end came in April, and it came largely from the air. On 9th April, *Admiral Scheer*, the regular fleet's most successful single raider, was capsized in dock at Kiel by RAF bombs. (She was buried under hundreds of tons of rubble when the dock was filled in after the war.) On the 16th, *Lützow* was knocked out by bombs at Swinemunde. On 4th May, she was blown up and scuttled there. On 30th April, the US Air Force sank the light cruiser *Köln* in Wilhelmshaven. Bombs also eliminated *Emden* at Kiel during April, and she, too, was eventually scuttled; the same went for *Hipper* in Kiel, for *Seydlitz* in Königsberg, and for *Graf Zeppelin* in Stettin.

When the war ended, only the light cruiser *Nürnberg*, the immobilised *Leipzig*, and the undamaged *Prinz Eugen* were still afloat, together with fifteen destroyers. The latter were divided between the Allies. *Leipzig* was subsequently loaded with a cargo of poison gas, towed out into the North Sea, and sunk. *Nürnberg* went to the Red Navy, serving as the *Admiral Makharov* until she was broken up in 1959. For the *Prinz Eugen*, last of the 'lucky ships' of Hitler's High Seas Fleet, a more Promethean fate was reserved. The British handed her over to the Americans, who expended her in their anti-shipping nuclear test at Bikini atoll in 1946. The following year, *Prinz Eugen*'s charred hulk was sunk at Kwajalein.

Thus by the time that hostilities ended on 4th May 1945, the surface fleet had ceased to exist. But the rôle of the German navy at the end of the Second World War was very different from that of 1918. Then the mutinies in the High Seas Fleet had been instrumental in precipitating the revolution which knocked Germany out of the war. Hitler's High Seas Fleet, in comparison, was astonishingly loyal. Its officers – apart from unique characters like Admiral Canaris of *Abwehr* (Security) had not been involved in the many plots against Hitler's life to anything like the extent of the German army officer corps. On Hitler's suicide, it was the C-in-C, navy, to whom were

The end of Hitler's High Seas Fleet. *Above: Hipper* at Kiel. *Below: Admiral Scheer,* capsized in dock at Kiel by RAF bombs

Below: Lightweight survivors – six surrendered German destroyers

bequeathed the reins of power. Dönitz, in fact, presided over a miniature Third Reich in Flensburg for three weeks before the British arrested him, together with his whole government.

Much of the navy's adherence to its sense of duty was the legacy of Raeder. He had always sought to infuse the navy with a sense of duty beyond politics, using the Nazi régime as the most efficient instrument to provide the wherewithal for the building of its warships. Naturally, he had striven to build a powerful navy which would help make the Reich a world power. For that he was indicted at Nuremberg as one of the men who were responsible for the Second World War, and imprisoned for life. Dönitz, on the other hand, the second Führer, wizard of the U-boat war, certainly the one German commander who had come closest to defeating Britain by his own efforts, received only ten years imprisonment.

Hitler's High Seas Fleet had gone the way of its imperial predecessor, albeit in a very different fashion. What was its legacy?

Admiral Scheer's verdict on the legacy of Scapa Flow in 1919 has

Sad echo of Scapa Flow: *Prinz Eugen* is escorted to Britain by the cruiser *Devonshire*

already been quoted. It is therefore fitting to remember the statement made by Dönitz after the 'U-boat atrocities' hearing at Nuremberg in 1946 had acquitted the German navy of the charge of having fought a dishonourable war:

'The conduct by Germany of the war at sea stands unblemished and immaculate. Every German sailor can hold up his head proudly. And, in the welter of accusations, both justified and unjustified, that have been hurled at the German people and Germany's conduct of the war, that is something of inestimable value.

'Compared with this victory won in the fight for the repute of the navy, my own personal fate is of no significance at all.'

He was speaking for Langsdorff of the *Graf Spee*, for Krancke of the *Scheer*; for the men who died so gallantly aboard the *Bismarck* and the *Scharnhorst* in battle against hopeless odds. In short, he was speaking the epitaph for Hitler's High Seas Fleet.

Bibliography

From the Dreadnought to Scapa Flow Arthur J Marder (Oxford University Press)
Yesterday's Deterrent Jonathan Steinberg (The Macmillan Company, New York)
Jutland Geoffrey Bennett (Batsford)
Coronel and the Falklands Geoffrey Bennett (Batsford)
The German Navy in World War II Edward von der Porten (Arthur Barker)
The Drama of the Graf Spee and the Battle of the River Plate Sir Eugen Millington-Drake (Peter Davies)
Action This Day Admiral of the Fleet Sir Philip Vian (Muller)
The Ship Busters Ralph Barker (Chatto & Windus)
The Russian Convoys Admiral B B Schofield (Batsford)
Loss of the Scharnhorst A J Watts (Ian Allan)
The First and the Last Adolf Galland (Methuen)
The Battleship Scheer Admiral Theodor Krancke and H J Brennecke (William Kimber)
The Secret Raiders David Woodward (W W Norton & Company Inc, New York)
The German Raider Atlantis Wolfgang Frank and Bernhard Rogge (Ballantine Books)
My Life Grand Admiral Erich Raeder (US Naval Institute, Annapolis)
Memoirs: Ten Years and Twenty Days Grand Admiral Karl Dönitz (Weidenfeld & Nicolson)
Führer Conferences on Naval Affairs – Brassey's Naval Annual, 1948 (William Clowes & Sons Ltd)
Dreadnought: A History of the Modern Battleship Richard Hough (Allen & Unwin)
German Warships of World War II J C Taylor (Ian Allan)
The War At Sea Captain S W Roskill (Her Majesty's Stationary Office)
History of the First World War (Purnell)
History of the Second World War (Purnell)